Hippocrene Companion Guide to
AUSTRALIA

Hippocrene Companion Guide to

AUSTRALIA

Graeme Newman
and
Tamsin Newman

HIPPOCRENE BOOKS
New York

For information, address:
HIPPOCRENE BOOKS, INC.
171 Madison Ave.
New York, NY 10016

Library of Congress Cataloging-in-Publication Data is available.

ISBN 0-87052-034-2

Printed in the United States of America.

Contents

Preface

This book is not about how to get around Australia on a budget, nor a guide to the best or cheapest hotels (although we suggest some that we have particularly enjoyed, whether they cost a lot or a little). One can find any number of books full of money-saving details at any bookstore. The cost-conscious consumer naturally hunts for bargains or at least a fair price for what he or she wishes to purchase, but determining if you got your money's worth out of a travel vacation is sometimes difficult. Tourists often confuse leisure with work, or to put it in a better way, they turn leisure into work. Those who really enjoy traveling will get tired and worn out, but they will not call it work. Leisure, like most sports, can be tiring, but if done well it can be enormously satisfying.

Too often books emphasize the cost of travel, as though this were the dominant factor to consider. It is important, but we would rather make sure that we get back the best return for every dollar spent. This means preparing for the trip well in advance (about a year, we think); reading the right books, knowing the right questions to ask. Above all, it means finding out about the people and places one is planning to visit. In this way, the personal experience of travel is maximized regardless of whether it is done on a shoestring budget or in style. If you do not embrace the ways of a foreign land, you will end up thinking only of the money to be spent or saved, the souvenirs to be bought, the fear of getting "ripped off."

In foreign lands where the language is not English, it may be difficult to blend in with the local populace. But in Australia, where the language spoken is English (well, sort of), there is a real possibility for the tourist to soak up some

Australian culture even during a very short stay. The success of the personal experience depends on the amount of preparation done beforehand by the traveler—and by the follow-up upon returning home. We have tried in this book to provide the traveler with a personal guide for getting to know Australia and Australians, and for making the best of a visit by linking the things tourists like to do (sightseeing, eating and relaxing) with the history and character of the Australian people.

Many Australian relatives and friends have aided us in this venture. Their hospitality, openness and advice have helped us craft this book in ways that would not have been possible without them. Amanda and Clancy Newman gave us a healthy kid's view of Australian life, sensitizing us to details that we may not have noticed otherwise. Joan Newman scrupulously edited the manuscript, saving us from many embarrassing errors. Her devotion to the task is much appreciated. Any errors remaining, of course, are those of the authors!

CHAPTER 1

Getting Ready
for the
Land of Oz

We have found that Americans have some misconceptions of
Australia and Australians, largely due to movies and media
coverage of Australia during the last ten years. They have also
been fostered by stories brought home to American families
by U.S. servicemen who fought in wars that took them to
Australia's shores, usually on R and R. Many Americans have
notions about Australia which are humorously incorrect.
Here are some common faulty impressions opposed by the
truths.

American Misconceptions About Australia	Truths About Australia
All Australians drive 4-wheel–drive pick-up trucks along dirt roads.	Some people in the outback do, but most Australians drive Fords and

The typical Aussie is a 21-year-old blond and tanned surfer.

Toyotas and Holdens (the Australian subsidiary of General Motors).

How can everyone in Australia be 21 years old, blond, tanned and a surfer? There are many immigrants and descendants of immigrants from the southern Mediterranean area, as well as a sizable population of Asians and South Pacific Islanders. Judge for yourself.

The "our" in "Melbourne" is pronounced aloud.

It's pronounced "Melbn," without the "our."

Kangaroos and koalas are as common to Australian households as dogs and Velveeta cheese are to American households.

Not true, though many Australians behave as if it were. One can hardly find an Australian children's book without either of these animals in it.

All Australians are descendants of big-eared convicts.

It's true that many Australians have big ears, and the old English stereotype of a criminal included this characteristic (not to mention the pictures used by Lombroso of the "born criminal"). Many Aussies are descendants from ordinary settlers who arrived in the 1800s and 1900s. It is also a fact that England dumped its convicts in the American

	colony before 1776, so don't be so sure of yourself, either.
Australians wear mostly tan and khaki safari clothing.	Consider yourself the victim of a smart marketing ploy: "If you tell people it's Australian, they'll buy it." Or, if you say something has to do with the outback, Americans will buy it, thinking that some of the adventure of the Aussie outback will affect them.
Australia is small.	It's actually bigger than all of Europe and compares to the continental U.S.
Nothing newsworthy happens in Australia, except maybe news about dwarf-throwing contests.	Dead wrong. Australia has plenty to match American and world news; there are terrible political scandals almost every month; police corruption erupts on a regular basis; celebrities say and do terrible things; the economy is in a shambles; crime in the cities is reported constantly; and acts of racism occur with reasonable frequency. Need we continue?
Crocodiles abound in Australia.	Now you are victim of Hollywood. They mainly hang out in the warmer northern regions of the

continent, and some of the West.

People walk around up-side-down in Australia.

Well, it depends how you look at it, doesn't it? We like the T-shirts they sell in Australia depicting Australia at the top of the world, and the rest of the Northern Hemisphere at the bottom. Trouble is Americans have watched Dan Rather too long and the image of Australia at the bottom of the world map is etched into their brains. It's a mere scientific convention that Aussies are upside down over there. Since Galileo, scientists should have realized that the world (and universe) could just as easily be depicted the other way up, with those of the Northern Hemisphere walking upside down. Get our point?

Australians do not speak English, or if they do, it's an amazing feat.

Then your humble authors have wonderful foreign language skills.

It is always hot in Australia and it seldom snows.

On the whole, it's true that the Australian climate is more temperate than that of, say, Massachusetts. But it does get cold enough to snow in parts of Tasmania,

	New South Wales, and Victoria.
In Australia, water empties out of a bath in counter-clockwise direction, whereas it drains clockwise in the U.S.	This one is true. We don't know why.

If you plan to engage the Aussies in conversation, it would be best to be prepared for a number of funny ideas that Australians have about America.

Australian Misconceptions About the U.S.	**Truths About the U.S.**
Americans are all loud and obnoxious.	Only true of a certain class of American tourists, most often found in Europe.
All Americans like to eat at McDonald's.	Well, it's all relative. Australians are the next most frequent diners at McDonald's after Americans. There are, though, quite a few Australians who will not eat, on principle, at McDonald's. But we've met quite a few Americans who are the same way. This rule does not seem to apply to children.
All Americans are money crazy.	Compared to Australia, it seems to be true. Or at least, Americans seem to let work take over their lives on the mistaken belief that one day they'll be

rich. Australians do not suffer from this illusion, since they have learned from way back that the government will keep them poor, no matter how hard they work. So, Aussies are much freer to enjoy life than are Americans.

If you go to America, you'll definitely get mugged; if you're lucky, you won't be murdered.

Recent crime statistics have shown Australian violent crime rates, as measured by counting those who are victimized, to be not too different from those of the U.S. (This study was conducted by the British Home Office, so it is suspect. After all, the Pommies have a vested interest in keeping Australia true to its convict ancestry.) Frankly, we feel safer walking around the rougher parts of Sydney than we do in any part of New York City. But Australians have only a vague idea of the American suburban life, which is very similar to the Australian. We recommend to Australia a season of reruns of "Leave It to Beaver" in

	order to re-assert the American suburban dream.
Americans are always adorned by cowboy hats.	Only true in Texas, guns included.
Americans are well informed about Australia.	They've only heard of Paul Hogan (and they're quickly forgetting him), and Mel Gibson (who is getting more American and less Australian every year).
Most Americans know where Sydney and Melbourne are located.	They sometimes know that Sydney is on the east coast of Australia, but they think Melbourne is in Florida. They're right. What they don't know is that Melbn is in Victoria.
Americans are familiar with kilometers and Celsius degrees.	Better get used to it. The older generation will talk to you in nondecimal language if you give them half a chance, but the younger generation hasn't the faintest idea what miles are let alone Faren . . . . what? And you had better not say anything about gallons at the gas station. Converting liters to gallons is impossible anyway. Best to try to learn this foreign system of weights and measures for what it means in every-

Most Americans live close to Disneyland and visit there several times a year on weekends.

day life, and quit trying to convert.

It's true, isn't it?

Getting There: The Feeling of Darling's Collar

It is some consolation that the convict ships used to take six months on the average to sail from England to Sydney. There were many interesting ports of call on the way, where the taking on of supplies was a must. Travel from America to Australia was not common until Australia's Gold Rush in the 1850s. As far as we know, no slave ships reached as far as Australia.

In fact, right up until the 1960s the most common way to visit Australia was by sea. One of us traveled to the United States from Australia on an ocean liner in 1968 because it was the cheapest way to travel. At that time it cost $250 for a single berth and took five weeks, with several exotic ports of call along the way. The route was across the Pacific, stopping at Fiji and/or Tahiti, Tonga or New Zealand, to Hawaii then on to the Panama Canal, Jamaica and to Fort Lauderdale/Miami. Young Australians by the thousands used to take a sea trip to Europe almost as a ritual, before settling down. Luxury cruises that leave from Australia's major eastern cities now cruise the Pacific for two to three weeks, but not too many people have the time (let alone the money) to take a sea cruise to Australia. Ships plying the seas between the U.S. and Australia are rare, although one can fly to Hawaii to pick up a cruise.

Air travel has become the cheaper and more efficient (by comparison) way to get to Australia. In terms of dollars per mile, fares to Australia are very reasonable in contrast to the fares within Australia, which are outrageous. As we write, Australian airlines are in the process of deregulation. Time will tell whether this will mean a reduction of prices.

Unless one is well prepared, the journey to Australia from the U.S. can be something of an ordeal. Depending on the route, you can be without a bed to sleep in for a couple of days. You will yearn for a shower and an opportunity to stretch limbs that have been bent for too long in a sitting position. You will be reminded of the suffering of a character of Marcus Clarke, 19th-century Australian author, best known for his novel *For the Term of His Natural Life*. Clarke wrote about the Darling Collar (named after the governor of Australia at the turn of the 19th century), which an unfortunate convict wore who was sentenced to work on a chain gang, building a road over the Blue Mountains just outside Sydney. He was weighed down with the 40-pound iron collar connected to leg irons by heavy chains which were short enough to keep the convict continuously bent, even when sleeping. And you may begin to feel like this man must have by the time your plane is half way across the Pacific no matter how well looked after you are (and they do look after you on those trans-Pacific flights).

There are a few ways you can reduce your suffering. Try to break your journey as often as possible. The airlines will allow stopovers for no additional cost or a small one. If you are strapped for cash and/or time, but can manage only one break, we strongly recommend a break in the journey coming home. There are two reasons for this. First, going on a trip, people are usually eager to get there. Breaking the journey seems to frustrate the purpose of the trip! One tends to have more free energy, and can withstand the trials of the journey better. On the return journey, by contrast, one is usually tired and needs a break! The other reason is that the body's biological clock seems to adjust better going against the rotation of the earth. Thus, flying to Australia (east to west) causes less jet lag than the return leg (west to east). A stopover in Hawaii, or better Fiji, will do wonders for a poor tired, confused body. Or, if you have far to travel within the United States, a stopover in Los Angeles or San Francisco will help. We recommend Fiji simply beause it is not American and it is, by comparison, much less commercially developed.

Next, don't overindulge on the excellent food and beverages the airlines to Australia provide so lavishly. We have found that the food, by and large, on the international airlines to Australia is much better than the usual fare on airlines within the U.S. It's easy to get carried away and overeat. Have the courage to skip a meal. Just say no!

While we are discussing excesses, one should be aware of a special temptation to those so inclined, while visiting Australia. Australians do like to drink beer, and more recently have begun to drink lots of wine as well. The airlines cater to this Australian inclination, so you may be tempted to drink more alcohol than usual. Australian beer (if it's not the export brew, but the real thing) is much stronger than that sold in the U.S. (see Chapter 4). So, be careful. You may find yourself **overimbibing, speaking gibberish** to the flight attendant, and have feet so swollen that you can't get your shoes back on!

Finally, make a point of getting out of your seat every so often and going for a walk around the plane. Fortunately, Australians are sports freaks, so it is not uncommon to see young men stripped down to their shorts and shirt, doing exercises in a spare space somewhere in the back of the plane. Stretch those legs—think of the poor convict in Darling's Collar! You're lucky compared to him! (You have much more **than the few square feet of space** in the hold provided to each convict on the six-month voyage to Sydney!)

One popular route to Australia is via New Zealand. We recommend this route only if you have plenty of time (more than three weeks). New Zealand, though often linked to Australia in the American's mind, is a vastly different country, with its own attractions and different people. It is well worth a trip in itself. While it may be tempting, given that you have paid a lot of money to get to the other side of the world, choose one or the other, and make a great trip of it. In trying to see both in a short time, disappointment may result. Or at least, there will be less personal satisfaction per dollar spent.

Getting Ready: What to Wear

A Warning to Men

If you want to blend in with the locals, or to, as in the Aussie vernacular, not "stand out as a bloody Yank," there are a few simple things to do. The most important is to leave untailored shorts at home. Australians think that the large billowy shorts (that older Americans wear) are very funny. The Australian way to wear shorts is with long knee-length socks or with sandals and no socks. If you arrive in Australia during summertime (December through March) you will see most public officials in shorts and long socks, even with short sleeve dress shirts and ties. This is considered quite formal and acceptable dress. But note the shorts. They are cut carefully to stay close to the contours of the body; the length is half way between thigh and knee, sometimes shorter. They do look nice. One suspects that they are modeled on the shorts worn by Australian Rules football players, very short and skin tight. (Tune in to ESPN sometime between March and September, the football season in Australia, and watch a game). In any case, if you like to wear shorts, we suggest buying them in Australia, or shopping carefully in the United States for a pair that fit snugly around the butt and thigh. One can find them, but it takes a little time.

Large billowy shirts are also not popular, and thought of largely as American. Again, an Australian sports shirt (casual open-necked shirt) will be worn either tucked in or left out over trousers or shorts. When one is at work, the shirt should be tucked in. At play, anything goes. Sun hats are common, and often very necessary. "Slouch hats" (the typical hat of the digger of World War I with one side turned up) are worn now mainly by tourists. Hats in wintertime are rare. They're just a bit too English.

Winter Clothing

The climate varies considerably across Australia. Remember, it's a continent as big as the U.S. But everything is upside down (or, if one is Australian—the right way up, after all), Australia's winter is during America's summer. Australia's summer is from December to March, basically America's winter. But extremes are not present in Australia. The coldest and wettest part of Australia is the deep south on the island state of Tasmania, the apple isle. But even there, there is rarely any snow, though the winters can be damp and dreary. Continuous below freezing temperatures are rare.

From Sydney to the south, the summers are hot (too bloody hot) during January and February, sometimes stretching into March. The temperature is measured and announced in Celsius, rarely in Fahrenheit. It takes a bit of getting used to, and we've found that even conversion charts don't help that much. One just has to get used to associating particular numbers with the way one feels.

So, for the winter, we suggest a raincoat with a zip-out lining, or a heavy wool sweater (buy one in Australia where, in contrast to just about everything else, they are a good buy and of high quality). If you plan to dine in a fancy restaurant, take a tie and jacket, as there are still a few places that require them (a bit like New York City in this regard). And, men, please, no plaid pants or jackets!

The months of June through August are the best in the north because of the subtropical climate. It is the dry season with warm days in the low 80s and cool nights in the 60 to 70s. Perfect weather! Coats are definitely not needed in this climate, which begins to emerge around Brisbane and the Gold Coast (more about this later). We would not recommend too long a visit to the north of Australia during the Australian summer (December through March) as this is the wet period. It is truly tropical—hot, humid, lots of rain—floods are common.

Other than what has been mentioned, men's fashions are generally the same for Australians as for Americans. Possibly the swimsuits worn are a little more brief and revealing. Those resembling shorts worn often by Americans are not common in Australia. But again, it depends which beach one goes to. There are some beaches on which no swimsuits are worn at all!

Australian women are very fashion-conscious. They are often dressed in European styles a season or so ahead of Americans. Women on the whole tend to be much more dressed up in fashionable blouses, pants, skirts, and expensive shoes. There are also a large number who are ultra-trendy and wear all black. We have detected some differences between Sydney and Melbourne. Dress in Sydney varies greatly—from businessmen and women in their fancy suits to the casual visitor in shorts and T-shirt. Generally, Sydney is more laid back than Melbourne, so you needn't feel that you must dress up for a leisurely walk. Outside of work, men often wear trendy button-down shirts with a pair of jeans.

These are very general observations. Australia is really a land of informal dressers; it goes with the climate. One can venture out in just about anything and not be too worried about whether heads will turn .

What to Expect: Flies

Little black bush flies have been a darned nuisance in Australia since they were first sighted by the great navigator and explorer William Dampier in 1686, as he described the first sighting of the Australian Aborigines:

> Their Eye-lids are always half closed, to keep the flies out of their Eyes: they being so troublesome here that no fanning will keep them from coming to ones Face; and without the assistance of both hands to keep them off, they will creep into ones Nostrils; and Mouth too, if the Lips are not shut very close.

While perhaps not quite as bad today as described by Dampier, flies can be quite troublesome, especially if one happens to be in the bush attending a barbecue. It is a good idea to carry a light hat, preferably one with a floppy brim. If with a really informal group touring the outback, one might be able to get away with doing what the old cockies (farmers) do on their stations (sheep or cattle farms), which is to tie corks on 3 to 4-inch lengths of string around the brim of one's hat so that they dangle down and keep the flies away. It works really well, although one may turn a little cross-eyed after a time! You can also always wave a handkerchief around your face. (Handkerchiefs are still common in Australia and commonly known as hankies).

Remember, if visiting an Aussie's home or if staying in a motel that has a screen door, be sure to see that it is shut behind you when you go in and out. Aussies have learned to keep their "fly doors" closed, just as Americans from the North know to close the door in winter to keep out the cold.

The creaking of wire screen doors is possibly the most pervasive sound one remembers after a trip to Australian suburbs.

There are other flies in Australia that can also be a nuisance. Blowies (blow-flies) are very large, about the size of a bee, and have a loud, low-pitched buzz. Do not leave any food uncovered. Do not attract that blowie! We need not go into details, but it's best if you get rid of these flies as soon as possible, in any way possible. Other flies that are a nuisance are march flies, which are rather large and shaped something like a yellow-back, but of a nondescript color. They do not announce their presence to the sunbather on the beach with a loud buzz. Rather, they prefer to sneak up on a nice patch of skin and apply a stinging bite. Fortunately, they are easy to swat. Keep an eye out for them and try to brush them off before they bite. They do not leave bite marks or itching, and generally are not a serious threat. Anyway, as we suggest later in regard to the sun, it's probably best if one does not lie in the sun uncovered too long. So, keep covered, and you won't be burned or bitten!

Driving in the Land of Oz

Driving in Australia can be a nerve-racking experience for the foreigner. The big problem is that Australians drive on the left side of the road, which means that the steering wheel is on the right side of the car. (That's right, not content to have just their seasons all back-the-front the Aussies went and reproduced the English road traffic system.) This wouldn't be quite so bad except that Australia's freeway system is not very well developed. Getting around by car, therefore, is quite an experience—not as bad as in Rome—though downtown Sydney isn't far from it.

Adapting to a righthand drive vehicle isn't as difficult as one would expect. In fact, because one drives on the opposite side of the road as well, everything seems to go together, and one adapts to the change almost instinctively. We say "almost." The problems arise, not while driving along the highway or on a busy street, but the mistakes are more likely to occur when driving out of a gas station. Since one goes in and out of gas stations in America to the right or left of the pump (sometimes called a "petrol bowser" in Australia), it is easy to forget that one is in a strange country and drive out onto the road going the wrong way! So, if you decide to drive, take special care any time you drive out onto a road from a drive-way, be it a gas station or drive-in bottleshop (yes, America may have drive-in banks, but Australia is in the forefront in drive-in liquor stores).

Another difficulty is that Australia's roads, by and large, are not of good quality. With some exceptions (sections of the Melbourne to Sydney Highway), most are single lanes, with two directions of traffic, each one pointed at the other, and traveling at 100k (60 miles) an hour! Australians drive fast and brake hard. And, in the cities, the affable Australian can turn into a monster once he/she gets behind the wheel of a car—not unlike drivers everywhere.

Driving in the Outback

Believe it or not, we think that driving in the Australian outback is much easier than driving in the cities. While the distances are enormous, the fact is that there are hardly any cars, no bends and no hills. Provided one keeps to the main sealed roads, we recommend this experience, though with proper preparation (see our chapter on Alice Springs). The only hazards are the wildlife and cattle that wander onto the roads at night (so don't drive at night in the outback), and the occasional road trains. These are huge tractor trailers, each the size of a train, and there's room on these outback roads some-times only for them, and not for you! But in all our driving, and we did a lot of it, we had absolutely no trouble with these trains. They were courteous and pulled over to the side to allow for passing. The one hazard we experienced was the tour busses. (More about them when we visit Ayer's Rock).

Gas. It's called petrol in Australia, and it's expensive. Even though prices have risen considerably in the U.S., plan to pay at least twice as much for gas in Australia. There's super and standard grades. Just about every car uses super. You can get petrol at a service station, and most of these will be familiar to you. They operate in ways similar to those in the U.S. Don't forget that fuel is measured in liters.

Cars. Most makes and models of cars you will recognize, some you will not. Ford and General Motors have manufactured cars in Australia for many years, although the models there are a little different from those in the U.S. One model, the Holden, now made by General Motors, is the original Australian car. There was a famous model called the FJ that is still running even though it is some 20 years old now. It has become something of a sacred object, a symbol of the good old days. Naturally, there are many Japanese cars of familiar makes and models.

Auto Clubs. There are major auto clubs in all states of Australia, each having reciprocal arrangements with the others. If you plan to drive for any distance or length of time, joining one of these clubs is strongly recommended. They provide superb maps and trip planning services, these alone worth the cost of membership. We asked various auto clubs in the U.S. whether they had reciprocal agreements with any Australian clubs, but were treated rather badly. There appeared to be no interest whatsoever. We found, however, that a number of auto clubs did recognize our U.S. membership in AAA, either with reciprocal services, or with special reduced rate membership. All supply emergency road service. They have different names in each state:

Royal Automobile Club of Victoria (RACV), (main office, 123 Queens Street, Melbourne, 3000, but there are many local branches; call 008-133527 toll free for the location of an office near you). Offers a complete travel service, many maps and handbooks either free or at a nominal fee to members. Best known for tailor-made strip maps which detail the journey over each main highway, complete with descriptions of sights at almost every mile along the way. The maps even include a complete listing of every radio station in Australia, and where it can be found on the dial. A valuable resource for the driver on a lonely road.

National Roads and Motorists Association (NRMA), 151 Clarence Street, Sydney, 2000 (main office 02-2609222, but many locations; call for the nearest). Supplies maps of main roads, also latest road condition reports.

Automobile Association of the Northern Territory. 79–81 Smith

Street, Darwin, 5790. Provides excellent maps and particularly useful synopsis booklets with background information on what to see in the Northern Territory.

Royal Automobile Club of Queensland (RACQ), 190–194 Elizabeth Street, Brisbane, 4000. Best known for its excellent multicolored regional maps of Queensland, beautifully produced and printed.

Royal Automobile Club of Tasmania (RACT), Patrick and Murray Streets, Hobart, 7000. Excellent handbooks on sights, bushwalking and camping facilities.

Royal Automobile Association of South Australia (RAA), 41 Hindmarsh Square, Adelaide, 5000.

Royal Automobile Club of Western Australia (RAC), 228 Adelaide Terrace, Perth, 6000.

Travel Sickness: Or Is It Homesickness?

We would not want to suggest that all travel sickness is psychological, but we do suspect that homesickness can strike even the most hardened of travelers. A dose of homesickness may especially strike one in Australia because of the feeling that one is really about as far away as one can get from the U.S.A. The yearning for something that is a clear link to home can suddenly attack. And we found that these symptoms could pop up at any time, usually in response to day-to-day living.

What about American news? Very little is reported in Aussie newspapers. American weather in Fahrenheit degrees? And Australians don't know what a real hamburger is, the kind without the red beets and actually cooked on the inside? Whatever happened to buffalo wings? And Hershey bars? And Ben and Jerry's ice cream? And REAL cookies, not the dried-up creme-filled, no-taste cookies? And what about American coffee with endless refills? And REAL orange juice, potato chips. . . .

Homesick remedies we recommend are:

Finding the real thing. Many newsagents in the major cities, especially the ones near tourist attractions, sell *USA Today*. It doesn't make the slightest difference what your opinion of this colorful, illustrated newspaper was prior to leaving the

U.S. Reading this newspaper about Supreme Court cases, Hollywood gossip, money and sports scores and everything else, is like being home again. Not that you want to go home—you're having a great time here Down Under—but it's wonderful to feel as though the U.S.A. actually still exists, and that you haven't dropped off the edge of the earth.

For a more vivid sense of home, watch the *NBC Today Show*. It's on late at night, usually after 11 p.m. on Channel 7 in Australia. There's nothing like seeing the smiling face of the President in your time of need!

Develop a keen eye for candy displays. Some chocolate stores carry international brands (although you'd have to be very lucky to find a Hershey bar). And finally, McDonald's hamburgers and coffee are the same all over the world, but keep in mind that the coffee is not bottomless—sorry!

Finding a substitute. First look for it under a different name. Rice Krispies are Rice Bubbles, and Oil of Olay is Oil of Ulan, etc. You'd be surprised how many things assume an alias when they come Down Under. We looked everywhere for American-style cookies and ice cream, but they simply do not exist in their accustomed forms here. But you can compromise. One can find chocolate chip cookies in Oz even if they are seemingly overbaked and brittle. Some cookie specialty stores are appearing in food courts selling chocolate chip cookies that are very close to those in America. They're not as chewy and they don't taste quite the same, but they're pretty good. Try to accept Australian ice cream as different from the American, and it's tolerable. Try something new like Gelato or Vitari.

Living with the gap in your life. Face it. Some good things in one life cannot be found in another. Once you realize this, often your longing will go away. Some cold, hard facts are that:

1. There are no Cheerios, Hershey bars, or American-tasting orange juice in Oz.

2. No ingredients are ever listed on products, so resolve yourself to the fact that what you're eating probably wasn't fried in vegetable oil, and the shampoo you're using probably does have that chemical your hairdresser said would straighten your perm.

3. No mail is ever delivered on Saturdays.

4. Very few banks are open past five in the afternoon.

5. There is no weather channel, headline news 24 hours a day, or HBO. In fact there is no cable TV. To make up for this lack, however, there is an amazing channel called the multicultural channel, which runs movies from all over the world in an incredible number of languages.

Do not feel guilty for being homesick. It does not mean that you are a failed traveler as long as you continue to try new things. Just remember to keep an open mind when trying new things, and you'll soon discover wonderful sensations which Aussies miss when they visit the U.S., i.e. cappuccino, crumpets, and Violet Crumbles (see the next chapter).

CHAPTER 2

The Romance of Australia

The Australian Mystique

Romance takes many forms: the American in Paris, a Roman holiday. We are enthralled by European accents, the grandeur of European history and architecture, the sheer age of everything. By comparison, America and Australia are the New World. What romance could one expect to find in Australia?

The North American traveler, jaded by the crumbling ruins of Europe and its churches, fed up with its predatory inhabitants, will find much to love in Australia. For here, one will find a population at once incredibly similar to North Americans, yet in almost every way vastly different. The language is English, though more difficult to understand than Ricardo Montalban's. But don't worry, you will not be spurned if you have trouble communicating with Aussies. Better yet, you won't be taken down for your money. The most important difference about being in Australia is that one doesn't have to be constantly on the defensive. The Aussies are not out to get every last penny from the poor tourist. In fact, they will treat you just like one of them—provided that you abide by a few simple, but important, rules of etiquette. Above all, a sense of humor is needed (more about this later).

In order to get the best out of a trip to Australia, one must enter the love affair of all Australians. It's an unshakable belief that everyone is equal, that people on top ("tall poppies") have something seriously wrong with them, and that the outback (one of the world's biggest deserts) is the source of energy and meaning for everyday life. Never mind that most Aussies have never been further than the edge of their enormously sprawling cities. Never mind that a huge portion of Australia's population today has migrated in recent years from Europe. Australians love their country and the idea of the rugged frontier more than anything else. This love of country is more than a shoddy nationalism. Rather it is a romantic attachment to a figment of the past. Just as Americans have been in love with the idea of the Wild West, and have exported this drama to all parts of the world through Western movies and novels, so Australians live out the drama of their wild past. The Western has had its day in America—or at least it awaits revival. In Australia, the romance has only just begun.

The Australian frontier has vastly different origins from its American counterpart, so it promises a rich and rewarding experience for the North American traveler. But first, we need to understand the historical factors that have fed into this growing Australian love affair. It is the history, the geography, and the special flora and fauna of Australia that all contribute to the romance. Some of it has been stolen from Australia's original inhabitants, the Aborigines—the general name given to the many different tribes that existed in Australia when it was first settled by Europeans.

It is the history of Australia as described by the aboriginal people that gives Australia its special mystique, and which also explains, as we shall see shortly, the special place that animals have in Australian culture and society. They are not just tourist attractions. They are an essential part of the Australian cultural experience.

Australia's Aborigines

About a thousand million years ago, Australia separated from the rest of southeast Asia. In time—near infinite time—

wind, rain and sun wore away the Australian earth, giving its mountains and hills their special rounded appearance. About fourteen thousand years ago (and possibly much more) the Aborigines moved down through the chain of islands from southeast Asia and Indonesia into Australia. There they found a strange collection of animal life which had evolved in isolation from the rest of the world, entirely protected from any of the fierce predators that lived in the northern continents. Aboriginal folk lore refers to this early period as the "Dreamtime," an apt way of coping with this enormous span of time, difficult to comprehend in the modern age when time is kept in minutes and seconds. The land, three-quarters of it desolate and flat with horizons seemingly reaching into the sky itself, conveyed a sense of vast emptiness as it does today. But more than being merely empty was the expanse of it all invoking a sense of awe and wonder.

The aboriginal tribes developed a harmonious relationship with the land and its animals. They saw their own history as simply part of the history of the land and its animals and vegetation. Individuals and groups, totems, were given names of animals, and even rocky outcrops had their own special names which also became totems. Stories were told of great giants of the earth who made mountains and chasms, formed animals in particular ways. Many of the stories were of the fall of these great giants who, after conflict among themselves, produced or were transformed into particular animal types or rock formations that were of this world. Everything around the Aborigines was sacred. As we will see, a knowledge of aboriginal folk stories adds to an appreciation of Australia's natural wonders.

At some point in time (or timelessness), these giants of the land receded or disappeared. What was left was a land of incredible beauty and harshness, of animals with distinctive and human-like characters, and rock and land formations exuding a character and atmosphere of their own. Sacred places evolved, many to become the source of great conflict in modern Australia.

The tools of the Aborigines were quite remarkable. Their boomerang stands today as an amazing contraption of aerospace. The woomera, a long stick that could be hinged onto a spear, was used as a lever to increase the speed, distance and accuracy. They developed a universal sign language that allowed them to communicate with all other tribes they met, even though many tribes spoke completely different languages. Today, it has become painfully clear that their treatment of the land as sacred was not a bad idea. Rather than hack and destroy the land and its bounty (however meager), the Aborigines lived with their surroundings as one. They were, in this respect, far in advance of modern civilization.

It is a shameful fact that the aboriginal culture and way of life was so completely shattered by the onset of modern civilization that it struggles to survive today. Where it has been able to, it has of necessity developed a kind of self consciousness that will take many years to overcome. Australian Aborigines today exist in anything but a sacred land, for they are in the midst of political conflict and a moral turmoil that seems to prevent any reasonable solution to Australia's racial unrest. For what can be said by a society that originated as a convict settlement, that did not choose to be there in the first place, yet is now held responsible for having stolen the Aborigines' land and way of life? The blame is easy to place on the English, for it is they who, by accident or design, saw Australia as an enormous dump where social trash could be conveniently kept out of sight and out of mind.

But we are getting ahead of ourselves. As badly as the Aborigines have been treated, and still are today, something of the reverence the Aborigines had for their country has come down to the interlopers, the modern Australians, from this Dreamtime. It is a special sentiment for the bush and its animals. Australian poetry and literature, especially children's literature, and many of her early (perhaps least sophisticated) movies feature the animals of Australia. There is a special feeling about things Australian: everything *is* different. The animals have pouches (and do other strange things), the trees don't lose their leaves in fall (and those that shed leaves do it in summer, and others shed their bark instead). And the birds laugh. We will never know whether or not this reverence for Australian wildlife comes from the aboriginal Dreamtime. It may simply be that the richness of the wildlife forces on people, no matter what their origin, a feeling of wonder and appreciation of things natural. However, if we are to judge by the way the first settlers treated the land, one must conclude that somewhere along the way, the more sensitive individuals began to see that the basically gentle aboriginals had it right.

The Wonder of Australia: Her Animals

In the Dreamtime there were two men, Mirram the kangaroo and Warreen the wombat. Mirram loved to enjoy life to the full, always jumping about, never bothering to build his house. He loved to sleep under the stars at night, and enjoyed the open spaces. "One day a storm will come and you will have nowhere to hide," warned Warreen, who spent all his time digging his house underground. And he was right. One day a fierce storm came, the rain driving down so hard it hurt Mirram's back. He pleaded with Warreen to let him in his house.

But Warreen said, "There is no room. You should have built your own house instead of having a good time."

The storm grew worse. Mirram pleaded and pleaded. Warreen cried, "Go away, Go away! Stop waking me up!"

Mirram became angry. "Surely you would not leave me outside to die?" he yelled, and at the same time lifted a huge stone and angrily threw it on Warreen's head. Warreen's head was flattened.

"You have learned your lesson," said Mirram. "You and your children and your children's children will forever have flat heads to remind you of your unkindness towards me."

Warreen said nothing. He planned revenge. One day soon after, he saw Mirram happily hunting a possum. He lifted back his spear and thrust it with all his might. It lodged fast in Mirram's buttocks and would not come out. "Let this be a lesson to you," spoke Warreen. "Your children and your children's children will always remember your cruelty."

And to this day the kangaroo must hop along, its huge tail making a loud thud when it hits the ground with each jump.

And the wombat lives in the ground, coming out only at night because it is ashamed of its flat head.

Of the marsupials, the kangeroo and the koala are the most famous. When you return from your trips to Oz, we guarantee someone will ask if you've seen a kangaroo or a koala. These animals are virtually synonymous with the word "Australia." Among the marsupials, the mother carries the young in a pouch-like fold of skin attached to her abdomen. When a marsupial is born, it must crawl up the mother's fur to the safety and warmth of the pouch—quite a long way for a joey (baby kangaroo), which measures only five centimeters (about 2 inches). Once there, it nurses and grows. Almost all marsupials live in Australia. Millions of years ago, marsupials were common all over the world. They gradually died out, and now the oppossum is the only known marsupial that does not consider Australia its natural habitat. The kangaroo, koala, wombat, and the wallaby (kind of a mini kangaroo), are all marsupials.

Kangaroos and Wallabies

Australians keep kangaroos and wallabies as pets, eat their meat, and use their fur for coats, right? Well, not exactly. Except under special circumstances, in Australia it's against the law to keep kangaroos as pets. They are protected in most parts of Australia, where they roam quite freely, and can be observed from short distances if one is quiet and still. There is a golf course in one of our favorite Australian towns in southern Victoria, Anglesea, where kangaroos roam freely over the course. Beleagured golfers imagine the 'roos sniggering at them as they try to tee off.

Kangaroos come in red and grey varieties, and are most frequently found in the dry forests of eastern and southwestern Australia. Their extremely powerful (and dangerous if you get too close) legs enable them to leap large distances, as much as 40 feet. Wallabies are very similar in appearance to kangaroos, except that they are generally about half the size, and almost always a mousey grey color. In the north, kangaroos have been hunted for their hides and meat. The controlled culling of kangaroos today is highly controversial. Farmers find them a nuisance because there is very little grass and they think that it should be for sheep and cattle. But there is concern that particular species of kangaroos may die out some day, especially the big red.

Koalas

Those cuddly things so many kids adore, koalas, are appealing, yet rarely accessible to man. The cute creatures are commonly referred to as koala bears. However, koalas are marsupials, and are in no way related to the bear family. If you drive past a "koala crossing" sign, don't get too excited; koalas are shy animals. They like to stay in the treetops of eastern Australia. At night, they roam in search of leaves and fresh shoots of a special variety of eucalyptus tree; they seldom drink water. Chances are you will not sight a koala in the wild, except in a nature reserve. A visit to Philip Island will virtually ensure a sighting (see Chapter 7), and, of course, there are plenty in Australian zoos.

Dingo, the Mystery Dog

Though it looks more ordinary than any of Australia's animals, the dingo is probably the most mysterious. It is a dangerous dog about the size and coloring of a golden labrador. More precisely, the dingo resembles a dog in all ways but two: it doesn't bark and it is quite aggressive. It was in Australia long before any European settlers or "imported" European animals like the rabbit or fox. Ever since the Azaria case (see Chapters 3, 4 and 9), Aussies have been especially fascinated by the dingo and its powers. Dingoes roam the outback, and most will not do any harm unless they are provoked. There is a special strain of them on Fraser Island (see Chapter 10).

Strange Birds

Many Americans have not heard of the emu, even though it is the second largest bird in the world. It resembles an ostrich, with long, powerful legs, and tiny, useless wings. Although the emu is incapable of flying, it can run up to 30 miles per hour. Its kick could rival that of any horse, mule or kangaroo. It lives in open plains, away from the more settled areas. An easy way to find out what an emu looks like is to look at the Australian coat of arms on all Australian dollar bills.

Australia's strangest sounding bird is the kookaburra, known to Americans from a familiar song of childhood:

> Kookaburra sits in the old gum tree,
> Merry, merry, king of the bush is he,
> Laugh, kookaburra, laugh, kookaburra,
> Gay your life must be.

If you are moved to break into song when in Australia, a word of caution: Australians sing this song a little differently. First, kookaburra is pronounced *cook-uh-bahra*, not *kue-ka-bare-a*. Second, don't make up extra verses about gumdrops, etc. (i.e., "counting all the gumdrops he could see"). A gum tree is the Australian term for the eucalyptus tree. It is a normal, all-natural tree, and it does not grow anything even remotely resembling chewing gum, or gumdrops, or candy. It has long, thin leaves (about 10 cm), and sheds its bark. Eucalyptus trees abound in Oz, and many animals eat their leaves and shoots. Aussies love to burn gum tree leaves and bark for their delightful aroma.

Just what is a kookaburra now that we know it lives in gum trees and laughs? It is white, grey, and brown, and it lives just as the song describes. It makes a sound that sounds like "Hoo-hoo-hooo-hoo-Ha-ha-ha-hahaha!!!!" The omnipresent cackling of the kookaburra is a sound which Aussies grow to love. Many kookaburras will become quite tame. We have had sausages stolen right off the grill by kookaburras! (This is understandable, since they live on small animals, their favorite being snakes.)

Platypus

Easily the strangest animal, the platypus, to Americans, might be living proof that things Down Under are a little bit wacked. It has been called a living fossil because it resembles many long-extinct animals all combined in one. Zoologists have trouble classifying this break-the-mold creature. It has the characteristics of a monotreme—that is, it is a mammal which lays eggs. However, the platypus suckles its young, and it also has a rubber-like duck-bill and a beaver-like tail. Males use poison in their hind paws to fend away enemies. Imagine eating your own weight of slugs and insects every day! That's what the platypus does. It lives in the fresh water of eastern Australia and Tasmania, but cannot breathe underwater and must resurface every few minutes. Don't set your heart on seeing a platypus in any Australian stream. And don't promise to bring one home for the kids. Platypuses are rarely sighted by tourists, largely because they are nocturnal animals and very timid. Incredibly, they were not a protected species until 1912. All major zoos now have a platypus display. We visit two in this book: the Melbourne Zoo and the Taronga Park Zoo in Sydney. Unfortunately, it has proven very difficult to keep platypuses alive in captivity, and next to impossible to breed them. As of 1988, there were only six scientists in all of Australia studying these rare and exotic animals. (See the excellent article in *Australian Geographic*, October/December, 1988.)

Another ubiquitous Australian animal is the sheep. This may not be too exciting to an American who sees them all the time. Well, even though sheep do not originate in Australia, nor are they rare anywhere else, they represent an important part of Aussie culture. Introduced to Australia early in the 19th century, sheep rapidly became an important part of Australia's growing economy. Many rural Aussies still make their livings from sheep farming, as the climate is ideal. And a significant part of Aussie folklore and songs is composed of stories from the sheep shearers of old. The most famous song is, "Click go the shears, boys. Click, Click, Click!"

The Land and Its Colors

The visitor's first view of Australia will be from the air, most likely approaching Sydney or Melbourne. The first sight of the great continent can be a bit of a letdown, we'll have to admit. No matter what the season of the year, the land looks dull; the browns seem drab, the greens a flat olive green.

The early settlers had an entirely different first view of the land from across the water, usually surf. It was a land slung low, without major mountains. Their perceptions were also colored by their experience of the rich green of the well watered north of both Europe and America. (It is true, however, that California and other parts of the West have a close

similarity to parts of Australia's drier center and western
coast. Much of California these days also looks like Australia
because of the eucalyptus trees. One of Australia's poets,
A. D. Hope, has described Australia as "A Nation of trees,
drab green and desolate grey."

The traveler, especially if used to the eastern coast of the
U.S. or northern Europe, will miss the rich green of spring.
The green of Australia's eucalyptus trees is not bright, or rich
as are the colors of many deciduous trees of the Northern
Hemisphere. Rather, the leaves of a gum tree are a deep
bluish green, usually darker in color on the undersides of the
leaves. The upper surfaces of the leaves, which turn following
the sun, glisten and shine, reflecting the light and protecting
the tree from the relentless heat. Of course, one cannot see
this from the air—a visit to the Australian bush is necessary.
The lack of richness in color is more a matter of what one is
used to. Australians love the colors. It is not so much the
hues, though, but the light of the country. The atmosphere
seems so clear (away from the cities, that is), the light so
brilliant, that bright color would frankly be blinding and out
of place.

A walk through the Australian bush is highly recommended—in fact as often as possible! The leaves of gum trees
have their own special rustling sound because they are fairly
hard and brittle. The gentle stirring creates an eerie background for the sounds of the bush. There's no mistaking that
these sounds are what convey the impression of being in an
exotic place—and that is truly what the Australian bush is.
One should try to take a walk just after it has rained because
this is when the trees release the strongest aromas of eucalyptus oils. Breathe in deeply . . . it is an experience one will
never forget.

Of course, there are many different kinds of Australian
bush. We'll visit these in later chapters. The wild flowers one
finds in the bush are truly unique and abundant.

Gum Trees. There are over a thousand different species of
eucalyptus trees in Australia, but they are all called gum
trees, or just plain gums. One can recognize all these trees by
the aroma of eucalyptus they exude. Usually, most gum trees

have leaves which are shiny on one side and dull on the other. Most are long, thin leaves, and tend to grow in clumps on long slender branches, although there are many bushy species as well. There are also many gum trees that are called flowering gums which in spring are ablaze with bright red and pink flowers. Along with gum trees are wattles of many different varieties, all of which are easily identified in the spring by their bright yellow, pin-cushion-like flowers.

The Emptiness of Australia

Another accurate impression when approaching Australia from the air is her emptiness. As Hope noted again, "She is the last of the lands, the emptiest . . .,"

There are vast areas of space with nothing in them. On the east coast, at least there is the Great Divide, a strip of small mountains that runs from North to South parallel to the coastline. They are mostly covered with Australian eucalyptus forests. But after one flies past these mountains towards the center of Australia, they quickly give way to a flat expanse of red and brown tablelands and later rocky flats with occasional scrub. The forbidding nature of the interior can be readily perceived. The emptiness and the desolate scrub of much of the land have played an important part in the history of Australia and the development of the national character. Certain elements are embedded in the Australian psyche just as the Bill of Rights seems to be inscribed in the brain cells of every American baby.

The Sun in Australia

Australia's sun is relentless, brilliant and sacred. Poets have called Australia a "sunburnt country," and this could not be more true. Australians, many of them, virtually worship the sun. Sunbathing is a practice that all people, especially young people, feel they must do, and a tan year round is something to be carefully cultivated. The dangers to the visitor, though, are great. We recommend very careful and strong precautions because one can get burned easily, often without knowing it, under the Australian sun. This applies particularly on the beaches where the sun reflects from the sand and the water. You should know that Australians have the highest rate of

skin cancer in the world. While this need not worry the
tourist too much, since that high rate results from early and
constant burning in childhood, nevertheless the tourist can
lose some valuable time in considerable pain with a bad dose
of sunburn.

We speak from experience, often unable to take our own
advice. Even the most "tannable" of us got sunburned after
two hours, through 25 SPF sunblock. The days that one can
be tricked are those windy blustery days in spring when the
sun shines brightly, but the wind is cool. Don't be fooled. It
may feel cool or even cold on the beach in this weather. But
unless one has taken precautions, either with a sunscreen or
protective clothing and head gear (although it is possible to be
burned through light clothing), one can return home at the
end of a day on the beach, and suddenly, upon retiring or
entering the shower, discover skin that is fiercely burned.

Speaking of the sun, one must also consider its central
place in Australian cultural life, particularly in art. It took the
English settlers a long time to adapt to the Australian light.
Early paintings by these artists tried to render Australian
countryside with the same coloring and textures of John Constable. The result was paintings that bore little resemblance to
the Australian landscape. It was not until late in the 19th
century that Australian artists themselves managed to portray
the light, the simple and harsh contours, and the expanse of
Australia's landscape. The Victorian Gallery in Melbourne
offers an excellent chronological display of the development
of Australian art (see Chapter 6). It was not until the 1950s that
aboriginal painters (the most famous Albert Namatjira) produced simple landscapes of Australia's hot interior, rendered
in delicate water colors, with fantastic hues of blues, purples
and reds. These have become a trademark of the country near
Ayers Rock (reputed to be the oldest and biggest rock in the
world—see Chapter 9).

Many Australian painters and artists left Australia for
France and Italy to learn their art, seeking inspiration from
the great masters of Western art. Many returned (some did
not, such as Leonard French) only to find that the quality of
the light back home was far clearer and more sparkling than

any they found in Europe. The result was a strong penchant in Australian landscape painting for light hues and streaming sunlight, and only more recently a tendency to stark and desolate scenes, and angular buildings made up of flat masses of rusty colors.

Water in Australia

There is an amusing poem that describes Australia's uncommon—and embarrassing—relationship to water, or the lack of it:

The place, my Lord, is much like Gideon's fleece
The second time he laid it on the ground
For by the will of God it has remained
Bone-dry itself, with water all around.

Yes, as a wheel that's driven in the ruts
It has a wet rim where the people clot
Like mud; and though they praise the inner spaces,
When asked to go themselves, they'd rather not.
—James McAuley, *Under Aldebaran*, 1946

Australia, a huge land mass, dry as a bone from the west to the east is surrounded by water. The people cluster on the well–watered edge of the east and southeastern coast. More than four-fifths of Australia's population lives in this narrow strip of land that has water and fertile soil. Of these, though, some 90% live in the four big cities of Sydney, Melbourne, Adelaide and Brisbane. We find a strange anomaly here. The bulk of Australians are urban or suburban dwellers, yet their cultural heritage, the very fiber of their character, is derived from and dependent on the lifestyle of the lone explorer and survivor in the outback. This is, of course, the great Australian myth. Ask any Aussie on the street of Melbourne whether he thinks of the outback each day, whether he gains strength to carry on his life each day by the idea of the great Australian bushman, and he will wonder what on earth you are talking about. Cultural myths remain unconscious. They must be resurrected and generated by artists, novelists and poets. So far, the only imagery of the Australian as urban dweller to successfully seep into the cultural life of Australia is the "ocker" who drinks beer and watches football (and sometimes cricket—more on this later).

In part, the water problem has been solved in the interior of Australia by the use of artesian bores, which tap the extensive underground river system. However, this is only a partial answer to the problem; the area needing water is so vast (about three-quarters the size of the continental United States), and the soil itself is of extremely poor quality. Since most of Australia's center was once an inland sea, there is the danger that with constant irrigation or watering, the salt will rise to the surface and become concentrated, making the soil even less usable.

Time in Australia

Eleanor Dark, one of Australia's greatest early novelists, called Australia the timeless land. The land, indeed, is timeless—its age only truly understood by the aboriginal lore. Many of the rock formations and outcrops in Australia's center are incredibly old—we're talking millions of years. Yet time can, and must, be measured in a different way by the traveler. There is never enough of it.

In a country where distance from one tourist attraction to another is measured in thousands of miles, with nothing inbetween but sheer distance, the challenge of deciding what to see is perhaps the most difficult task for the tourist in Australia. Yet one long trip may be necessary if the visitor is to try to gain a semblance of the Australian outback. Otherwise, one's tour may end up being largely a tour of big cities, which, let's face it, are getting more and more the same the world over. So, while most of one's travel in Australia will be up and down the east coast, there may be a few trips that are well worth the investment, into the center, or away from the urban strip. There are train rides that are really worth the effort: on the *Ghan* from Adelaide to Alice Springs, the *India Pacific*, or the *Queenslander* from Cairns to Brisbane across the Nullabor from Adelaide to Perth. We recommend at least taking one of these, for they offer a chance to share a little of the awesome challange faced by some of Australia's great (though in some cases foolhardy) explorers. These men (perhaps the only great men in Australia's popular history) prob-

ably set the rock on which the Australian's love of travel now
rests.

The Explorers

The first penal settlement at Sydney Cove was shut off for
25 years by the Blue Mountains (so called because of their
distinctive blue tinge, see Chapter 8). The mountains seemed
impassable, and as well, the English were basically sailors,
not landlubbers. It is no surprise that much of the early
exploration of Australia was done by sea. Matthew Flinders
circumnavigated Australia and charted its entire coastline.
He, along with George Bass, established that Van Dieman's
Land (Tasmania) was in fact not joined to Australia. It was not
until 1813 that the Blue Mountains were crossed by Lawson,
Blaxland and Wentworth, and the rich Bathurst plains were
discovered. After that, during the next several decades, most
of Australia's eastern river systems were explored.

But the biggest mystery still remained for some 30 years:
what was in the center of Australia? A huge inland lake
perhaps? In 1844 Ludwig Leichardt managed to travel over-
land from Sydney to the Gulf of Carpentaria (the North), and
in an attempt to cross Australia from Sydney to Perth, his
entire party perished—disappeared and were never seen
again. In 1844 Sturt set out from Adelaide and managed to get
as far as the present border between the Northern Territory
and Queensland, but lack of water and food forced him to
turn back. So, the country had still not been crossed from
south to north. Finally in 1860 the Victorian and South Australian governments began to compete for the honor. The
doomed excursion by Burke and Wills (perhaps the explorers
best remembered by Australians, about whom there are
many jokes and popular expressions) was made in the summer of 1860–61. Both Burke and Wills made it from
Melbourne to the Gulf of Carpentaria, but failed to make the
return. They died presumably of exposure and thirst somewhere near Mount Hopeless.

In 1843 Edmund Kennedy led a major expedition to explore
the Cape York Peninsular (northeastern point of Australia),
planning to meet up with a supply ship at the end of his trek.

It was a doomed expedition pretty much from the start when the large wagons were bogged down in swamps. They also met hostile aboriginals, missed supply drops, and generally succumbed to the rugged and harsh terrain. Nine of the 13 men in the party died; Kennedy was speared by an Aborigine just 20 miles from his destination.

Edward Eyre, after various attempts to reach the center of Australia, turned his attention to a trek from Adelaide to the western Australian port of Albany. (If you look at a map, you will see that this is an enormous trek over virtually barren desert.) Food and water were non-existent. His companion Baxter was killed by their aboriginal guides. But luck smiled on Eyre, as he chanced upon a French whaling vessel in Rossiter Bay. He thus managed to complete his journey. To-day the modern Adelaide-Perth railway, the longest stretch of straight railway line in the world, now covers much of his route. The large (often missing) lake in Australia's center has also been named after him: Lake Eyre (saltwater). (There is a colorful article with a detailed map about Eyre's explorations in the *Australian Geographic*, Oct.–Dec., 1989.)

Exploration continues. There are still parts of Australia so isolated and so uninviting that they have not been explored— or at least Europeans have not set foot there for 100 years or more. Expeditions are still carried on, one recently partly retracing Kennedy's route.

CHAPTER 3

Australians as They Used to Be

Discovery and Settlement of Australia

If you have traveled in Italy or Spain, drifted through their
dank churches and crowded galleries, you have experienced
the power of Christendom. For many centuries the Church
was the sole source of knowledge in the Western world.
When explorers in the 16th and 17th centuries finally began to
break loose from the geographic confinements of the Christian world, they were unable to break loose from its preoccupation with evil. The Inquisition pursued evil and found it
everywhere—even, not coincidentally, in strange places like
Central and South America that turned out to be full of gold,
spices and other commodities cherished by the world of
Christendom. Indeed, it is little wonder that evil was found so
easily, since it cohabited in the form of greed with the search
for new lands where beaches were said to be bathed in gold.
This land was the fabled *Terra Incognita*, first spoken of by

Ptolemy in 300 B.C. Fear of the unknown was slowly chal-
lenged by the lascivious demand for riches.

In the 17th century explorers of the Dutch East India Company were sent on many expeditions. The most famous was
that of Abel Tasman who discovered Van Dieman's Land, now
known as Tasmania. Others came from Spain and Portugal
(Magellan and later Torres). They sighted various parts of
Australia's dry western coast, only to report back that they
had found a land of depressing sameness, inhabited by
wretched people hardly even worth saving in the Christian
sense. It seemed a land of inhospitable coastline and poor
soil. And no gold.

The great English explorer William Dampier reinforced this
early vision of Australia describing it as destitute of water or
trees that bore fruit, as well as animals, save what we now call
the dingo. In a famous passage he wrote of the Aborigines in
his log of 1687: "They have no houses or skin garments . . . or
fruits of the earth . . . they differ but little from brutes."

This description of Australia remained the dominant view
of the land until it was settled by white men. In fact, it may
have been this image of Australia that unwittingly caused it to
be settled in the way it was, as a place of punishment for
convicts. It was beyond the wildest stretches of imagination to
regard the country as in any way beautiful, a potential garden
of Eden or land of refuge. Unlike the other new world, America, Australia was not settled by those seeking to establish a
new life, one of hope and refuge from tyranny. In contrast,
Australia was first settled with the absolute intention of making it a place of tyranny and anything but a refuge.

The emergence of Australian society from its origins as a
police state, created out of the bodies, lives and souls of
convicts must be one of the most amazing human and social
experiments of all time. Certainly it was an idea to which the
English in the 18th century never gave the slightest consid-
eration.

Children in Australia's schools are taught that the
discoverer of Australia was Captain James Cook. On April 29,
1770, he dropped anchor in Botany Bay, a small inlet just
south of Australia's largest city today, Sydney. Captain Cook

had on board Joseph Banks, a botanist who made extensive studies of the fauna and flora of Australia. In contrast to other explorers of Australia, Cook reported back to England that there was rich black soil, excellent for supporting crops. His was a rosier picture. The conflicting views of Australia—at once rich and at the same time harsh and punishing—provided a perfect political scenario that allowed Australia to become a dumping ground for social trash while politicians talked themselves and others into believing that such a convict settlement could become self-sufficient by working the land.

While there were many reasons for the final selection of Botany Bay as the first convict settlement for England's criminals, one thing is sure: with this settlement the first deep wound to Australia's collective psyche was embedded in her fiber, the tyranny of distance. It took some six months for the journey from England to Australia. The use of Australia as a convict dumping ground meant criminals were out of sight and out of mind. The ills and suffering subsequently reported by officers and convicts alike could be disregarded easily; the convicts deserved to suffer anyway, and at the same time they were better off there than crowded into the rotting hulks of ships in England's harbors which were used as makeshift prisons. Certainly deportation to Australia was better than being hanged for stealing.

We relate this because Australia's penal history helps explain much about the Australian character, the way Australians view the English, indeed, the rest of the northern world. However, we must be careful in drawing comparisons here. North America is part of the New World too. But the difference between the history of the two countries is dramatic. America had her revolution against the British—yet historical and social conditions were such that Australia had much more to revolt about. Australians are perhaps a little embarrassed at this, and sometimes try to elevate a small uprising, called the Eureka Stockade, to the level of revolution (of which more later). In actual fact, Australia still remains a member of Britain's Commonwealth of Nations. It even accepted (not without difficulty) the sacking of Prime

Minister Whitlam in 1974 by the Governor General Sir John Kerr (the Queen's representative). Australia has not shed her official and legal ties to England.

Australians, therefore, have become acutely sensitive to what the English think of them. And the English view of Australia has been something like Professor Higgins's view of Eliza Doolittle in the musical *My Fair Lady:* a coarse, wayward child, disobedient, foul-mouthed, verging on the primitive. As an Oxford professor observed of Australians in 1958: "To hear an intelligent, critical, sardonic conversation in an accent which, in England, one associates with near-illiteracy, is a startling experience."

So it is worth remembering that, for the first 100 years or so of its short history, Australia was an actual police state, ruled by a military dictator (and at times a military *junta*), appointed by the reigning English monarch.

Liberty in Australia

Somewhere, somehow, this unholy mix of prison guards, military police, convicts and middle class Englishmen (who came later as free settlers) turned into a society. It was not just any society, but one in which there was an overwhelming feeling of personal freedom. It is of great significance that Australian society essentially emerged after the French and American revolutions. Liberty was to many of the convicts a concrete, tangible commodity, not an abstract symbol for revolution as it was in France. Yet once the convicts obtained liberty—whether through a ticket of leave (the first use of "parole" as we know it today), or having served that sentence—the question of liberty and freedom took on a new significance.

This particularly applied to the "currency," the offspring of the convicts who, unlike the children of slaves, were born free. There arose in the early 18th century a deep social division between those stained by convict family and those who were free settlers. The free settlers, largely petty bourgeois who would be insignificant on the social ladder in England, were able to command with their newly found affluence the respect due the upper class. They were treated far more favorably in terms of land grants and other privileges than the children of the convicts.

It was out of the very feeling of being free that the indigenous currency developed a sense of owning Australia, seeing the free settlers from England as the interlopers. As well, many currency and ex-convicts (called emancipists) worked and accumulated large fortunes and thriving businesses. Their power could not be ignored. Many of the large land holdings granted the free settlers could simply not be run without the know-how of the locals. Thus there developed a certain class conflict, one might say, or at least a resentment of one class towards the other. The free demanded respect, which they certainly did not get. For if nothing else developed as typical of the Australian character at that time, and lasting to the present, there was the disdain of "side"—airs and graces put on by anyone, not just the upper class. The Australian character became one that was sullen, resentful, and belligerent. Today the sullenness has become a peculiarly quiet manner; the resentment an inferiority complex; and the belligerence, tempered with a penetrating sense of humor, a characteristic that borders on the insulting.

Anyway, such was the distinction between the currency and the free, that one observer was moved to note:

> It is sometimes said that in Australia there are no class distinctions. It would probably be truer to say that in no country in the world are there such strong class distinctions in proportion to the actual amount of distinction between the two "classes."

This English observer went on to note, though, that Australian workers showed a distinct lack of deference to their employers, "who have grown to tolerate and perhaps in some cases secretly rather to like [them]. . . ."

While we are talking about freedom and the formation of the Australian character, we should pause for a moment to examine an important rebellion that occurred in the early colonial time, for in many ways it highlights what is perhaps one of the most important roots of the modern Australian lifestyle. It was called the Rum Rebellion and occurred against none other than William Bligh, the notorious captain of the *Bounty*. Bligh was governor of the penal colony from 1806 to 1808. A group of officers had banded together and cornered the rum trade. Their monopoly gave them immense power over pricing and many other aspects of colonial life, for rum was perhaps the most prized commodity. Those who suffered from this monopoly were the people who had little money and no power. Bligh sided with them, seeing both the injustice of the rum trade and of the opinion that trading in rum was not appropriate for officers of the realm. On January 26, 1808, the Rum Corps with band playing and banners flying, marched on Government House and arrested Bligh who, some wags say, was hiding under his bed. The leader of the Rum Rebellion was John Macarthur, an accomplished man in his own right. Macarthur's punishment for this treason was that he was returned to England for a period, but never punished. He acquired vast holdings of farmland in Australia and is credited with having originated Australia's fabulously successful merino sheep farms.

England was prompted by this brazen act to at last take the government of Australia seriously and the somewhat more reasonable government of Macquarie followed. But it was during his reign that the problems of class distinction became acute. Macquarie, perhaps more than any other ruler of Australia to that time, recognized the uncommon industriousness and ingenuity of the convicts and former convicts. Those who were not so stained resented the attention and access to his offices that he gave convicts and their currency.

It is against this background of late colonial times—in fact possibly during most of the 19th century—that snobbishness and pseudo-class distinctions were mixed with a belligerence toward authority and those who claimed to be part of it, a denial of status in any of its forms, and a resentment toward foreigners of any kind, but especially the English. Particularly when working the land, it was easy for the indigenous Aussies to demonstrate to the ignorant Englishmen just how little they knew about farming and surviving in the Australian bush, which required special skills and knowledge that were not to be acquired in England.

Today, the foreigner will note a certain underlying belligerence among Australians. It is not a hostility to each other or
to outsiders, but rather towards authority. This is easily understandable given the origins of Australia as a police state.
Australians resent being told what to do by anyone. They are
suspicious of those in authority—and great historical figures
are hardly revered at all. The contradiction is that the society
is essentially socialist in outlook, and expects the government
to protect the security of all individuals, which requires that
the authority of government be exercised frequently. The
visitor will find dealing with Australia's bureaucracies a
strange experience. On the one hand they can be very courteous and helpful, even caring. But there is a strain of of-
ficiousness that comes with a view, on the part of the public
official, that he/she holds a position of great importance and
that the government knows what is best. Questioning a public
official is, therefore, a risky undertaking. This imperious attitude will be justified to the foreigner through an excessive
pride in the Australian way of doing things. It is an attitude of
"Well, you might do that in America, but we don't do that sort
of thing here."

These observations apply mainly to the federal government. The visitor is unlikely to come into contact directly with
state or local governments which tend to be less formal, and
staffed by that ubiquitous Australian middle class. Members
live a quiet suburban life, comfortable, unperturbed and
focused on buying a house and two cars, and raising a small
family, enjoying weekend sports, and taking holidays.

Equality in Australia

It is puzzling to some that out of this early preoccupation
with class distinctions arose an ethos, more or less real, depending on the historian, of egalitarianism. One ideal that all
Australians say they cherish is that everyone is equal. By this
Australians mean *really equal*, not as in America where lip
service is paid. Australians really believe that people are
more equal in Australia, no matter what yardstick (whether
salaries, status, privileges, etc.) is used, than in any other
country.

The spheres in which this egalitarian ethos dominates is in everyday life and social relations. Airs and graces are not tolerated. People readily address each other by first names and people, even strangers, will openly chat in any chance meeting place. If you try to impress an Aussie with your superior knowledge, contacts or whatever, you will quickly find yourself the butt of wry, insulting humor, called in Australia "knocking." In fact, Australians go one step further with this and often make fun of themselves as part of this egalitarian mentality. Thus, egalitarianism to Australians is more a way of dealing with each other, rather than how much money one has, or how big a house one lives in. There are exceptions, however. Universities, for example, tend to be much more formal and exclusive than in America. There is a strong tradition of private schooling which fosters the English ways of social intercourse and more formal address, uniforms and the like.

Tipping is an excellent example of a practice where the Australian egalitarian attitude presents problems. One has to be very careful tipping. Many take it as an insult and refuse a tip with some annoyance. "We don't do that sort of thing here," they will say. As American hotels spread throughout Australia, though, this practice is unfortunately changing. The main reason for the antagonism toward tipping is the egalitarian ethos, but there is also pride in the Australian basic wage, a minimum wage set by the Commonwealth Government. It is something like two to three times the minimum wage in the United States.

In theory, the idea of egalitarianism extends to the Aborigines, but in actuality this has been rarely practiced. Given the enormous disadvantage that the Aborigines have to begin with, it would seem that something more than equality is needed; perhaps a cultural change.

It is a strange anomaly that in actual formal working conditions, Australian women fare far better than their American counterparts. Equal pay has been recognized in Australia for many years, and women receive very generous maternity leave (men receive paternity leave, as well). But a woman's place is a special one in Australian society, which cannot be understood until we talk about one other major Australian trait: mateship.

Fraternity in Australia

There is a continuing controversy among Australian historians and writers as to whether the "mateship" ethos is real or just a myth. Russell Ward is perhaps the most persuasive historian who argues that the mateship ethic has several different roots, but that its primary one is in the outback. Ward goes further and suggests that Australia's endemic socialism can be traced directly to this mateship ethos. Whether or not this is true, we do not know . . . especially as many would object even to the suggestion that Australia is a socialist society. Though in comparison to the United States, it certainly has many trappings of socialism: a well established pension program, a national health scheme, a minimum wage, government monopoly over utilities, transportation and communications, and extensive welfare programs, particularly for the unemployed. This is all the more puzzling when one considers that the dominant political party of this century has been conservative and only in the most recent decade has the Labor Party held sway.

The mateship ideal originates with the demands of outback life. In Australia during early settlement and development of the land, small homesteads, such as those established in America's westward settlement, were not usual or possible. Rather, because of the necessity to farm huge portions of land in order to support a reasonable herd of cattle, fewer people were owner-farmers, and the distance between each farm was enormous. The majority of people in the frontier, or outback as it was called in Australia, were therefore actual laborers, not owners. These men moved from one station or spread to another, offering their skills and labors. Comprehending the isolation and loneliness of this life is difficult. Because there were fewer owners, so the argument goes, unlike the Wild West of the U.S., rabid individualism did not develop. Due to the harsh and lonely conditions of the outback, it was necessary for the itinerant workers to depend on each other, so they developed a collective ethos, a spirit of mateship.

The second important factor that fueled the mateship ethos were the simple facts of convict life. These men were in the same lot, equally and collectively oppressed by their jailers. There were also hardly any women (or at least for many years until well into the 19th century, men outnumbered women by at least 2 to 1), nor were there many families. The outback was *lived in* primarily by convicts and former convicts, and a few of their children. There was little to compete for, thus competitive individualism did not develop. Loneliness virtually forced the men to look to each other not only for help, but for social survival. Indeed, it was commonly thought at the time that to be a shepherd—the loneliest of occupations in the bush, for the weeks and months at a time tending cattle, sitting and sleeping under a makeshift lean-to as primitive as that of the Aborigines—led these fellows to the point of madness. It was the lowest paying job, and taken only as a last resort. Perhaps, some say, it is from these shepherds that the Australians developed their manner of speaking—with chin almost on the chest, as though mumbling to themselves. Certainly, some observers have suggested that Australians as a whole are a distinctly silent and noncommunicative lot, as noted by Brian Fitzpatrick, a distinguished Australian historian:

> But perhaps the majority (i.e., male) Australian approach to articulation is best indicated by a generalization: utterance is better not done at all; but if it is done . . . it were well it were slowly and flatly and expressionlessly, to betoken the subject, any subject, is hardly worth talking about.

If this observation is true, it is only true to a point, or at least, it is compensated for by one other aspect of mateship that dominates all others: the rowdy, raucous extremely male behavior in an Aussie pub.

After months of isolation in the wilderness, the workers were paid. They would ride for several days to the nearest town, and spend it all on—yes—booze. Australian pubs quickly developed a character of their own. At first modeled after the English pubs, they gradually became larger and larger public bars, accentuated by their own distinctive architecture: low roofs of galvanized iron rising to a point, sweeping verandas surrounding the entire structure; profuse decorations of fine lacey wrought iron. But the wrought iron was the only fine thing about them—inside they were virtually all male, coarse dens of drunkenness.

To experience authentic Aussie pub life is a must for every tourist. Would one visit Tahiti and miss the ritual feast of the islanders? Or visit Italy without experiencing its restaurants? The Australian pub—the authentic pub, that is—is part of Australian cultural life. There is much to be learned about Australians in these places, as we will see. The Aussie pub has become a kind of idealized institution of mateship. They have changed tremendously over the last ten years. But what they stand for in Aussie mythology remains essentially the same: the focal point of mateship. The rituals of beer drinking are the Australian way of denying class distinctions of any kind. None are recognized in the idealized pub. Here everyone is equal, and it's mateship that counts above all else. The popular novels of Nino Cullota (*They're a Weird Mob*) published in the fifties are hilariously funny renditions of this mateship ideal, describing the difficulties a foreigner (in this case an Italian immigrant) has in understanding the folkways that are attached to it.

The Good Life

Australia's standard of living is one of the highest in the world. The percentage of home ownership is probably the highest, certainly higher than in the United States. This is a remarkable achievement given the beginnings of Australian society as we have described them. What is the good life in Australia? This is a very special view of life, and makes Australia's achievements all the more remarkable. Australians value leisure probably more than any people of the developed northern world, in contrast to America, where, in order to make it to the good life—that is, a house, two cars, etc., etc.—the work ethic is paramount. The majority of Americans work long hours, and take relatively few and short vacations. Not so in Australia. Australia has more public holidays than any other country. The pace is nowhere as keen or intense as in the U.S., not even in her biggest cities of Melbourne or Sydney. Everywhere one hears that wonderfully casual expression, "She'll be right, mate," that is to say, "Give it a go;" but if things don't work out, well, there's another day tomorrow." Achievements are simply not of that high order. It's wonderful to achieve and to succeed, but it's as good or better to take it easy, and not let the rat race get to one. Weekends and long weekends therefore abound. Australian beaches and sporting grounds are almost always full and in use. In fact, there is only one aspect in which the Australians are fiercely competitve and admire achievement, and even here they show a special coolness in their dedication: sport.

The national passion in Australia is sport of any kind, though primarily footy (football, three varieties, Australian Rules, Rugby and Soccer); in the summer, it is cricket. The television is dominated by these, plus tennis and swimming and golf in season. The passion is coupled with one other— perhaps even more pervasive, and with deep roots in Australia's past—gambling, especially on horse racing.

Australia's love of horses is understandable given their importance to the settlement and survival in the bush. Physical achievements were early valued, and these are well expressed in Australian folk tales and songs. The movie *The Man from Snowy River*, though somewhat based on the formula for an American Western, shows the eminence of horses and masculine accomplishments, especially as the mystique of the bush is made part of them. Australia's love of horse racing and breeding of great horses continues today. There are several important horse races in Australia, of which the most famous is the Melbourne Cup, which demands a national holiday. The movie *Phar Lap* depicts Australia's reverence for a great horse. The most revered item in the Victorian museum for decades was the stuffed Phar Lap—sought out by visitors even before they went to look at the dinosaurs.

But where did Australia's love of gambling come from? We think that the discovery of gold in 1851 had a lot to do with it. Gold was a mixed blessing to the young and growing economy of Australia. It made an already severe shortage of labor even more scarce. Life on the gold fields was tough and primitive. The establishment worried that the complete breakdown in law and order was imminent. Draconian laws (the Master and Servants Act) were passed in an effort to prevent employees from forsaking their employers. But these laws were useless, since the constables, police and other officials went along with everyone else to try their luck. This kind of crowded free-for-all life of the gold fields contrasted drastically with the calm life of the pastoral society.

It did, however, provide in a relatively painless way much needed capital formation for Australia. She was able to develop her economy more easily when mining fees became a lucrative source of income for the government.

The easy gold ran out by 1854. By then there were few miners left who could afford to pay the hefty license fee of 30 shillings a month. It was this that provided the issue for revolt and gave rise to Australia's only violent rebellion: the Eureka Stockade. A small group of miners built a stockade just outside Ballarat, the main town of the gold fields, about 70 miles west of Melbourne (in the state of Victoria). They barricaded themselves in, proclaimed the Republic of Victoria, and hoisted a blue and white flag with the Southern Cross. They vowed to defend their liberties and privileges, and pledged to defend and protect each other. Unfortunately, their devotion to the cause was not as strong as the tradition of having a beer at the pub. On Saturday, December 2, 1854, the majority of the armed men sallied forth to the local pub. Troops and police knew well that those who returned to the stockade after a serious Saturday's drinking were in no state to defend themselves. They attacked at 4:30 A.M. on Sunday, killing 22 diggers and losing six of their own. The majority of those killed were Irishmen, only one was Australian born. The leader, a well educated Irishman called Lalor, lost an arm. He and his comrades were tried for high treason, but public sentiment was so strongly in their favor that they were acquitted. Lalor eventually became Speaker of the House for the Victorian legislature.

Historians view this as the only battle ever fought on Australian soil. One can see, though, that it was hardly a battle in the sense of a real rebellion, and that the behavior of the rebels fell short of absolute devotion to the cause. One could say that in spite of the many attempts by historians and politicians to sanctify this event, the bottom line was that the diggers would rather have a few beers with their mates than carry on a war with the authorities—even though they had been bullied and suffered horrible injustices.

This is not meant as a criticism of the Australian character. On the contrary, it is the most endearing trait: Aussies refuse to take anything too seriously, least of all themselves (with the exception of competitive sports). It is what makes living, visiting or working in Australia relaxing in comparison to America. The pace is definitely slower. One takes things as they come. One doesn't worry about anything too much. "She'll be right," as Aussies say, even in the face of the most difficult challenge.

After the Stockade, reforms in the gold fields followed, but Australians continue to revere the Eureka Stockade as the time when a few diggers thumbed their noses at the authorities. They were men who were trusting their lives to luck—they were underdogs "having a go," hoping to strike it rich.

In many respects gambling has always been an important way for Aussies to prick the soft sides of the authorities. Taking bets in bars remained illegal (and still is), yet one can almost always place a bet in most working class pubs. The relationship between these back room bookies and the police remains one of the amusing aspects of Australian pub life. And the sacred place of gambling in Australia's cultural and political life is also very important. Australia's great opera house would never have been built without Australia's love of gambling. The opera house was financed completely from the proceeds of a lottery. Nowhere else in the northern world can one find such a mind boggling mixture of high and low culture.

So the good life came before the committed life. If the Australian had to choose between having a beer, and defending principles, he'd take the beer any day. There were some, though, for whom the good life never came. And these people found themselves constantly on the other side of the law. These were Australia's bushrangers, much revered folk heroes in Australian life.

From Bushranging to Nationhood

The folk law of bushranging in Australia dates to the first convict settlements. Naturally enough, enterprising convicts tried to escape from the penal colonies. The problem was where to escape to. Many perished in the wilderness of Australia's harsh outback environment. There were terrible stories in Tasmania of an infamous bushranger who became a cannibal in order to survive the bush. But as land was settled and farmed, outlaws ranged over huge tracts of land throughout Australia's history from early settlement until the late 1800s. It was virtually impossible to control them as the distances were so great, and the population so sparse in the bush.

These bushrangers, as they were called, became heroes. They developed a kind of Robin Hood reputation—robbing from the rich and giving to the poor. The most famous of these aroused public hysteria in 1880s. He was Ned Kelly. This notorious bushranger eluded authorities for years because he was so popular with local inhabitants who shielded him. Kelly and his gang developed a way of operating very similar to that of Jesse James—he robbed banks, held entire towns hostage while he harangued them with speeches. In short, he appeared larger than life. Kelly constantly belittled the authorities, his speeches shot through with resentment and hostility toward England (being Irish himself, of course).

Unlike Jesse James who was shot in the back of the head by one of his own collaborators, Ned Kelly went out in a blaze of glory. He was eventually trapped in a railway station in the small Victorian town of Glenrowan. A hail of gunfire ensued, and the constables were amazed to see Ned Kelly emerge clothed from head to thighs in a homemade suit of armor. Unfortunately, once the police saw his legs were unprotected, they managed to wound him several times. Kelly recovered from his wounds and was found guilty of murdering a police officer. He was sentenced in 1880 by Judge Barry who said,

"Edward Kelly, I hereby sentence you to death by hanging. May the Lord have mercy on your soul."

To this Kelly replied, "Yes, and I will meet you there." Ned's final words were, "Such is Life."

To this day, fearless sportsmen and reckless children are described in endearing terms by Australians to be "as game as Ned Kelly."

The demise of Ned Kelly was the end of the era of bush-ranging. His legend lives on in Australian popular literature and art. But at the end of the 19th century important things were afoot. Australia was about to grow up.

Australia did not become a nation until 1901, much later than her American counterpart. And the events that led to her nationhood are quite different, although Australian historians tend to regard the period as somewhat similar to the exciting establishment of America in Philadelphia in 1776. By the time the last British soldier left Australian soil in 1870, each of the settlements in Sydney, Melbourne, Brisbane, Adelaide and Perth had gone its own way with a fierce independence. Because of the enormous distances between them they had always been largely separate communities. Each developed different sets of laws, particularly in regard to trade. Smuggling became a big problem. With the departure of the British soldiers, it became apparent that sooner or later a way must be found for the defense of the entire country. Many books have been written about the events leading to Australia's federation. Historians look back upon it as something akin to America's framing of her constitution.

Certainly, in the 1890s there was an incredible rise in nationalistic fervor. Australia had already established an impressive public education system (she was the first in the modern world to introduce compulsory education), so that literacy was approaching a high level. Many of Australia's greatest poets flourished during this period (Henry Lawson from 1867–1922 and "Banjo" Paterson, 1864–1941). Joseph Furphy ("Tom Collins"), 1843–1912, in his novel *Such Is Life* captured the new Australian spirit, which he described as, "in temper democratic, bias offensively Australian." It was "offensive" in the sense that Australia's discovery of her own, individual spirit and nationhood was not only a process of self discovery, but one of almost angry resentment towards England's superior and imperious attitude. As Sir Samuel Griffith, scholarly premier of Queensland, observed at the Federal Convention of 1891: "I am tired of being called a Colonist . . . used at the other end of the world . . . The colonist is . . . regarded [as] inferior . . . not quite entitled to the same privileges as other members of the Empire."

Other speeches aired similar views, attempting to throw off the English class system, echoing that strong Australian egalitarian sentiment:

> By the term Australian we mean those . . . who come to these shores with a clean record . . . who leave behind them the memory of class distinctions and religious differences of the old world . . . all men who leave their fatherland because they cannot swallow the worm-eaten lie of the divine right of kings to murder peasants, are Australians by instinct . . .

Yet while many lofty speeches were made, and Australia's nationhood was asserted in popular literary magazines like *The Bulletin*, there was nevertheless a strong element of downright Australian earthiness to the movement. One very popular speech in favor of Federation, for example, went like this:

> Gentlemen, if you vote for the Bill, you will found a great and glorious nation under the bright Southern Cross, and meat will be cheaper. . . .

Lest one is tempted to interpret the Australian ability to reduce lofty principles to earthy epithets as shallow, we hasten to add that other events in Australian history suggest that this is certainly not the case, although the standards by which the depth of national character are popularly judged leave something to be desired. That is, rightly or wrongly, the depth of national character is by some twisted standard measured by how many men have been lost at war. Thus, the contrast of Australia's Eureka Stockade with various of the great battles of America's revolution or Civil War are used to show how insignificant was Australia's battle. Other historians, though, have likened Australia's loss of life in World War I to the horrors of the American Civil War, and there may be something to this, in the senseless loss of life, and the seeming willingness with which the men threw themselves into battle.

Australia at War

The innocence of Australia's fighting men—and subsequent loss of innocence—is beautifully portrayed in the movie *Gallipoli*. Having just achieved nationhood through federation, and as we have seen, much of the thrust for this arising from a kind of anti-British resentment, it is amazing that Australia volunteered such a massive army to fight for the English. By the end of the war, over 330,000 soldiers had sailed from Australia to fight in Europe, and all of these were volunteers. It was on April 25, 1915, that Australia experienced her worst defeat in all her brief history. Because Australians tended to be somewhat more physically developed than their European counterparts, and were volunteers, they were more often used as crack troops to lead an offensive. On this day, they were used along with other allied troops (the Australian and New Zealand Army Corps—ANZAC) to attack a Turkish post at Gallipoli. They were put ashore and had to claw their way up perpendicular cliffs. The enemy was well dug in and reinforced. The ANZACs suffered the most horrendous losses, some 65% more than other British Empire troops. This day is celebrated in Australia as a kind of national day of identity crisis. It was the point in Australia's history when, given the macho view of what it means to be a man—to risk one's life in violent confrontation with others—Australia came of age.

The period between the wars was difficult for Australia as it was for most other countries that weathered the Great Depression. And when war came again in 1939, it was met with a good deal less innocent enthusiasm and some fear because of the Japanese involvement. Australian troops were once again (this time conscripted) sent to the Northern Hemisphere to fight for the mother country. But when Japan attacked Pearl Harbor on December 7, and then took Singapore, thought to be an impregnable garrison with 15,000 Australian troops defending it, Australia lay completely vulnerable to Japanese invasion. Australia's wartime prime minister, John Curtin (Labour Party) insisted against Churchill's wishes that Australian troops be used to defend Australia from Japan. It was at this point that Curtin made a significant speech pleading with America for help: "Without any inhibitions of any kind, I make it quite clear that Australia looks to America, free of any pangs as to our traditional links or kinship with the United Kingdom." Eventually, as we know, there were a number of battles in the Pacific, the major one known in Australia as the Battle of the Coral Sea. It was widely believed that America saved Australia from the Japanese. It was certainly a very close call. The Japanese had bombed one of Australia's northern cities (Darwin, the city in the northwest of Australia) and small submarines had surfaced in Sydney Harbor.

Many older Australians remember and appreciate the American influence during that time. Many Australian girls married American servicemen and returned to America with them. Today, the attitude toward Americans is somewhat more complicated, largely because of the Vietnam war, in which Australian troops through a lottery-based conscription fought alongside Americans. The war was also accompanied by severe domestic upset and antiwar sentiment, not only because of the issues surrounding the war itself, but because of the perceived failure of American presidents to consult adequately with Australia concerning significant decisions. The view of young Australians towards Americans today is therefore very mixed. There is some of the typical antagonism that one encounters in many other countries of the world; a tendency to blame America for all the ills of the world. On the other hand, one can see immediately upon stepping off the plane that much of Australian commercial life is very similar to American. (More about that later.)

A very important series of events after World War II helps explain the complexion of Australia's society today. The Labour government during the final years in power, that is, during the final days of World War II, enacted some strong and very typical socialist legislation: university scholarships

for able young people and ex-servicemen, help for the unemployed and sick, free prescription drugs for the needy, increased subsidies for hospitals, as well as many other social
benefits. Led by Prime Minister Chifley, the Labor Party also
staged an attack on private enterprise, nationalizing Australia's air services and attempting (unsuccessfully) to nationalize her banks. The legacy of this Labour era remains
today. The heavy hand of government lies everywhere in
Australia, yet Australians do not feel it.

A good example of the government's hidden hand is the
way in which sales tax is collected in Australia. Americans are
used to the shopkeeper adding on whatever amount of tax is
applicable. In Australia, the advertised price of any item
always includes the tax, and the rate of such tax remains
unknown. Ask any Australian what the sales tax is on any
item, and he will be unable to tell you. Furthermore, they see
absolutely no reason to know such details. Yet, we have seen
Australians in America, when a shopkeeper added on a few
cents to the price of a postcard for sales tax, get extremely
irate. They act as if only a thief would add anything on to the
advertised price!

During the war labor unions increased in strength and were
heavily influenced by the Australian communist party. The
Soviet Union, after all, was an ally. It was in the midst of these
immense political reforms that Robert Menzies (leader of the
conservative party, to become known as the Liberal and
Country Party Coalition) was able to come back from an
ignominious defeat during the war to regain leadership. He
managed much of this on a platform of anticommunism, and
when elected, legislation was passed banning the communist
party. The government now had the right to declare anyone a
communist, with the onus on the individual to prove otherwise. Australia's High Court found the bill unconstitutional
in 1951. Menzies put the question to a national referendum,
and the Australian people voted it down (with a narrow
margin). The Australian people had spoken—and the country
was spared the McCarthyism that so blotted America's politics
of the 1950s.

But perhaps the most significant program enacted by the

wartime government was a plan for large scale immigration. It was realized that in time of war or crisis, Australia was going to be left to herself, because her greatest handicap was lack of population to defend and develop a enormous land area. From 1945 to 1965 over two million immigrants came to Australia. Her population increased from 7,500,000 to 11,000,000 during that period. Probably it has been the massive immigration that makes Australians what they are today, and what has added a dimension to Australian life that makes it an even more fascinating place for the visitor. Australia has her own version of the melting pot.

Boom and Bust

One can imagine the commercial activity generated by the enormous increase in population. The familiar Australian problem of shortage of employment held sway for the next two decades. The sixties were especially a period of expansion and economic development. It was during these two decades that Australia's economy also began to expand into heavy industry with the development and discovery of an incredible wealth of mineral and oil resources. She no longer had to be dependent on wool as a single major export (though Australia is still the world's leading producer). And Prime Minister Robert Menzies ruled Australia almost as though he were another English king.

Times change. A recession came in the seventies. The Vietnam war divided the country. Menzies retired and the Liberal government was unable to find a leader anywhere with anything like Menzies' charisma and popular appeal. Menzies' successor Harold Holt (who disappeared while swimming in the surf—a most Australian way to end one's life) embarrassed Australia with the cry "All the way with L.B.J." and Prime Minister Gorton staggered the incredulous American and Australian press when he offered to go "Waltzing Matilda" with Richard Nixon to fight aggression throughout the world. And McMahon, the last Liberal prime minister before the new labor government, embarrassed Australia by his obsequious behavior in Washington. As in America, the

Vietnam war had torn the moral fabric of Australia to shreds. To aggravate the situation, Johnson made decisions concerning the bombing of North Vietnam and not seeking re-election without informing Australia. The Liberal government lost credibility, and was quickly voted out of office at the next election in 1972.

Labor was elected into parliament with a narrow majority under the leadership of a fiery, articulate lawyer, Gough (pronounced Goff) Whitlam. Whitlam's government, dictatorial and decisive—quickly pardoned draft resisters and others who had been in various ways punished by the former government because of their opposition to the war. In a flurry of activity, the Labour government passed some 103 bills in the 1973 sitting alone! These ranged from the abolition of British titles and abolition of tax on contraceptives to massive spending on aboriginal welfare and on education, abolition of Australia's racist immigration policy, recognition to China, equal pay for women, and abolition of farm subsidies. Virtually all of these changes produced near hysterical reaction on the part of the conservative opposition, both because it meant taking away some of their perqs (the farm subsidies) and also heralded a drastic change in foreign policy for Australia, which since time immemorial had been based on anticommunism.

The conservative (the Liberal party) held the balance of power in the upper house (also as the result of political shenanigans), and refused in a series of fateful votes to support supply, that is to allocate any money for the government to continue operating. A political crisis followed. Surreptitiously, Sir John Kerr (whom Whitlam himself had appointed), the Governor of Australia and the Queen's legal representative, called Whitlam to the government house and fired him. Many books have been written about this event and what would have happened if Whitlam had refused. What would the military have done? The leader of the opposition was waiting in the wings. When Whitlam was ushered out one door, Fraser was ushered in the other and sworn in as interim Prime Minister and asked to form a government.

Australian politics, indeed Australians themselves, would never be the same again. Although a general election was immediately called on the basis of a non-confidence vote in parliament, Whitlam's government was soundly defeated by the greatest margin since federation. The change in the Australians' view of themselves was dramatic. Almost over night Australians began to talk about politics openly and heatedly. Before, politics was treated by ordinary Australians as something that one voted about, but was not worth discussing. It was rare to encounter an animated political discussion within ordinary circles. This was the kind of talk that was only carried on among the academics. But now, ask any Australian about Kerr's coup and see what response you get. Don't try it in a public bar though. That is not the place for politics. Horses and sports are the topics there.

Historians have worried about this series of events for a long time. Some have compared the arbitrary power exercised by Kerr as greater than that exercised by the monarchs prior to the French revolution. Even more worrying was the fact that the Australian people voted against the Whitlam government—the very victim of the governor's tyranny. Others point to the control of economics over any Australian election. While it would appear that the majority of Australians disapproved of what Kerr did, they also were concerned by the deepening crisis: inflation was getting out of hand, the government was spending too much (even though there was much to show for it, such as a national health scheme), and unemployment was rising.

Years of bickering and incompetent leadership followed under the conservative government of Malcolm Fraser. His party, immediately on taking office, moved to eradicate many of the reforms enacted by the Labor government; especially reinstating the farm subsidies. Almost all domestic programs were cut drastically, and there were massive increases in defense spending. The only domestic bodies to receive increases were Australia's beleaguered secret police (ASIO) and Sir John Kerr's salary, which increased by 171%!

With Menzies gone, Australians seemed lost. They yearned

for a star politician with charismatic qualities. And this wish was granted in 1983 when Bob Hawke emerged to take over the leadership and save Australia. An unusual person indeed was Bob Hawke: Rhodes scholar, experienced unionist, and one-time holder of the Guinness record for skolling a pint of beer. In many ways the period has been Australia's most difficult. She has been dogged by strong inflation, a severe trade imbalance, unemployment of levels hitherto unknown in Australia, and a problem of what to do with her youth. While the older generation in Australia complains a lot about Hawke's government, in actual fact pensioners especially have benefited from the labor socialist orientation.

Hawke turned out to be much more the pragmatic politician than the left wing ideologue that some of his supporters had hoped he would be, and that many of the conservatives feared. In fact, he has over the years followed much of the American way: encouraging free enterprise and shying away from the old Labor demand to nationalize large commercial establishments such as banks. There is constant talk of selling Australia's national airline (Qantas) to private interests.

But the cost of living for Australians has increased tremendously. Cars cost almost twice as much as in America because of the 90% sales tax. Food is more expensive. And salaries have not kept up with prices. There is a large increasingly entrenched group of unemployed youth. Higher education is strapped to the limit, inaccessible to all but the very few who do well enough in their exams in the twelfth grade. By 1991 Australia's economy was in the middle of a deep recession. Hawke's popularity dropped to its lowest ever, and by November of that year, the Labor Party removed Hawke from leadership, appointing Paul Keating, the former Treasurer, as Prime Minister.

In spite of these problems, Australia remains, along with New Zealand, the most egalitarian country of the Western world. Roughly 3% of all families in Australia have no assets, compared with 20% in Britain and the U.S. The richest 1% of Australians control only 9% of the nation's wealth, compared with the same proportion controlling 33% of the wealth in Britain and 26% of the wealth in the United States.

But the visitor will by and large see none of this, and just as well, for the clear and striking aspect of Australia is its love of sport and leisure—just what a tourist is looking for.

CHAPTER 4

Australians Today

The Australian Character

A friend of ours some years ago described Australians as pre-Freudian. By and large he meant that Australians as a group are an unreflective lot, taking life as it comes, their personalities unsullied by neuroses and self doubts. Much of this Australian character derives, as we have seen, from the convict past and the challenges of the natural environment the early settlers faced. The loneliness, distance and isolation of the early settlers produced a kind of inner quiet without the self promotion from which Australians recoil when they travel abroad, especially in the U.S.

Events of the last two decades, however, have changed much of this. Australian politics and society have undergone drastic change, causing much more reflection about what kind of Australia Australians would like. As well, Australia is a far more cosmopolitan country today than any time before.

71

About 40% of the population is now composed of first and second generation immigrants from England and the Mediterranean countries. This is obvious especially in her large cities, where there are populations of Greek and Italian speaking peoples, often in concentrations greater than any of the largest cities in their home countries. It is claimed that more Greeks live in Melbourne's Greek section than in any other city outside Athens. The European based ethnic diversity is now an established ethnicity, if we may call it that. But the new ethnicity, most clearly developed over the last decade, is that of Asia.

The abolition of the White Australia policy very soon after the Vietnam war opened the doors to the migration of more and more Asian peoples, particularly to the major cities. Australia's cities have become wonderful places to explore with a fantastic variety of restaurants and ethnic fare that cannot help but delight the tourist. One can eat well and differently in all Australia's great cities, experiencing the food and ambience of most of Europe and large portions of Asia. And while the Asian influence is most clearly seen in Sydney and Melbourne, Asian cuisine has reached into many country towns. In fact, one could say that Asian food has penetrated the very heart of Australian eating-out culture, the country pub. Unthinkable some ten years ago, there are now pubs that have handed over their entire food–serving trade to Asian cooks. We found one such pub in Bacchus Marsh, for example, as we explored the Victorian countryside (Chapter 7).

Children of the established immigrants have soaked up the Australian ethos of leisure orientation, mateship and the derision of pretensions. Politicians are suspect by definition. Corruption of political officials is assumed, and usually proven in endless scandals and revelations. Police are frankly not particularly liked. Social commentators deplore the fact that people in the street pointedly do not help police when they are in need. There have been many instances when bystanders have stood and watched police being beaten up. And much of this attitude, while again probably deriving from the distant past

of Australia as a police state in colonial times, is also somewhat justified, as there appear to be endless scandals and
police corruption—with one currently under investigation in
New South Wales, following hard on the heels of one in
Queensland.

On the other hand, the visitor (or Australian for that matter) can walk up to a policeman, just as in Britain, ask the way
and be treated most courteously and kindly. Australia's officially recorded crime rate, though high, is nowhere near as
high as that of Britain (a little higher in some respects). There
are a few neighborhoods in the big cities in which one would
be advised not to walk, but these are very few. The tourist is
usually very safe and, more importantly, feels safe in Australia (except driving a car on narrow two-way roads).

Are all Australians like Paul Hogan? The character played
by Hogan in the *Crocodile Dundee* movies is rather like the true
Australian. (Obviously, Hogan does not represent that other
Aussie type, the ethnic immigrant. To obtain a picture of an
established immigrant, read one of Nino Culotta's novels,
particularly *They're a Weird Mob*, which portrays the stereotype of the Italian immigrant of the 1950s.) Hogan portrays
the quiet, unassuming, seemingly innocent fellow whose inner strength derives from a hard life in the outback. Of
course, few Aussies have ever been to the outback, much less
lived there. But there is a worship of the physical way of life—
the outdoors, sport, the beach—that parallels the drama of
Crocodile Dundee's persona. Other characters in that movie,
though stereotypes, are not too far from the mark. The characters in the outback pub in the movie's opening scene—
especially the one that says "Get stuffed" to just about everything—are typical of those called "ocker" in Australian slang,
a term equivalent to "red-neck." Both types like to drink beer
(but then so do most Australians, except "wowsers"), are
preoccupied with sport and love gambling. Unlike their
American counterparts, it is doubtful if ockers have any political opinions one way or the other. In the crowded constantly funny Australian pub, there is no room for politics.

The egalitarian ethos of Australia is carried to an extreme in the working man's pub, that is, if one ignores the fact that women are not welcome. It is a complicated topic, however. Although these days, women more often frequent the public bar (for uncouth working men only), but they are still a rare sight. There are usually formally or informally designated bars or lounges to which Australia's women go to drink. As we will see in one of our Sydney walks, there are some wonderful watering spots to visit, and in which perhaps partake, if one is so inclined.

Critics of Australian culture have also observed that it is male dominated, or to put it bluntly a macho society. Reviewers of the first Crocodile Dundee movie hailed the character played by Hogan as refreshingly nonviolent and by implication, nonmacho. The reviewers complained that it was a pity America's screen heroes could not be heroes without being so violent (the obvious contrast is to the Dirty Harry roles played by Clint Eastwood—whom Hogan likes to satirize). Other historians have shown with great pride that Australia has achieved great societal change and progress largely without serious bloodshed, the Eureka stockade compared to the American Civil War, for example. The wildness of Australia's frontiers has also been compared to America's Wild West and found less violent, in spite of the overwhelming evidence for banditry just as violent and endemic as it was in America. Zane Grey found it easy to set one of his Western novels, *Wilderness Trek* with classic violent Western plot, in the Australia outback. The difference lies in the fact that the American movie industry constructed the myth of the wild, violent West, while in actual fact, life there was largely nonviolent and devoted to the daily toils of trying to tame a wild land. The great Western novelist Louis L'Amour has remarked on this on many occasions. But both frontiers had one type of violence in common: the systematic destruction of the native people, in America's case the Indians, and in Australia's, the Aborigines. The only difference lies in the fact that there were probably more Indians than Aborigines to defend the land, and the tribes were perhaps better organized and able to turn to war. The Australian Aborigines, because tribes were so small and sparsely scattered due to the essentially nomadic existence they led in the harsh outback environment, were easily defeated by the white man.

The second Dundee movie, made particularly for the U.S. market, suggests that our interpretation is accurate. The amount of violence is much greater in that movie—probably a response to the fact that the movie was directed at an American audience. The screenplay was also written by Hogan, with the result that the portrayal of women is much different than in the first movie. In the first, the female reporter is portrayed as more than capable of taking care of herself in the Australian bush. The stereotype of the helpless female was avoided. But in the second movie, this was not the case; the return to Australia brings with it a strong and intense dependency of Dundee's woman on his cunning, but violent, achievements. There is one very strong theme that runs through both movies: the Australian love of making a fool out of their opponents. Dundee makes his opponents look like dolts. Both movies also do much to promote the mystique of the outback, to reinforce that old and entrenched belief that Australians have in themselves, that their pride, strength and determination reside in the wilds of the bush even though 90% of Australians (all of whom live in large cities) have probably never spent one night in the outback!

Unreflective as they may be, Australians love a real life mystery. The popularity of the movie *A Cry in the Dark* reflects this national interest well. The movie is about an Australian woman (Lindy Chamberlain, played by Meryl Streep with a perfect Australian accent) and her husband who are accused of murdering their baby Azaria, which disappeared one night while they were camping by Ayers Rock. In defense, the mother and father claim that the baby was stolen by a dingo, an indigenous dog-like animal. The family, strict Seventh Day Adventists, were accused by an irresponsible media of having killed the baby in a satanic ritual. There were many unexplained details surrounding the case. The mother was tried, found guilty, and gave birth to another child while still in prison. Subsequent new evidence surfaced, resulting in a new hearing, and eventual release of the mother. Australians will spend much more time arguing about and discussing such events than they will over politics. There have been many cases, perhaps not quite as celebrated as this, in Australia's history.

Uncharacteristically, though, Australians tended in the Azaria case to consider the mother guilty. Usually the Australian personality champions the underdog and supports individuals who are being "done in" by the authorities. Australians like nothing better than to see the underdog win, and the persons in authority have "a rise taken out of them." One could argue, though, that they did support the underdog because many defended the dingo that Lindy Chamberlain had accused. Many debated as to whether the dingo was a dangerous animal and capable of carrying off a baby. Nor was Lindy's husband liked by Australians—we suspect mainly because he was a minister, a representative of authority.

The irreverence for public officials, formality and social ritual remains. Australian openness in this respect is refreshing, and their informality much like that of Americans. In this way they are much different from their English and European ancestors.

Because they are not preoccupied with social graces, Australians make wonderful hosts for tourists. They are approachable, easy to talk to, and will help you on your way with pleasure and with a smile. In this they are truly genuine, and have been known to be quite annoyed at what they see as inauthentic niceties, such as the McDonalds' dictum "Have a Nice Day," now commonplace in the restaurants of Australia. When Australians say, "G'day mate, 'ow yer goin' awright?" they really mean it. It's the way friends and relatives talk to each other. (One doubts that friends and relatives in America say "have a nice day" to each other.) And because of their happy-go-lucky attitude about life, their great sense of humor (sometimes disarming to the point of alarming to Americans—in this respect Australians are more like their English forebears), you cannot help but have a great time—no matter where you go or what you do.

On the other hand, the leisure orientation of the society can have its pitfalls for the tourist. If one harks back to the union campaigns of the 1950s, the placards that were carried by demonstrators read: "8 HOURS WORK—8 HOURS REST—8 HOURS RECREATION." Australian society believes in this deeply. Shops and other conveniences are therefore often closed on weekends especially, and often by 5:30 p.m. in the evening. The only establishments that are always open somewhere in a city are pubs and milk bars (more on this shortly). One must plan one's activities to fit in with the rhythm of Australian life—just as the tourist in Italy plans to visit the churches during the afternoon siesta hours and the museums in the mornings.

Perhaps the most visible evidence of Australia's leisure oriented society is her beaches. These are virtually sacred to Australians, in the sense that they are all public beaches (with some very rare sections where land is owned down to the shore line). While the United States has coastline to the east and west, because Australia is an island continent, she has a fantastic coastline to the north and south as well. There are literally thousands and thousands of miles of unspoiled beaches. In summer, the most popular beaches are crammed full of pleasure and sun-seeking Australians of all ages. These places are treated as though each and every individual owns them. Australians who travel abroad, especially to the Mediterranean, are deeply shocked when they find that they must pay to get on to a beach. To Aussies this seems tantamount to a horrible fascist tyranny. Beaches are public property to Australians. They are sacred territory. (Unfortunately, this has not stopped pollution from hitting Australia's more frequented beaches; recently Sydney's Manly Beach was closed due to many syringes in the sand in a similar incident to the Long Beach Island pollution of 1988. There are other beaches that are still virtually unspoiled in every state of the country, and within an hour of any major city).

It is no accident that D. H. Lawrence chose a beach as the scene in which two of his characters talk about feeling free in Australia:

> Freedom! That's what they always say. "You feel free in Australia." And so you do. There's a great relief in the atmosphere . . . an absence of control or will or form.

The sky is open above you, and the air is open around
you. Not the cold closing-in of Europe. . . .
—From *Kangaroo*, talking on Manly beach, one of Australia's most famous surf beaches near Sydney.

The Peculiar Language of Strine

How is it possible for two people to speak the same language and not be able to understand each other? Australians
speak English all right, and their newspapers look just like
those in the U.S. But Americans have a lot of trouble understanding Australians, though Aussies can usually understand Americans. (Not always, though. When at a check-out
in an American supermarket, after having been in the U.S. for
only a month, we had an embarrassing scene when the
young person at the register asked us whether we had any
"kew-pons." We simply could not understand him. Finally, he
showed us what he meant—coupons, of course.) Apart from
the unusual accents of Australian drawl, there are many expressions and words that simply do not exist in the U.S. The
Australian accent is almost always mistaken by Americans for
an English accent—don't make this mistake in Australia, as it
will be taken as quite an insult to an Aussie. Australian vowel
sounds are very distinctive. "Paper" is pronounced *pie-pa*,
although the word "mate" is pronounced somewhere in between *mate* and *mite*. Accents do not differ greatly among
Australians, at least by region, as they do quite drastically in
England, and between North and South in the U.S. Country
folk probably speak a little more slowly. But all Australians,
especially the men, tend to speak without moving their lips
much, and tend to mumble into their chests.

Women and children speak differently from men, though
the vowel sounds are the same. Women will generally speak
more loudly than men, and both women and kids tend to
raise the pitch of their voices towards the ends of their sen-
tences, especially if they are relating the details of an important incident. A favorite phrase used by Aussie mums is "Did
you?" spoken with a lilting voice that starts with a high pitch
on "Did," and wavers with a drawn out "you." Educated
Australians (that is, those who have gone to a university and

finished an undergraduate degree) may display a somewhat different accent in which there are attempts to distinguish clearly between the *a* and *i* vowel sounds, and emphasize the *ah* in such words as "part" (rather too like the English). "Plant" may be pronounced as *plarnt*.

Aussies also like to truncate many common nouns with an *ee* sound. Thus, the barbecue is a barbie; television, telly; football, footy; Christmas, Chrissy; biscuit, bikkie; just about any other common noun can be shortened in this way. Many cockney expressions are still preserved in everyday speech, so that to "have a Captain Cook" is to "have a look," and the "dead horse" is the "sauce" (Australian for ketchup).

Here are a few words that you might strike in your travels, and find it necessary to understand in order to get the most out of your experience:

abo—common but insensitive term referring to aboriginal.

alu<u>min</u>ium—note spelling and syllable stress here; pronounced exactly as it is spelled, meaning aluminum (obviously).

arvo—afternoon.

'ave a go yermug—most often heard at a cricket match, usually urging a batsman (batter) to " 'ave a go" and hit the ball.

back a Bourke—part of the outback, where no sensible person would go (as Bourke perished in the desert); a long way away, close to nowhere. Bourke is a town in the New South Wales outback. Bourke is pronounced without the *o* or *r*; that is, it sounds nothing like the name of the rejected American Supreme Court Justice nominee.

banger—an Australian sausage, commonly cooked over the barbie; see also **snag.**

basic wage—legally required minimum wage set by the federal government.

barbie—barbecue (certainly not a teenage doll).

barrack—cheer on your team.

bathers—your swimsuit; see also **togs.**

black stump—the beginning of the outback, used mainly in Australian folk songs and novels; not common in everyday speech, except among older people.

blowies, bloody blowies—blow flies; they do nasty things to food foolishly left out in the open for just a few minutes.

bewdie mate—you're doing a fantastic job.

bickies—cookies.

billabong—not used in everyday speech; known because it was in one of these that the protagonist (a bum) in Australia's national folk song drowned himself rather then let the cops take him; a pool of water in a dried-up bend of a river.

billy—tin can with wire handle used to boil water on a campfire; and then make *billy tea.*

bloke—fellow.

bludger—lazy freeloader.

blue (have a blue)—have an argument, often violent; these occur in workingmen's pubs quite a lot.

bluey—roll of blankets and belongings carried by a bum (see **swaggy**); not common in everyday speech, but mainly in folk songs and stories of the 1890s.

bluey (get a)—get a speeding ticket.

bonnet—could be worn at Easter, but also refers to the hood of one's car.

bonzer, bonza—nice, great, as **a bonza bloke,** a genuine kind person.

boot—might refer to one's shoe, but can also mean the trunk of a car.

bubby—affectionate term for your baby; **My little Bubby.**

bull dust—fine red dust on outback roads; used by men in front of women when they'd rather say "bull shit."

bumper bar—not a fantastic bar, but certainly a bump is likely; these are fenders of a car.

bunyip—Australia's mystery bush animal; if you're having a *really* good time, you might see it.

BYO—bring your own booze to a restaurant or party.

cappuccino—coffee drink available all over Australia, made especially with froth and chocolate on top; served in a café atmosphere unparalleled in America.

caravan—trailer one takes camping; no camels or covered wagons.

chatting up girls—the usual pick-up routine, the same all over the world.

chips—as in fish and chips; the term "french fries" is understood, but looked down upon because it symbolizes American fast food.

chook—chicken

chunder—throw up, vomit, also known as technicolor yawn; many expressions pass in and out of usage quickly for this well known consequences of excessive drinking.

city (go to the)—to go downtown

cobber—mate; not common, though perhaps the most well known Australian word outside Australia; older people may use it to refer to their grandchildren's friends.

cockies—farmers, large or small.

cordial—non-carbonated sweet drink (kids drink gallons of this), obviously nonalcoholic, unlike its American counterpart.

crook (feel)—feel sick.

dag—dirty wool of a sheep's rear end; a person who does crazy things might be called a **bloody dag;** may be a term of abuse or endearment, depending on how it's said.

daks/underdaks—men's trousers/underwear.

damper—bush bread made from flour, water and salt; Not common in everyday speech though known by folklorists and Boy Scouts who have to cook it to pass their tests; sometimes called a **twist** when the dough, instead of being made into a loaf, is twisted around a stick and cooked above the campfire, rather than in the coals.

didgeridoo—aboriginal musical instrument; a twenty-foot or longer tube which emits an eerie deep monotone.

digger—original term for the Australian soldier of World War I, who dug a lot of trenches; if used today (not all that common), it means almost the same as **mate;** very sentimental.

dill—a real bloody dope; a **ning-nong.**

dingo—native Australian wild dog, famous since the Azaria case in which the dingo was accused of stealing a baby in 1981.

dinkum/fair dinkum—truly authentic, honest, genuine; not used much these days, except to assert that one is a **dinkum Aussie.**

dinki-di—abbreviation of dinkum; archaic, known from a song with the line "dinki di I do."

drongo—a larrikin or hooligan, a bloody no-hoper.

duco—paint on a car.

dunny—outhouse; not too long ago toilets were all out back in the yard; Aussies are amused when American call the toilet "the bathroom."

entree—Australian appetizer, or half serving.

fair go!—have a heart, mate; give us a break.

fair few—more than a few, and more than several, but not too many.

fanny—most private female part; NOT rear end; not used in the presence of nice ladies.

fireplug—fire hydrant.

flake—shark meat served as fish and chips if you don't specify the kind of fish; Aussies eat a lot of it, where it is not banned because of high mercury content.

flat—apartment, or any living premise which has just one floor.

flick—film, or movie.

flog—what went on in Australia's early penal settlements; but today it more often means to sell, usually a hard sell.

footpath—sidewalk.

footy match—Australian Rules football game; if you like noisy crowds, going to one of these games is quite an experience.

galah—a rowdy cockatoo; noisy young hooligans are galahs too.

garbo—not an actress, but the man who collects trash.

get stuffed—the mildest of the verbs referring to sexual activity, often used between mates as an expression of endearment; much depends on the way it is said.

g'day—well, everyone knows this one, but saying it with the right accent is difficult for Americans; try not to pronounce any of the *ood* at all following the *g*, and practice saying day as if you were calling Di (the princess), but don't hang on the *i* too long.

g'donyer—(good on you) well done; very good job.

good-o—right you are; O.K.

grog—perhaps Australia's oldest word for liquor; one may also **grog on.**

head—not the john (an expression unknown in Aussie); rather, it refers to the amount of froth on a glass of beer.

holiday—vacation; "I'm going on holiday."

icy pole—popsicle; comes in hundreds of artificial flavors and colors, enjoyed especially in the summer.

joey—baby kangaroo, often seen peaking out of its mother's pouch.

jumper—also known as sweater, pullover, or windcheater.

kiosk—common Aussie term meaning anything from a refreshment stand to a café.

knock—criticize constantly; Aussies like to knock those in authority; knockers, however, are those who constantly criticize and everyone gets sick of them sooner or later.

lamington—spongecake cubes covered with chocolate frosting and dried coconut; unmatched anywhere!

larrikin—hooligan and *drongo*, probably a juvenile delinquent.

lemonade—fizzy water with a lemony taste, such as Sprite or 7-Up; American "freshly squeezed lemonade" does not exist here.

lift—elevator (and the first floor is the one <u>above</u> the ground floor—confusing!)

lollies—candy

lolly, doing your—having a temper tantrum

lollywater—soda

loo—affectionately adopted English expression for toilet.

lurk—tricky arrangement bordering on a con game, the kind of thing you do when you **take a sicky** (pretend to be sick for a day) or figure out a way to beat the tax man.

middy—medium glass of beer (New South Wales)

milk bar—small corner store that tends to be open when everything else is not; try their milk shakes and snow balls.

mozzies—mosquitoes—no shortage of them.

nappie—diaper, NOT napkin.

ning-nong—dill, **drongo.**

ocker—red neck Aussie

passage—hallway

pasty—(pronounced *pah-stee*); Australian fast food made of chopped beef, vegetables, and sauce, wrapped in pastry—delicious!

pavlova—mouthwatering Australian meringue dessert.

petrol—gas, as for your car.

pie'n' sauce—meat sauce of various kinds, wrapped in pastry, available everywhere; Australians eat these like Americans eat hot dogs.

pissed (get)—to get drunk.

piss off—doesn't mean getting someone upset as it does in America; rather, you tell someone to **piss off** if you want them to get the hell out, right now!

pom, pommy—somewhat derogatory term for an Englishman; Australians do not call them limeys.

poofter, poof—male homosexual; may be spoken in falsetto voice, which is, perhaps, overdoing it.

poser—one who shows off, a snot or snob.

postie—mailman

pot—might mean marijuana, but in a pub it's more likely to refer to a large mug of beer. And while we're at it, in Australia you ask for a jug of beer, not a pitcher.

potato cake—slice of potato deep fried in batter; if soggy french fries (chips that go with fish and chips) are not your bag, then potato cakes may be just what you'd like; they're usually crisp and tasty.

power point/plug—electrical outlet.

prawn—what Americans call shrimp.

ratbag—bit of a **larrikin,** but probably not a delinquent.

rapt (I was)—thoroughly enraptured.

rubbish (to)—to criticize another in good humor, very much like media "roasts" celebrities.

school—group of drinkers in a bar in which each takes a turn "shouting" (i.e., paying for a round of drinks); don't get in a big one, or you'll end up very drunk, because you CANNOT leave before your shout.

serviette—napkin for keeping clean at restaurants; "napkin" is sometimes used now, especially in American fast food chains.

sheila—a girl, usually young and unattached.

shout—turn to pay, a common expression in pubs, and if it's your shout, be prepared to buy everyone in your group a drink; needless to say that everyone has a turn to shout, so if yours is a large group, you could get quite **pissed.**

sloppy joe—store term for jogging sweatshirt.

smoke-o—coffee break (tea, actually); Australians take two a day at least.

snag—sausage, banger, weiner, whatever you call it.

spanner—wrench.

strine—Australian language, harsh contraction of "Australian."

stubby—small squat bottle of beer, a **glass can.**

sultana—an American raisin.

sunnies—NOT Cher partner look-alikes; simply an abbreviation for sunglasses.

swaggy—a **swagman** or bum, common in Australia during 19th century, up to the end of World War II; often seen walking with **swag** (roll of gear) and **billy;** rare these days, only known in folk poetry and stories. Romantically referred to as "the Sundowner" played by Robert Mitchum; the only bums left now are the same as in the U.S., called winos.

tanked up—drunk.

tea—"**What's for tea?**" "What's for dinner?"

thingo—whatchemacallit.

thongs—worn by most Aussies in the summertime, NOT to be called flip-flops unless you are hoping to be laughed at.

togs—your swimsuit, or **bathers.**

toilet—the room where you pee; do NOT say "Where is the bathroom?" or "I have to go to the bathroom" because Aussies will laugh at you. Many houses have toilets and baths and showers and sinks in separate rooms; your asking them where the bathroom is implies that you are about to take a shower or even worse pee in one.

track suit—jogging suit.

tram—noisy clanging streetcars, "noisy as a Bondi tram," was a widely used saying.

trousers—common Aussie term for pants.

tube—can of beer.

tucker—food.

two up—traditional Australian gambling game using two pennies, illegal just about everywhere (except in casinos), which is strange for a country that is a leading gambling nation of the world.

uni—college.

unit—common living quarters for the elderly, consisting of a small, one level apartment with a small garden. Often surrounded by identical **units.**

Vegemite—thick dark paste made from yeast and vegetable extracts; every Australian eats this spread lightly on buttered bread or toast; also good on crackers. Spread it lightly though—we can't emphasize this enough.

videoplayer—VCR; American videos do not work on Australian videoplayers.

wag (to play the)—play hookey.

walkabout—to get away from it all, originates from aboriginal practice of **going walkabout** as part of their ancient nomadic lifestyle.

wog—any flu-like virus.

wharfie—dockside worker, always a union man.

whinge—complain, like Mr. and Mrs. Whiner on *Saturday Night Live.*

whinging pom—just about all Englishmen.

wowser—a teetotaler, usually of strict puritan religious beliefs, disapproving of other people's pleasures; a killjoy; not a popular person in Australia.

yabby (yabbie)—small crayfish found in inland streams throughout Australia.

yooz—more than one of you.

Pub Life: In Search of a Bar

There are no bars of the American type in Australia (except, of course, in American-run hotel chains). All drinking is done in a pub, which may have within it several bars, possibly a dining room, and maybe (though less and less these days) a residential side.

Australian bars are usually large, much larger than American bars. In a pub, there are usually public bars, saloon bars and sometimes lounges. In public bars the beer is usually a few cents cheaper, and the social experience that goes with it much more earthy. Here you will find, at the peak hour (depending on the locality) the ockers and other Australians. The talk will not be particularly profound, but it will certainly be loud, funny, and probably coarse. There may be a few women in the bar, but by and large, this bar remains the refuge of men. The saloon bar (or any other bar that is preceded by a fancy adjective) is meant for those who consider themselves a "cut above" the workers. You will pay a little more for your beer there, and it probably will be quieter, unless dominated by Aussie Yuppies. Women are not out of place here. In the lounges, rock groups and other entertainment are the norm. Dancing and bingo are common. But a lot of beer flows through all the pipes.

If you do take a beer now and then, you should certainly stop at one of Australia's pubs. On the walks we will recommend later on, we will direct you to some particularly historic pubs and those that serve good quality beer. Australians are very picky about their beer. While it's all good, they will say, some beers are much better than others. The draft beer especially varies widely from one pub to another, even though they may pull (pour) the same brand. A lot depends on how well the publican takes care of his facilities.

If you choose a public bar, and you are on your own, there are a few guidelines to follow. First, it is probably safer to be a little unsociable and refuse an invitation to join a school (i.e., a group of drinkers, usually standing up at the bar, who take turns shouting—paying for a round of drinks). It is an iron rule of the pub that one must NEVER leave before one's shout. This means that if you join a large school, say five or six people, you will either have to drink five glasses of beer, or pay for five glasses and leave having had less than that. Australian beer is very strong! Be careful. The neophyte may not realize what has happened until he hits the street, and finds that it keeps coming up to hit him in the face! Nothing amuses Aussies more than to see a foreigner fall foul of this trick. One solution if caught in a school is to ask the bartender (barman or barmaid) to serve you a small beer (in some localities called a pony). In this way, it is possible to withstand the round, though it may cost a little more.

It's acceptable to be particular about beer. If a beer is served with more than a half inch head (froth), ask for it to be topped up. On the other hand, if a beer is served without any head on it at all, ask for the beer to be livened up.

Beer is an essential part of Australian life. Australians are the third biggest beer drinkers in the world, following hard on the heels of the Germans and Belgians. They drink more than 130 liters per man, woman and child a year. (And since children don't drink, or aren't supposed to, and women drink far less than men, this means that the majority of men must be tanked up a lot of the time). In Darwin, Australia's northernmost city, where it's very hot and dry, the rate is almost double that. In fact, in Darwin, they have a boating regatta solely for boats made out of beer cans. One gang of dills even sailed a beer can boat to Vietnam and claim that they were the inspiration for the Vietnamese boat people! While England is probably better known to America as a nation of beer drinkers, as consumers, they rank in 10th place, some 25 liters per man behind the Australians.

And let us repeat. Australian beer is strong—stronger than most beers in Europe, much stronger than that of England, and far stronger than beer in America. (Australians fondly refer to English beer as dog's piss because it is so flat, and served unchilled.) There was once an unfortunate monopoly on beer manufacture in Australia, so that the range of beers available was very narrow. Nowadays, there is much more competition, and one can try any number of different kinds of beers. However, the most popular, and best known, is still the beer that was the major product of the monopoly (Carlton and United Breweries), which is Fosters. This is available in the U.S. as an export beer. But believe us, it's only a pale replica of the real thing—both in strength and taste. There are some interesting beers that one can taste—we'll mention them when we visit the best places to either buy or drink them.

Not Quite Prohibition. The pub hours in Australia have gone from the ridiculous to the sublime (or the other way around, depending on one's attitude toward drinking). Back in 1914, during the First World War, the fledgling federal government decided that the pubs should close at 6 p.m., as a war time emergency. How this would help fight the Germans in Europe is hard to figure out, but anyway the pubs were made to close at 6 p.m. The hours remained in force for another 40 odd years! In those days, the good old days, people would stop work ("knock off work" as they say in Australia, no insult implied) at 5 or so, rush to the pub, and put away as much beer as they could before "6 o'clock closing," which was harshly enforced by the police. The publican was allowed 15 minutes to get his hundreds of customers out of the bar and lock up. This period of craziness was known as the "6 o'clock swill." The various state governments tried at times to change the laws, but an unusual alliance between the wowsers (as we have noted, an unpopular type in Australia) and the publicans and beer manufacturers managed to delay any changes. You see, the publicans realized they could sell only so much beer and customers had only so much money to spend, whether they had one or several hours to spend it. It was not until the late 50s that the hours were liberalized, and in the state of Victoria not until the 60s. State referendums didn't do it. Finally, the state governments simply did it on their own. The hours by the 70s were usually from 10 a.m. to 10 p.m. Today there is virtually no control on pub hours. In the big cities especially, licenses can be obtained for almost any combination of hours a publican wants, so long as he abides by the law that he remain open for the given number of hours each day or week. One may laugh, but at least Australians never had Prohibition!

Counter lunches (meals served at the bar) can be bought at pubs, and are solid meals, usually of meat and two vegetables, and almost always with a choice of red meat or fish. The English traditional fare of shepherds's pie and steak and kidney pie are common, as are the ubiquitous pies and pasties. These lunches are reasonably priced, as far as meals go, but they can vary considerably in quality. Publicans used to use them to entice people in to drink their beer. In fact, when these lunches were first introduced some 20 years ago, individuals who ordered soft drinks (sodas) to go with their counter lunch were frowned upon, as though they had no right to be in the bar in the first place! But now there is less money to be made on a glass of beer than there is on the food, so the quality may be lacking sometimes. On our city walks, we'll suggest some good places to try the counter lunches.

About buying beer in Australia. Beer can be purchased at some supermarkets, but is mostly available at bottleshops attached to hotels, or in free standing shops. There are even drive-thru bottleshops! Supermarkets tend to be the only places that sell beer at discount prices, which can be substantial, though one will never buy beer in Australia that is as cheap as in the U.S. Aussie beer is beaut, though, and well worth trying if that's where your taste buds and brain cells express their craving. Try some of the following (only a small example of what is possible):

Powers Bitter—a bitter, light tasting beer, with a kind of champagne consistency.

Balmain Dry—a light ale, with a slightly aromatic flavor.

Fosters, Victoria Bitter, Melbourne Bitter—made by Carlton and United Breweries, the giant of brewing companies. Fosters is probably the most popular beer in Australia. It's a nice beer, but we can't understand why everyone goes crazy over it. It is hard to distinguish the taste from the other beers that C & UB produces. Possibly the beer that is most similar to U.S. beers (which is probably an insult to Fosters). Certainly it is not as sweet as the U.S. beer; in fact all Australian beer is more bitter than beers of North America.

Coopers Red Label—easily the best beer going. Has a slight sediment in the bottom of the bottle—this is normal; beer afficionados will pour the beer out and leave the small amount of sediment. Greedy people like us will drink the beer sediment and all, which adds to the delightfully full bodied, heavy flavor. A great taste; one can distinguish the hops, barley, and roasted grains separately on the palate.

Swan—a very strong flavor, perhaps of hops, but hard to identify. Not to our liking, but many swear by it.

Coopers Stout—this full bodied stout is a match to *Guinness*.

Both are great; we prefer the Australian brew because we're part Aussie after all.

Tooheys "New"—a dry ale, tasty as well. Tooheys also makes a light beer (2.2) which has half the alcoholic content of regular beers. It has a nice strong taste too, which is more than can be said for Fosters Light, its direct competitor.

Black Snake—the snake is great, and the brown bottle attractive with its green label and sticker of a snake entwined about its neck. But the beer is no special taste sensation. Most common along the gold coast of Queensland.

Meeting People

Australians are open, friendly, hospitable people. One can strike up a brief conversation with anyone, anywhere, without too much trouble. In a pub, you're almost assured of finding someone with whom to spend a few hours chatting and drinking. There's even a good chance of being invited home to meet the family. Or, if the person is single, you may be invited to join a group of friends who are probably going to partake of some sporting event the next weekend.

If you are not a drinker, then the best place to meet friendly Australians is at a local church. Find out when the service is, and go. In no time, you will be invited to someone's home for a cup of tea, (and if you're lucky, some of those delicious homemade Australian cookies). Be warned though. Striking up these friendships is very likely not a short term affair. Aussies are great travelers, so there's a good chance that some time a year or even more in the future, one or more of these hospitable Australians will show up on your doorstep. In fact, Aussies have a habit of exchanging names and addresses of friends of friends that they meet from foreign lands. So, if you have enjoyed the hospitality of an Australian during your visit, don't be surprised if a friend or cousin of this person calls upon you some time in the future. It's expected that you will show the same hospitality in return.

And if someone asks you home to tea, don't make the mistake of thinking that this means a cup of tea (which it might mean in England). It means dinner! While it's not really necessary, it would probably be a good idea to bring with you a bottle of wine (if the person is a professional or educated person), or in other situations, a couple of bottles of beer. Certainly, if one brings a bottle of beer to any gathering to which one is invited, it will always be welcome! (Except, of course, to a church group that does not approve of alcohol, of which there are quite a few. On such occasions, a plate of cookies or a trinket or souvenir from your native land is more welcome.)

Women and Children

Even though Australians insist that things have changed dramatically in the last ten years or so (which they have), the roles of men, women and children are rather separate in Australian society. Depending on the social circles, children are expected to be obedient, to play outdoors whenever possible, to be "seen and not heard." Women tend to congregate in the kitchen, or wherever meals are prepared. Men will gather away from the women and drink beer. Women drink much less beer than men. A foreign woman may have difficulty joining this entrenched social arrangement, without seeming to make a spectacle of herself. Since things are not going to change as a result of you in particular, it's probably best to go along with established social patterns. The two sexes are not as segregated in educated and professional circles, but generally the more beer that's drunk, the more the men get together.

In settings where no alcohol is available, the division can be just as clear cut, though these social gatherings are usually a little more formal, and one has to manage both saucer and teacup along with another small plate. Polite talk about sport, weather and travel experiences of a simple nature are about all that one can expect here. If you like gardening, though, you will have no trouble having a lengthy and animated conversation, because many Australians, as one can see from their houses and gardens, are avid gardeners, since the climate is so conducive to it. One will often find that this topic cuts across all Australian social barriers; that is, both drinkers and nondrinkers like gardening, as do both men and women.

Another sure winner for a topic of conversation is sport.

But this offers the visitor quite a challenge, since the popular sports of cricket and football (Australian Rules) are sports foreign to the American (see our visit to the footy in Chapter 6).

Food and Restaurants

What fantastic variety awaits the palate in Australia! Restaurants, though not cheap by American standards, offer a tremendous diversity of ethnic fare. Large cities and even country towns have many restaurants that could not fail but to satisfy even the most demanding of diners. The best tradition of Australia's restaurants, however, is the practice of BYO—bring your own bottle or bottles of wine and have them with your dinner. Most restaurants will charge a small corking fee, but it is certainly a way to have a good meal with fine wine inexpensively. And Australia's wines these days are among the best in the world, and growing rapidly in popularity in the U.S.

We searched Australia in vain for the equivalent to the American diner. We found nothing even remotely similar. There are many coffee shops that have a clientele that sometimes reminds one of the level of diners at the somewhat better class of American diner, but the range of foods in these places is nothing like that in the U.S. On country roads, especially main highways, one finds roadside stops attached to service stations. These are, however, meant for transient people, and rarely have a regular lot of patrons, as do most American diners, even those that double as truck stops. There is little or no atmosphere in these road stop cafés either. It is as if they were added to the service station as a bit of a nuisance. It may be that Australia has such a variety of BYO restaurants and takeaways that the diner is just not needed.

How to Order from an Aussie Menu. There is a slight difference in menu terminology. An entree in an Australian restaurant is not the main course, as it is in the U.S. Rather, it is an appetizer. So, pay attention to the menu. The main course is usually called a dinner or simply main course.

Waiters and Tipping. Australians these days have a strong, ingrained feeling against tipping. Many still are insulted if given a tip. We experienced this marvelous Aussie attitude when we ordered room service from a gourmet restaurant to be brought to our suite in a large condo in Surfers Paradise. Aussies would complain that Surfers is the most Americanized of all Australia's cities. The meal was delivered, placed on our table, and we prepared to pay. We worked out 15% of the price and gave the individual the appropriate total. He looked at the money, counted it a couple of times, then looked at as, somewhat annoyed, saying that we had given him the wrong amount—it was too much. He seemed puzzled that we had given him such a strange amount. No tip was given that night!

Yet as more and more restaurants are staffed by European immigrants who also wait on the tables, tips are seen as not especially sinful. Of course, unlike America, waiters are paid at least the Australian basic wage, which is about double that of the American minimum. There is no obvious assumption, therefore, that the waiter needs the tip to make up an already pathetically low wage. On the other hand, tipping is more often than not indulged in at the most reasonably priced Australian restaurants. Some places even add the service onto the bill, as in Europe.

About loud voices. For some unknown reason, Americans and their accents stand out in restaurants. Americans are also used to speaking clearly and saying directly what they want, without mincing any words. Sometimes this comes across to Australians as bossy and ugly. It is hard to know why this image of Americans abroad has emerged, since having lived in America for many years, we are hard put to say that most or even a few of the Americans we know are bossy loud mouths. Perhaps the contrast to the Australian reserved and self-consciously modest way of presenting the self is enough to exaggerate the cultural differences between the two. In any event, an American has to be careful how requests are made of a waiter or waitress. If one is perceived as bossy (and as we have seen, Australians, because of their special origins, don't like authoritarians), then service will deteriorate. And certainly, money will be the last thing that can fix it.

Fast Foods. Australians call fast food restaurants "takeaways." Although McDonald's, Kentucky Fried Chicken,

Pizza Hut and other well known chains seem to flourish in Australia, they have fortunately not overtaken the little independent fast food stores, usually with a sign such as "Takeaway" or "Hot Bread" or "Bakery" or "Milk Bar" or "Fish and Chips" or "Chicken and Roasts." The food in these stores is certainly different from the usual American fare, though it may look familiar: dim sim (dim sum) and chicken rolls, for example, or chips (french fries). These foods are almost always deep fried. The Chinese and Asian food offered at many of these stores tastes more authentically Chinese, and there is a much wider variety available, including Indonesian satay chicken kabobs (small chunks of chicken marinated in a spicy peanut butter sauce), a variety of fried rice dishes and Chinese vegetables and noodles, Indian tandoori chicken, not to mention the omnipresent Greek dishes including mousaka and souvlaki. Of course, there is a strong Italian influence, and pastas, especially bolognese, are made with a very distinctive sauce, quite different from that found in America (or Italy for that matter), usually with much more meat.

The usual fare of Australian fast foods is meat pies of various kinds and sauce (ketchup), sausages, hot dogs and Cornish pasties. Hot dogs taste quite different, and in our view are more succulent than the American counterpart (can't guarantee how much meat is in them, though). Hamburgers bought at places other than the chains can be quite an experience in themselves, especially one bought with the works. We won't mention just what is in them, but if you're interested, the book by Graeme Newman, *The Down Under Cookbook*, has considerable detail on this topic.

The fish and chip shops are the most tempting with their deep fried goodies including a wide variety of fish; in Victoria, gem fish, whiting, flounder, shark, scallops, shrimp (prawns) and potato cakes (sometimes called potato scallops—large thin slices of potato deep fried in batter). Further north in Barramundi, bream and grouper are found. The french fries may take a bit of getting used to. They tend to be heavily salted, and larger than the usual fries in the U.S. However, the major difference is in texture rather than taste; the inside of the fry is somewhat grainy and soft because most of the french fries sold in fish and chip shops have been half cooked a couple of days before. When the order is given, they are deep fried once again. Vinegar is sometimes offered to go with the fish and chips. Try it. Some like it, some don't.

The mecca of takeaway stores is Sydney. Beneath the heavy, stolid bank and insurance buildings which rise into the Sydney sky to provide a backdrop for the visual lines of the harbor is a literal rabbit warren of food courts and takeaway shops. In Chapter 5 we have described some of the delights that await one there. To find anything similar to Sydney in other cities, one must visit the newer shopping malls. We recommend the new Chadstone in Melbourne, an enormous mall, with two huge food courts offering food almost to match Sydney's for variety and quality. Chadstone may be reached from the South Eastern Freeway, and is about ten miles east of the city, about half way to Dandenong.

Australian pizza. Order with care. Hawaiian pizza was popular when we were there, along with a boast that pizzas could be served in six minutes. Not a good sign. Unless we were taking pizza in a distinctly Italian restaurant or bistro, we found the quality, or should be say character, of pizza to vary enormously. The definite tendency was for pizza makers, especially in outlying country areas to be rather skimpy on the sauce. Ham was almost always liberally sprinkled on. The six-minute pizzas had that undeniable taste of the frozen pizzas we have bought in American supermarkets. But occasionally we were agreeably surprised. If a meal full of suspense is what one wants, then pizza is the meal.

Pies and pasties. The "flag food" of Australian fast foods is the meat pie, maligned by foreign gastronomes (described as watery meat sauce in cardboard), and voraciously devoured by true blue Aussies. So try one, though we suggest you wear old clothes, or at least find somewhere to sit (standing is better) outside where it won't matter if you spill half the contents. These pies are devilishly difficult to eat without their contents spurting out the sides with each bite. Many a necktie and dress has been ruined by meat and sauce stains! (Oh, yes, you will be asked if you want sauce on your pie, which means ketchup).

The pie's twin is the Australian pasty (in gourmet areas sometimes called Cornish pasties). These vary considerably in taste, as the types of vegetables in them differ depending on the maker. They are generally pockets of pastry filled with chopped beef mixed with diced potato, onion, turnip (sounds strange, but it's great), sometimes swede or rutabagas, carrot and other vegetables. A very healthy fast food! Comes with sauce too. All-vegetable pasties are also common. The quality of these varies enormously. One has to take potluck at getting a good one. The all-vegetable pasties tend to be very spicy, in our opinion, and a little dry—definitely needing sauce. Probably the best pasties we ate were bought in Balmain at Diana's Bakery (Chapter 5). They had a delightful center of meat and several vegetables, blended and mashed into a nice consistency, and a slightly puffy pastry shell that was crunchy and brown.

A typical Aussie lunch might include a pasty and a pie as well. Pies are more uniformly good, although again we recommend Diana's for a wide variety of pies of different flavors (steak and onion, steak and bacon, steak and tomato, etc.). In Sydney, The Pie Shop in the food court underneath Australia Square (on George Street) is also excellent, and offers a wider range of pies. However, their pasties have too much meat in them for our liking. (Pasty is pronounced *pah-stee*.)

Fish and chips. Once the domain of Greek immigrants, fish and chip shops have been slowly modernized and have infiltrated large chain stores and shopping malls. The real fish and chip shop will have a half dozen or so varieties of fish, two big vats of oil, a huge pile of half-cooked large-size french fries. You order your fish, and (as we say, in a genuine shop) the fish will be taken from the display, dipped in freshly prepared batter, and cooked before your eyes. At the same time, you will be asked how much chips you want, to which you reply, not in weight (confusing anyway, because it's all metric in Australia), but by the amount of money you want to pay. It is safest to say, "A piece of fish and a dollar of chips, please, mate." As we noted in our small Aussie dictionary, if you don't specify the fish, you'll get flake, which is shark. We urge you to try it, it's the cheapest, yet one of the tastiest. If you don't like the idea, then you can't go wrong with Australian whiting (much better than the frozen whiting you get in the United States.)

Milk Bars. For a selection of foods somewhat more limited than take-outs, go to a milk bar. One can almost always obtain a pie and sauce, and there's a good chance that a round of sandwiches will be available. Don't expect a sandwich like those obtained in a U.S. deli. Australian sandwiches are dainty and restrained compared to their U.S. counterparts. The filling is rather light. In fact they are intended as a light meal, rather than as a filling meal. There are a lot of other goodies to be had in these little independently owned shops, including a terrific range of candies for the sweet tooth, milk shakes (not as thick as those in the U.S.), and a variety of popsicles that leaves America for dead. In a milk shop, basic ingredients for making one's own sandwiches or lunch can be purchased: milk, soda, butter, bread or rolls. Sometimes even hot water for a thermos, or perhaps a cup of tea if one asks nicely. These are basically mom and pop stores with a little of just about everything. They are worth a visit, if one can stand the temptation of the lollies (candy).

Coffee and Cappuccinos. Thanks to the influx of Italians to Australia after World War II, there are many Italian coffee shops (though few typical Italian bars, except in some small very Italian areas in the big cities). Cappuccino and coffee shops have become a part of the Aussie cultural landscape, but we urge close scrutiny.

On drinking cappuccino. There may be only one correct way to drink a cup of tea, handed down to Australians by the people of Victorian England, who spoke with a plum in their mouth—as a casual scrutiny of pictures of Queen Victoria herself will prove; one can see the bulge of the plum in her cheek (or else she posed tongue-in-cheek). But Australia, or at least Sydney, has been liberated from this stuffy nonsense into what can only be described as cappuccino heaven. In any of the coffee shops we describe, one can sit and learn how to drink a cappuccino. The delights of this drink make it such that a wide variety of ways to experience its special character have emerged in Australia. One might add that there are no such rituals in the country of cappuccino's origin. Italians are never still long enough to savour a cup of coffee. They stand up at a bar, whisk it down and away they go on their busy days. Furthermore, the Italians will generally only take cappuccino in the mornings, often on their way to work.

Not so in Australia. The Aussies have embraced this delightful drink with a vengeance, so to speak. And they have added their own special touches. There are, however, a couple of things to remember about Australian cappuccino compared to the Italian (in Italy that is). First, it is almost always too hot to drink straight away. Never will one get a cappuccino *tiepido* as in Italy. So watch the tongue and don't get it burnt! Second, some coffee shops get a little carried away with the froth. They will serve huge mounds of it. Third, Australian coffee shops sell cappuccino to take out in plastic cups. It takes a bit of getting used to for those travelers who have languished in the morning Roman sun, sipping a cappuccino, enjoying the surrounding ruins. But hold on now! We have found that the foam cups maintain the froth much longer. We have even noticed enterprising Italian coffee shop operators using large styrofoam cups in which to froth up the milk from their machines. But they do make for one problem: how to extract the froth from a cup when the coffee is half or more consumed?

Look around the coffee shop, wait, and watch. It is the froth on the top of the cappuccino that dominates the drinking styles. The older ladies, used to the rigors of tea drinking, surreptitiously raise their spoon and, can you believe it, scoop up the froth from the bottom of the cup and place it in their mouths! The guilt! Tea dinkers know that the spoon, once used to stir the sugar into the tea, is to be left sitting in the saucer. It is a most dreadful crime against Victorian manners to scoop anything out of one's teacup. But one of the greatest delights of cappuccino drinking is to finish the coffee, then consume the froth as dessert.

Older men will not use the teaspoon. They are more rebellious, so they think. Watch how they lift the cup, not by its handle, but often with the left hand grasped round the body of the cup itself. There is method in their mad rebellion. The froth sticks to the sides of the cup, especially styrofoam cups. The tongue becomes important. The tongue can be stuck out and down, the cup lifted up to the nose, and turned around slowly. Ah! Now the froth can be licked off the sides except for the part of the cup next to the handle. This is why it must be turned around, and not held by the handle, so the tongue can reach behind it.

Australian women are more open and decidedly unphased by the public display of their tongues. Out comes the tongue—definitely longer tongues than men, and certainly tongues longer than non–Australian women (although this is admittedly hard to prove).

Other methods of coping with froth can be used, but in our experience are not as effective. If it is a large mound of froth, the easiest is to place the bottom lip on the edge of the cup, open the mouth as if to take a deep breath inbetween swimming a stroke of the Australian crawl, then push forward with the top jaw, scooping back the froth into the mouth, which works until the froth is below the level at which the top lip can reach. Take care—a dob of froth on the nose is not uncommon.

To stir a cappuccino. There is much disagreement about this. If sugar is added (sometimes necessary if the cappuccino is particularly strong), the way it is done is important. We suggest that the sugar be lightly sprinkled on the froth so that little crystals will touch the tongue when the froth is licked, and provide starry gustatory delights. If more sugar is needed for the coffee itself, make a small opening in the froth with the spoon, then pour the sugar in a stream into the hole so that it immediately sinks, not taking froth with it. Stir carefully, with the face of the spoon facing upwards, and a small shaking motion. Do not stir in a circular motion around the entire cup, or you will lose much of the froth.

There are probably many other ways to drink a cappuccino. Look around you in Australia's coffee shops. This is cappuccino heaven! On our traverses we will be sure to point them out to you—they are our favorite hangouts! In fact, in Sydney, we will take you on a special walk to try them all.

Supermarket Wonders

One of the most interesting and enjoyable pleasures for the traveler is to peruse the foods that ordinary people buy for their everyday life: the shelves of the supermarket. Markets are bustling places, the more recent laid out along much the same lines as their American counterparts, complete with fancy electronic check-out gadgetry. While a superficial glance at the shelves will reveal much that is the same— cornflakes, Coca-Cola and the rest—there is much that is different. Apart from the extensive variety of candy which we have already recommended, some of the other unusual foods that might be tried are:

Thickened cream, which, when whipped up produces cream of delicious consistency.

Apricot pies, the same as apple pies except made with stewed apricots; try them with the thickened cream.

Salamis, an enormous variety of salamis equalled in America only in specializing Italian stores.

Lemon saline, a powder which combined with water produces a refreshing sparkling drink somewhat reminiscent of a certain aid to digestion.

Vita-Brits, now a health food cereal, a kind of thick biscuit made of compressed wheaties; great with milk, but better with butter and eaten dry; do stick to one's teeth, however.

Vita-wheats, tough, crisp dry biscuits with a delicious toasted flavor; once favored by those on diets, now a favorite health food; great with vegemite and butter.

Boston bun, a round loaf of bread of very light consistency, with raisins mixed throughout, and a buttered creme on top, topped off with coconut; great sliced through the middle and filled with cream, or just cut a slice and spread with butter; available in bakeries too.

Vegemite, the famous spread made from yeast extract; rather salty, so spread lightly on a cracker or thick slice of bread and butter.

Black and/or white pudding, a slightly spiced sausage which is fried; tastes not unlike "scrapple" of Pennsylvania fame.

Milo, Australia's version of Ovaltine.

Passion fruit, a flavor rare in the U.S.; one can find this in all kinds of products: spreads, toppings, sodas, drink mixes, frostings; or buy the fruit which should be a deep purple (not unlike eggplant) and slightly wrinkled when ripe.

Crumpets, guaranteed to convert the light breakfast eater into one whose first thought in the morning is to toast a crumpet; these round, thick, spongy, doughy things have a brown toasted back and a front that is full of small holes, not unlike a honey-comb pattern. After toasting, smother with butter which soaks into the dough; Some like to sprinkle salt on the butter, others douse them with honey; either way they are irresistible.

Orange juice, the strangest commodity in all Australia, since it comes in many different varieties, all of them claiming "all natural" or "no sugar added," Australian orange juice can taste dreadful and unrecognizable or superb. We recommend S-R juice, available only in gourmet food delicatessens and very pricey (about $2.50 a liter). This juice has the genuine flavor and consistency of freshly squeezed juice.

Raspberry lemonade, if you find yourself in a pub for lunch and have the kids tagging along, ask for raspberry lemonade. This is a drink made from a dash of raspberry flavoring (called raspberry vinegar in Australia though it is incredibly sweet and nothing like vinegar) and Australian lemonade (the same as American 7up). The bright red concoction never fails to keep the kids happy and quiet. Cheap too.

Cordials, non-alcoholic flavorings used to make a wide variety of drinks for kids; they are very sweet, come in many flavors.

Candy, Violet Crumbles, Polly Waffles, Cherry Ripes, Snowballs, Minties, Columbines, Thirst lifesavers, Fantales, Jaffas—we could extend this list a hundredfold. Try these fabulous taste sensations! Most of these are unavailable in the U.S. And we assure you, many of them are very different from American candy and chocolates.

Shopping

Sales tax is already added to the listed price of an article. No one knows, and doesn't seem to care, how much of a price is to sales tax. What you see is what you pay. There are no extra charges. Bargaining for prices, as is a favorite occupation in other countries, is frowned upon in Australia, although Australians when they travel abroad quite enjoy doing it.

Aussie Sports: Peculiar and Common

Australia is a nation obsessed with sport. Everywhere there are tennis courts and ovals (football fields, called ovals because of the shape of the field used for Australian Rules football). The evening news is as dominated by lengthy accounts of the day's sporting activities as it is in the United States. Though Australians are best known in America for their prowess in tennis (mainly Cash Rose, Newcomb, etc.), and currently in golf (Greg Norman), sports are avidly watched and generally practiced by a large portion of the population. One can drive through the suburbs of any Australian town or city and find playing fields, courts of all kinds, with men, women, girls and boys going hard at it. One sees the squares of neatly manicured green grass with white uniformed men and women playing lawn bowls (see below) in every town and suburb. All churches have some form of sporting activity, usually tennis and sometimes cricket. People playing tennis and bowls well into their 70s are not uncommon. Here is a brief capsule of the major sports, and which ones are the best to watch and/or partake of yourself.

Aussie Rules Football

Perhaps one of the most spectacular body contact sports is Aussie Rules football. No protective clothing is worn (well, almost none). You can catch this sport on various cable channels in the U.S. (there's no cable in Australia, by the way), usually broadcast in the wee hours of the morning. You might have to record it to watch later. The game is nothing like rugby, the other game of football played in Australia (particularly Sydney) and New Zealand, which is identical to the English game. Rugby, in some respects resembles American football. To the outsider, Australian Rules football looks as though it is completely out of control, with players running wildly at each other and in all directions at once. The distance covered on the field (oval in shape) is about twice that of an American football field. There are 18 men on each side, and at kick-off (called the bounce by Aussies) each player on each side is paired with his opposite all over the field. Goals are scored by kicking the ball (without it being touched on its path by an opponent) through the gap between two large goal posts, not unlike the posts on an American field. However, these posts are flanked on each side by two smaller posts. Getting the ball through these gaps gets the team one point. There are six points in a goal.

The spectacular part of Aussie Rules is the high flying and catching of the football (shaped somewhat like an American football, though less pointed on the ends). Players kick the ball (the most spectacular move the drop kick, in which the player drops the ball so that it hits the ground on its point, then kicks it just as it is bouncing back up. In this way, the ball can be kicked enormous distances of 80 to 90 yards). The fun part comes when a bunch of players try to leap above each other to mark the ball, that is, catch it before it bounces. Doing so, makes one invulnerable to attack. (More correctly, it is against the rules for another to attack a player who has just marked the ball). There are strict and complicated rules about how one can tackle another player. Those without the ball, or not going for the ball may not be tackled. Generally, you can't push anyone from behind. Heavy bumping from the side is encouraged.

This game inflames the passions of millions of Aussies every year, especially in Melbourne. In October of each year, footy passions reach an insane, fever pitch. If you're lucky enough to get tickets to see one of the final play-offs, do so by all means—but take along earplugs. Very little can be talked about in Melbourne during these final weeks, except who will win, and what mistakes were made by the umpire (referee) whom rarely anyone likes and who is made the ritual object of abuse. (And when we say abuse, we mean *abuse!*)

Cricket

As a game, cricket is very much the opposite of Aussie Rules. It is slow, quiet, systematic, studied, intellectual, and mostly very bloody boring! However, during the summer months, Australian news and leisure time is taken up with a lot of cricket playing and watching. Test matches, as they are called, occur according to a set ritual of schedules between the major teams of Australia, England, the Windies (West Indies), India and Pakistan. There are usually five matches in all, and each has a limit of five days. Yes, that's right. A test match can run for as long as five days, and Aussies will watch the telly (TV) for five days in a row. If you decide to attend a cricket match, we suggest that you go to see one at the Sydney Oval, and select the hill as your vantage point. You will find that the spectators are very able to lighten up the serious game of cricket, and during the dullest moments (most of the time) they will more than entertain you. Enough said! At the height of the season there are also now one-day matches (games) which make the play a little more exciting, and at least provide some closure at the end of the day.

To explain the game of cricket in a paragraph is pretty difficult. Suffice it to say that there are 11 players on each side, one lot bats (as in baseball) and the other lot bowls (pitches) and fields (again, a bit like baseball). But that's where the similarity ends. Balls are delivered in a straight-arm-over style, according to quite strict rules. There was a scandal one year when an Aussie captain bowled a grubber (an underarm delivery which rolled along the ground), for certain tactical reasons. (They said, "That's not cricket!"). Each bowler gets eight deliveries which make up an "over." The pitch is closely cut, heavily rolled grass, and 22 yards long. The batsman (batter) must defend his wicket (three-foot high posts called stumps, belted into the ground so the cricket ball can't fit between them). If the ball hits his wicket, or if any of the fieldsmen catch his hit, the fieldsman (sometimes down on his knees, arms outstretched like a supplicant) will cry, "Owzzat?" to the umpire. The ump must give a decision on whether the batsman is out or not.

The batsman (batter) must hit the ball, and run up to the other end of the pitch, to the point where the bowler delivers the ball. At the same time, the batsman's partner, who has been standing, waiting by the bowler, must run to the opposite end of the pitch. If it's a good hit, they may run back and forth as many times as they can, before the ball is thrown back to either end of the pitch. If the batsman hits the ball into the stands, he automatically gets six runs, and doesn't have to run back and forth at all. Similarly, if the ball reaches the edge of the oval, having bounced, he automatically scores four runs. The five-day match allows for two innings (chances to bat) per team. In practice, though, anything can happen. Since the batsman does not have to hit the ball if he does not want to (unless it is going to hit his wicket), and does not have to run even if he hits the ball, the game can often get bogged down in a cat and mouse affair. Many hours may pass without much happening. That's why the ratbags on the hill at the Sydney oval turn to a few tubes (cans of beer), and are never lost for words when it comes to giving advice either to the players or the umpire. The team with the most runs, and the last batsmen out, wins, unless, of course, there's no time to complete all innings in the five days, in which case it's a draw (tie) as it often is. Ho-hum!

Other Sports

Swimming. The best place to see Australians swimming, and the most interesting, is to go to the major surf beaches. If you swim yourself, just observe one major rule: SWIM BETWEEN THE FLAGS. The beaches are carefully watched by an incredible volunteer organization called the Australian Surf Lifesavers Association. Many young boys and men join this group, and give their leisure hours. In return they are taught how to swim in the surf; they take part in national competitions of a fascinating variety of events (from marching to surf swims to spectacular boat races through the surf, not to mention the more familiar board riding). These dedicated young people patrol the beaches, and are available to rescue swimmers should they get into difficulty. And believe us, they're greatly appreciated. Australia's surf is renowned for its treacherous undertow (a strong current of water that tugs at your legs below the surface), which can sweep a swimmer, even a good swimmer, way out in minutes. The lifesavers survey the beach, and mark out the safest section, with least undertow. They also police the separation of swimmers from board riders, so that the two do not collide. Watch the local

papers for a surf lifesavers' carnival, and don't miss it. You'll
see a side of Australia not too many are aware of—and the
flower of Australia's youth besides!

Tennis and Golf. Tennis and golf are international sports, so
we don't have to describe them to you. There are many
beautiful golf courses in Australia, some truly memorable
because of their wild life (on one in particular, kangaroos
abound, and slyly watch the player tee off. See Chapter 7 on
Victorian car trip and Great Ocean Road). Major events are
the Australian Open golf tournament, usually held at a major
club in one of Australia's cities. This event is attended by all
the major golf pros. The Australian open tennis tournament
is held every year, usually in either Melbourne's Kooyong
(with its amazing new center court that has a solid roof which
can be opened or closed according to the weather). Also,
American and English tournaments in tennis and golf will
invariably be broadcast live on Australian TV. Sorry, but
American football is ignored, though baseball has a small and
dedicated following.

Lawn Bowls. This is not the fastest of games, quite different
from ten-pin bowling. The object is to bowl one's bowl—
which has a weight or bias on one side—so that its curved
path comes closest to a small white ball at the other end. Two
teams compete. It is the popular sport of older persons. We
have seen this game played in Florida and parts of California.

Soccer. This sport is very popular in Australia, and has a large
following comprised naturally of European immigrants. Tem-
pers flare and passions rise among the spectators, just as they
do in England and Europe and South America, though pretty
much without the violence, fortunately.

Jogging. Do it anywhere! Australians are hooked on it.

Sailing. Depending on the season and locality, sailing is possibly the Aussies' favorite outdoors activity. Available through
various clubs, a visitor can partake of the sport. And if you are
an experienced sailor, you might like to tackle the exciting
experience of sailing a catamaran through the surf. Not for us,
thank you, but if you have the adventurous spirit, the Aussies
will love you for it. Nothing like seeing a bloke 'ave a go!

Hunting. Shooting rabbits used to be the major form of hunting for the common man in Australia. Since the rabbit is widely regarded as a pest (and not even Australian, because the English introduced it) many attempts have been made actually to eradicate it with all kind of lethal poisons. Foxes also may be hunted. But they are rare (also introduced to Australia by the beloved English). If you seek real hunting excitement, you might try an excursion up north to hunt crocodiles or in the center of the continent to shoot buffalo (also introduced into Australia early in the 19th century). But again, we'd rather not. In the small amount of time one has to cover the enormous distances in Australia, we would prefer to use it looking, savoring, tasting, sunning and swimming, rather than killing. But if hunting is your thing, please, don't shoot the kangaroos, even if you're told you can. Leave it for someone else. Australia's natural beauty has been torn apart enough already by 200 years of civilization.

Fishing. No end to it. In 1936, Zane Grey rented a specially fitted boat in Bermagui (Chapter 8) so he could fish the waters off the Australian eastern coast. Among his huge catch were a 480-pound black marlin and a tiger shark weighing 1,036 pounds. For the lesser of us, one can rent small dinghies in tiny villages around the coasts and bays. One fishes for whiting and flathead in the south. One can also fish off the wharfs in the big cities around the bay areas, but we would not recommend it. Unfortunately, the bays around Australia's big cities have gone the way of Boston harbor. The Great Barrier Reef, of course, offers the greatest opportunities to fish, although once one is in this glorious environment, one feels the urge to look and learn, rather than to catch and kill. Inland fishing is also pleasant, though can be time consuming. There are a number of tasty fish such as the Murray cod (not really a cod, but found in the Murray River). And one can always use a piece of string and some red meat to catch a feed of yabbies (small crayfish) in any of the brown and muddy streams. Fishing in these streams late at night is especially rewarding. The sounds of the bush become amplified, and one may, if lucky, sight a platypus which only comes out at night, and are present in many of Australia's southern streams.

Australia—The BIG Country

There are many jokes about everything being big in Texas. In Australia, we're not sure whether it's a joke or not, but there is definitely a big craze to have things that are the biggest in the world. We have made a small list of them and where they can be found. It's probable that there are others that we missed. Here they are, all of them claimed to be the biggest in the world:

The Big Banana. This is a huge banana that stands at the side of the winding Pacific Highway on the way from Brisbane to Sydney, just outside Coffs Harbor. Everything to do with bananas can be bought here, including chocolate-coated frozen bananas. One may also take a tour of a banana plantation on a small train.

The Big Fish in Caboolture, Northern New South Wales, just off the Pacific Highway.

The Big Pineapple in Gympie, at the Sunshine Plantation, 60 miles north of Brisbane on the Bruce Highway. Everything to do with pineapples, including a tour of a pineapple plantation, and a ride on the nutmobile.

The Big Sheep in Goulburn, on the Hume Highway between Sydney and Melbourne. This big merino (the biggest in the world, of course) is actually a fancy roadside stop and service station. It's here because it's in the heart of some of the best sheep farming country in Australia.

The Big Tangerine in Bundaberg, Queensland, in the heart of the Queensland citrus growing area.

The Big Bull in Wauchope, New South Wales. Redbank Road, Redbank. Farm tours. World's biggest man-made bull, five stories high.

The Big Oyster is Port Macquarie, New South Wales, a small side trip from the Pacific Highway.

The Giant Crocodile, Wyndham, north of Western Australia; biggest crocodile in the world, of course.

The Biggest Knitted Flag, Toowoomba Council Chambers, New South Wales; knitted with the aid of school children to celebrate Australia's bicentenary.

The Biggest Teddy Bear: Teddy Bear Fantasy Gardens, Beauty

Point, 35-minute drive from Launceston, on Tamar River, Tasmania.

Biggest House of Bottles in Tewantin, Sunshine Coast, Queensland, built in 1966 by bottle collector George Clifford; constructed from 35,000 bottles, and houses a museum of 7,000 bottles. (There's also a "little house of bottles"—an out-house—functioning outside toilet).

Biggest Collection of Salt and Pepper Shakers, found at the Biggest Teddy Bear (above) in Tasmania; one finds here a collection of 6,000 salt and pepper shakers.

Biggest Live Tree House, Herbig's tree on the way to the Barossa Valley, outside Adelaide, South Australia; 150 years ago Johann Herbig and his young wife Anna Caroline set up house in this tree after arriving from Silesia with no money. They had 16 children, two of them born in the tree, which is now nearly 20 feet high and as wide, with a burned out hollow center trunk in which they lived.

The Biggest Cockroaches, giant rhinoceros cockroaches of North Queensland are the biggest in the world; fully grown they are the size and dimensions of a business card; of the 4,000 cockroach species in the world, 450 of them are found in Australia.

The Biggest Letters, biggest letters in the world are found in the Nullabor Plain, West Australia, near East Belladonia; 600 feet tall and spell the words READY MIX, which can be read from the sky quite easily.

The Tallest Tree Ever Recorded, unfortunately someone chopped it down, but it was felled in Watts River, Victoria, and measured 435 feet; it was a eucalyptus tree, of course.

The Biggest Opals, the biggest rough black opal was 1,500 carats, mined in Lightning Ridge; the largest cut black opal (The Empress of Glengary) was also mined here; the largest white opal was mined at Coober Pedy and called the Jupiter.

The Biggest Dry Lake, Lake Ayer, of course.

The Biggest Rock, Ayer's Rock, of course, which is a monolith 1,430 feet above sea level; however, Australia has the biggest rocky outcrop as well: 1,273 feet high Mount Augustus, 200 miles east of Carnarvon, West Australia, and twice the size of Ayer's Rock.

The Biggest Coral Reef, the Great Barrier Reef is 1,260 miles long.

The Biggest Sand Island, Fraser Island (see Chapter 10).

The Biggest Bar, at the Workingmen's Club in Mildura, Victoria, built in 1938, is a 290-foot-length counter, with 27 pumps.

The Biggest Gold Nugget Ever, the Welcome Stranger nugget, 2,280¼ ounces, discovered in 1869, at Moliagul, Victoria.

The Biggest Main Street, in Mount Isa in the far western edge of Queensland; Main Street is actually the Barkly Highway, stretching for 120 miles, the longest in the world (see Chapter 9).

The Biggest Stretch of Straight Railway, across the Nullabor desert from Nurina, Western Australia, to Ooldea, South Australia, the Trans-Australia railway runs dead straight for 297 miles.

The Biggest Stretch of Straight Road, across the Nullabor desert in Western Australia is a road that is dead straight and goes forever.

And for sheer Aussie craziness, we recommend:

The Humpty Doo Hotel, home of the most famous Aussie beer drinker, Norman the Bull, 36 miles southeast of Darwin, this amazing Brahmin bull downs a two-liter bottle of beer in 44 seconds, an undisputed world record. See it on the Arnhem Highway to Kakadu, Northern Territory.

The Ettamogah Pub. Once a figment of cartoonist Ken Maynard, now come to life, this pub is complete with 1927 chevy parked on the roof, and looks as though it came straight out of an illustration for the nursery rhyme, "There was a crooked man who had a crooked pub. . . ." The pub is located on the Hume Highway between Sydney and Melbourne, just five miles north of the Albury-Wodonga turn-off.

CHAPTER 5

Sydney: The Jewel of the East

Two hundred years ago, a visit to Sydney was seen as a terrible fate. Most visitors were criminals being deported from England, and they hardly saw the distinction between Sydney and hell. Australia was a strange, savage, land. What you could eat or how you could get it was certainly a mystery. Consequently, the white settlers were on the verge of starvation for many years, while the Aborigines survived easily on what they considered to be relative abundance.

Today, a visit to Sydney is hardly a punishment. Two hundred years of Australian history have transformed this once struggling, half starved colony into a glittering, sensual city. Its beautiful harbor and landscape are unique assets. In addition to its special historical and aesthetic features, Sydney is the business capital of Australia, brimming with skyscrapers both old and new. The commercial area resembles London or Boston. Everything in Sydney, however, is much newer, and there is a squeaky-clean feeling to much of it. Old winding streets and classic buildings combine with a growing world business center, all within the context of one of the most beautiful water settings in the world.

Oh, the view! The harbor consists of many nooks and crannies which now host a spectrum of suburbs and cozy beaches. Eucalyptus trees abound above the rocky shores. Changes to the scenery introduced since settlement include new vegetation such as palm trees, and new buildings and structures such as the Opera House and the Harbour Bridge. Unlike many other world cities, man-made scenery nicely complements natural features, to give Sydney its own special character.

Everyone benefits from the harbor, which is the focus of Sydney. On dry days, it is spattered with private yachts and sailboats, and sometimes even canoes. Many Sydneysiders use the public ferry transport system to get to work each day, or travel across the harbor over the bridge by train. Some lucky people have (expensive) houses which look out upon the harbor, including the Prime Minister of Australia. And there are hundreds of restaurants with harbor views.

Be prepared to walk in Sydney. It is the thing to do. If you're a suburbanite used to driving everywhere, don't panic. . . . it's not all that bad. Many of the most intriguing aspects of Sydney are better discovered on foot. And maps of Sydney are deceiving, as one city block (though they are no means uniform) is much smaller than a usual city block in New York or Philadelphia or even Melbourne.

The Rocks

A historical section of Sydney, The Rocks is probably the best place to begin an acquaintance with this beautiful city. On January 1788 the First Fleet and several hundred convicts landed here. Many of the convicts spent their whole lives clearing away the rocky sandstone which covered the area and made it difficult to build roads and drains. The Rocks prevailed as Sydney's most shady section for some years.

Today, The Rocks has much to offer to the history buff, but due to unfortunate razing in the past, it does not have as much as it could. Beautiful examples of early Australian architecture once existed here. However, the plague of the 1900s spurred the burning of many of these buildings in an effort to rid the area of disease-infested rodents. Still others were razed with the construction of the Sydney Harbour Bridge in the 1920s and the Cahill Expressway in the 1950s. In 1970, the government finally put a stop to the destruction of these symbols of Australian heritage, and now The Rocks is one of Sydney's greatest attractions. It has been renovated and re-built, and today it is famous for its colonial atmosphere.

We felt this colonial atmosphere to be largely superficial. Many of the historical sites must be admired from the outside with no possibility of entering; others are modern buildings with notations "at this site, there used to be. . . ." True, the lines of the buildings are preserved, but they are highly spruced up and modernized and somehow they seem just too well kept. This is not old Sydney, and it's hard to imagine it so. (Instead, check out Old Sydney Town, a tourists' village outside of Sydney. It seems much more authentic. See Chapter 6.) The fact is The Rocks is more of a shopping haven than anything else. Once one makes this adjustment, The Rocks can be enjoyed because shopping for Australiana here provides an enormous variety of choice. The area is overrun with fancy and pretentious shops, with prices sky high to snare rich tourists. The wares are beautiful, no doubt, particularly the Australian tapestries, aboriginal art, opals and jewelry. Stray from the beaten path to peep into delightful narrow courtyards and alleyways for pleasant dining or peaceful cappuccino sipping. Eateries include pubs, elegant restaurants and quaint tearooms. Choose carefully or your pocketbook will feel the pinch.

Begin by visiting *The Rocks Visitor Centre* on 104 George Street. See the film about the history of The Rocks area, which is most informative and evokes some of the atmosphere of days gone by. You'll find literally hundreds of brochures promoting almost everything. We especially appreciated the free *The Rocks* (self-guided) walking tour booklet. It directs one through the various high priced commercial establishments and points out the occasional historical building. Walking tours are also available with a guide and include yarns and stories about Sydney's seamy past. Call 247-6678 for information. These take about one and a quarter hours and depart from the ground floor in the Argyle Center (corner of Playfair and Argyle Streets), or at the Visitors Centre. One can also rent a narrated tour of The Rocks on a tapeplayer with headphones for a small fee.

The Rocks offers something for everyone, depending upon one's interests, time and money. Here we'll mention a few worthwhiles, but it would be best to look through the self-guided tour booklet (from the Visitors Centre) to decide what offers the most interest.

Cadman's Cottage on George Street was built in 1811 and is the oldest building in Sydney (and therefore Australia). One can still see the steep rockface which is its foundation. Cadman's Cottage is now occupied by the National Parks and Wildlife Service. On Hickson Road is the Australian Steam Navigation building, constructed in 1883 for sighting ships. Climb the tower and look out; the harbor is so beautiful today, it is hard to imagine what the view must have been like for the early settlers. Dawes Point Park, located underneath the Sydney Harbour Bridge, is yet another great photo opportunity. Go there and you'll see why (a prime location for photographing the Opera House). Nearby, the ugly, cement block buildings are public housing apartments. The tenants probably have a better view of the harbor than you do from your expensive hotel!

Sydney Harbour Bridge Pylon Lookout has the second best view of Sydney's waterways and the city after the Centrepoint Tower. Before the tower was built, this was the place to go. Enter from Argyle Street (traversed during The Rocks walk) and climb the 200 steps. There are historical displays of the bridge's heritage, and a small gift shop at the top. Admission is less than two dollars, and one can enjoy the magnificent view for as long as one wants.

Circular Quay

As the center of Sydney's public transport system, there's nowhere quite like Circular Quay. In 1788, this was the place where Governor Philip and the First Fleet arrived in tall-masted ships. Today, things have changed somewhat. There are six ferry wharfs, a train station, a main bus stop, several cafés and takeout eateries. And, there's always a musician playing a violin or mandolin on the sidewalk. (This form of work is called "busking" in Australia, a word widely understood but rarely used in the U.S. Australian city dwellers love buskers. City councils even put on busking competitions. It has become a great Australian tradition.) One of our favorite pastimes while in Sydney was sipping a leisurely cappuccino at Café Gelato on Wharf 5, while watching the people walk by.

First, a little history. Outside the quay is Customs House Square. Park benches are everywhere, seemingly placed for the tourist who needs a moment to look at his map. If you've ever aspired to taking a public bus, visit the Bus Information Centre, a little box-like building on the corner. Here one can obtain schedules for any bus route.

And of course there are the ferries. They are lots of fun, and for the view they offer of the harbor, the price is amazingly cheap. Ferries run to many of the northern, eastern and western suburbs, as well as to the popular fun spots. You might want to visit Manly, the Taronga Park Zoo, or Darling Harbour, to name a few (see below). The ferries are very big, and there are usually seats inside and outside, upstairs and downstairs. There are even toilets on board, and sometimes there is a booth selling coffee and hot chocolate. Ferry staff are usually men in the typical Australian garb of shorts and long socks. They are very friendly and like a good joke.

Leaving the quay by ferry, one cannot help but enjoy being a tourist as the incredible Opera House slowly passes by on one side, while on the other is the massive overseas passenger terminal and Harbour Bridge. Many Sydneysiders take ferries to work and school everyday! (A Sydney local is easily identified as the person reading a newspaper, and not noticing the beautiful scenery in the least bit.) On fine Sunday afternoons, our favorite Sydney outing was to take a ferry to the eastern suburbs to enjoy the view of hundreds of sailboats out for weekend races or pleasure cruises. One can easily see that the boats inspired the design of the Opera House. The colorful sails dance across the small bays such as Watsons or

Rose Bay, their masts stretching up to the bright sky. The skippers wave warmly. Who would want to live anywhere other than in this paradise?

Getting Around Sydney

We highly recommend Sydney's Public Transport System because it is inexpensive and not at all difficult to figure out if one has a map. It is also more fun to travel among real Australians, rather than tourists. But if learning a new public transport system is too much, another option is the red *Sydney Explorer Bus*, which runs exclusively for tourists. The Sydney Explorer buses are run by the State Transit Authority, and the route stops at 20 of Sydney's top tourist spots. Cost is $10 a person ($5 a child or $25 for a family), and this covers unlimited use for one full day, 9:30 to 5:00. Buses stop every 15 minutes at designated areas. For more information, phone 954-4422, or visit the New South Wales Travel Centre.

In terms of the regular public transit system, both buses and ferries cost $2.20 per adult and $1.10 concession (at the time of writing), which adds up if you take many trips. There are, however, special rates available which make frequent public transportation use cheaper. The MetroTen ticket is by far the best; it saves 40% on ten rides, with no time limit (combination ferry/bus/train MetroTens are also available). MetroTens are sold at most newsagents; ask which one would be most suitable to your needs.

Taking a Public Bus. Bus stops are identified by yellow signs. Remember that buses, like all other traffic, drive on the left, so after you have decided which direction you want to go, stand by a bus stop on that side of the road. Some bus stops have a bench for waiting passengers, and some have schedules posted. The schedule either lists the specific times (to the minute) buses will come, or it lists the frequency that buses will come. Aussies enjoy talking about transport timetables (schedules) if you need help. Remember, buses are almost always on time even in the heaviest of traffic. This is another one of Sydney's marvels.

Taking a Train. The railway station is located directly inside the Circular Quay terminal. A train ride costs only one dollar and can take you virtually anywhere. Follow signs to the platforms, where trains arrive almost as frequently as American subways. Some trains are actually double-decker!

Taking a Ferry. Buy four tickets at the counter opposite Wharf 3. They cost $2.20 one way; $1.10 for children. The price is slightly more to Manly. The times of the ferries are listed on TV monitors. As is the case with most of Sydney's public transport, ferries are always exactly on time. If you get confused, don't hesitate to ask for help from the attendants at the information center located next to the ticket booths. We found them very helpful.

Taronga Park Zoo. Catch the Taronga Zoo ferry from Circular Quay and during the 12-minute ride admire the views of Mosman, Cremorne Point and the northern suburbs. We recommend that when you alight from the ferry, don't immediately go into the zoo. Instead, walk to the right, up the hill, until you see a sign to the park, off to the right. This is a pleasant half hour's walk (round trip) along the cliff face, with fabulous views of the harbor. At the point, children enjoy playing on the rocks and sand and waving to the ferries as they ply their way close to the shore from Manly and Watson's Bay.

Taronga Zoo itself is an old-fashioned zoo set into a beautiful hillside, overlooking Sydney's fabulous harbor. Efforts have been made to make this zoo look less like a prison for animals, and these have succeeded in some respects. There is an excellent display of Antarctic elephant seals in a habitat that simulates their natural surroundings. They use water drawn from Sydney Harbour, though, and there is some doubt that the water is safe. (For more information see the article in *Australian Geographic*, April/June, 1990) The zoo is always crowded, and there are hills to climb, so wear comfortable walking shoes. Enjoy the views of the harbor—they are some of the best. Open 9 a.m. every day.

Manly. Manly is a popular surfing beach which has been developed into a popular resort and tourist center. The ferry ride there takes 45 minutes and leaves from Jetty No. 2; a hydrofoil takes 15 minutes and leaves from Jetty No. 3. Predictably, since Manly is significantly farther, ferry and hydrofoil tickets are more expensive than those to other suburbs. But getting there is certainly half the fun, and we feel the price is worth the experience.

Pulling out of Circular Quay, one first sees the Opera House, the Royal Botanical Gardens, and Government House. Watson's Bay is next, well known as the home of the famous Doyle's Seafood Restaurant. Even if you can't afford to eat here, at least look at it. Many of the mansions which line the shore are only visible from the water.

Manly Wharf was under renovation during our visit, but it will someday resemble Circular Quay in its offerings of cafés and other eateries. The beach is certainly picturesque, especially if one enjoys Norfolk pines or topless sunbathers. Also, mind the seagulls which are especially friendly; either share a little or carefully guard your fish and chips! The outdoor pedestrian mall is lined with retail stores, souvenir shops, pubs and restaurants. Manly is especially alive on weekends. A craft market with cute Australian jewelry and trinkets lines the beach. Numerous buskers fill the plaza, offering everything from a marionette show to a lewd comedy act. Sometimes there are special surf or volleyball carnivals on the beach itself, adding an extra Aussie touch to the festivities.

The Sydney Harbour Bridge. Before the Opera House was built, Aussies went to Sydney just to see this bridge, sometimes called the "old coathanger" by Sydneysiders. (Sydneysiders have an affinity for nicknames, this being one of the least offensive; read on about a certain fountain in Kings Cross). Completed in 1932 at a cost of $20 million, the Harbour Bridge is the largest arch bridge in the world, reaching 134 meters (1659 feet) at its highest point. Although a continuous process, repainting has only been accomplished a few times. Painters (once among them Paul Hogan, of Crocodile Dundee fame, so the rumor goes) start at one end, and by the time they reach the other, it's time to start over again.

The Opera House. We've all seen the Opera House in pictures, if not the American Express commercials. Nowadays, this architectural masterpiece tends to hog the Sydney limelight. Danish architect Joern Utzon won the 1957 international competition with his design for the building, which was supposed to cost $7 million dollars and take five years to build. After the outer shell was completed, no one could figure out how to fit everything inside. The solution and the finishing touches actually took $102 million and sixteen years. Utzon had long since given up on the project and on the country completing it;—he has yet to see the building in its finished form. In 1971, Queen Elizabeth II officially opened the Opera House, and today, yesterday's opponents to the construction of this famous symbol of Australia seem to have vanished. Everyone admits that all that trouble and money were definitely worth it.

The Opera House is somewhat of a misnomer: in addition to the Australian Opera, it also hosts the Sydney Dance Company, the Australian Ballet, the Sydney Symphony Orchestra, and contains several restaurants and theaters. Its halls are used for a variety of occasions—even some school concerts take place there. The sails and the shell-like roof of the Opera House form an eyecatching counterpoint to their sisters on the harbor, and soar up to 67 meters (220 feet) in height.

On the whole, touring the Opera House can be quite expensive. Tours are about $5 a person, and the restaurants are expensive. We were quite content to stroll freely about ourselves, and read a tour book about the history without paying any money for a tour. Concerts are a good opportunity to see the inside of the Opera House. They occur quite frequently and sometimes the prices are not too outrageous. The Concert Hall is breathtaking and occupies the largest "sail" of the building. There is no balcony, but seats seem to slope up into a lofty horizon. There are even seats behind and to the sides of the stage. Clear, big acoustic "donuts" hang from the ceiling above the stage. Indeed, this place is literally state of the art—you won't find a more modern or beautiful concert hall anywhere else in the world. Look for the pipe organ, which is complete with television monitor so that the organist can see the conductor! There are also TV monitors in the lobbies, so everyone always knows what is going on. Backstage, the dressing rooms overlook the harbor—a truly "Sydneylike" experience for any performer!

The Royal Botanical Gardens. A haven for walking and relaxation, the Royal Botanical Gardens are located behind the Opera House next to Macquarie Street and embrace Farm Cove. Established in 1816, they are the site of the first Aussie farm. The Gardens are open at 8 a.m. and close at sunset, and admission is free. There is a vast collection of exotic flora from Australia and around the world, all clearly marked with names and countries. (However, Melbourne's Royal Botanical Gardens has a much better and well-tended variety of plants.) If you are not interested in the gardens, a trip here is worthwhile just for the view. Set along Farm Cove, they offer a perspective of the harbor and the entire city skyline.

The people who visit the Gardens are also interesting. Joggers frequent the paths at almost any time of day—one wonders if they have jobs or if they jog for a living. Mothers and grandmothers and babysitters like the peaceful setting. Children are especially common by the duck ponds and kiosk. Packs of schoolchildren can also be seen roaming about on science field trips.

Within the Gardens lies a stately, stone building: Government House. Admire it, but don't knock at the door. This is the home of the resident governor of New South Wales, and demanding a tour of his house might be asking for your visit to Sydney to be cut unexpectedly short! Close by are what used to be the Government House stables, what were established in 1817 as a Conservatorium of Music.

Walk the periphery of Farm Cove until you reach a thin peninsula called Mrs. Macquarie's Point. This is where they take all the postcard pictures! Hopefully you've brought a camera. This spot is undoubtedly one of the top five tourist photo opportunity spots in the world, if not the best! On the other side of Mrs. Macquarie's Point is Woolloomooloo Bay (that's two *l*s the first time, one the second). Just around the point on the Woolloomooloo side of the peninsula is a big rock carved in the shape of a chair, the result of the lifelong labor of some poor convicts! There are similar rocks throughout the Gardens. This particular rock, titled "Mrs. Macquarie's Chair," is the spot where Mrs. Macquarie, Governor Macquarie's wife, used to sit for hours in awe of the view.

The Domain. The road which traverses the Botanical Gardens and leads to Mrs. Macquarie's Chair, Mrs. Macquarie's Road, eventually turns into Art Gallery Road (after it crosses the Cahill Expressway). The Royal Botanical Gardens are now replaced by the Domain. It's the public's domain, actually, and you are welcome to frequent this beautiful park whenever you want. The Domain is especially exciting on Sundays, around two in the afternoon. At this time, the righteous and the curious congregate for a soapbox meeting. One can hear opinions about everything from local politics to nuclear power. This is an event which is very entertaining and fun. Art Gallery Road, predictably, leads to the Art Gallery of New South Wales, located right in the Domain.

The Art Gallery Of New South Wales. Admission to the Art Gallery is free. The collection is varied and fascinating. Perhaps the most obvious aspect of the collection on display is the preponderance of lesser known English painters of the 19th century. In the halls of period paintings, there are some classics of Australian art, an excellent collection of the Australian Heidelberg School (the Australian impressionists), particularly pieces by Tom Roberts. In contrast to the Victorian Gallery in Melbourne, which is well organized but noticeably cramped, the New South Wales gallery display lacks organization. Pieces are displayed for effect rather than for chronological importance. The halls are large and convey an airy feeling, much more in keeping with an Australian sense of openness and space.

Upon entering, one finds the period exhibits on the right side of the large hall. On the left side are the modern pieces, many of which are also stunningly displayed. There are many wonderful exhibits of Australian 20th-century painting here, including pieces from Sydney Nolan's Ned Kelly series, along with those of other well known 20th-century Australian artists. There are coffee shops in the back of the gallery which overlook the harbor. The fare is a bit over priced; simple though, and wholesome. Across the road is another restaurant looking out over the Domain. Again, rather overpriced, but tables are outside. On a pleasant spring or autumn day, this is an excellent place to pass an hour or so.

Macquarie Street

Skirting the Domain is Macquarie Street, named and built by Governor Macquarie, who was possibly one of Australia's greatest governors. It was Macquarie who virtually built the new Sydney Town, both in terms of buildings and in spirit, at the beginning of the 19th century. In 1810 Macquarie took what was left from Governor Bligh's administration (which had ended in the Rum Rebellion of 1808) and established a thriving community of people and buildings. Much on this street is the result of his inspiration and leadership. Today Macquarie Street is the site of significant Australian historical buildings.

The Conservatorium of Music is the castle-like building at the northern end of Macquarie and Bridge Streets. In addition to providing professional music education, it also houses a secondary music school. Many of the students of the Conservatorium go on to be members of major Australian orchestras and opera companies. Check the *Sydney Morning Herald* for lunchtime recitals and night time performances. There are usually performances on Tuesday at lunchtime and Friday evening.

Continue down Macquarie Street, and just past the Royal Botanical Gardens, on the left is the *State Library of New South Wales*. The building itself is one-half stately stone, and one-half modern, with glass walkways. There is a good bookstore that sells Australian titles in addition to the actual library. The library houses some important historical documents. In fact, it holds the major compilation of written records and illustrations of young Australia's heritage. The large reading room of the old library is permeated with the stateliness of learning and knowledge. It is somewhat reminiscent of the New York Public Library. The new library at first impression appears quite small, until one realizes that it descends seven floors into the ground.

Further down Macquarie Street, the impressive building on the left is the *New South Wales Parliament House,* said to have been designed in part by Mrs. Macquarie. Parliament House is open to the public, but it doesn't exactly welcome you. Although it has a gift shop, it was deserted when we visited and the security officers gave us funny looks. The best part was the visitors' log, in which we signed our names (and did not put "exciting!" in the remarks column). If you really wish to see an Australian parliament house, we highly recommend the one in Melbourne, which offers excellent tours and commentary.

Next is the *Sydney Hospital*, which, along with Parliament House, was originally part of the old Rum Hospital, so-called because Macquarie contracted with two Sydney merchants to import 45,000 gallons of rum in exchange for building the hospital. The hospital is now guarded by a bronze boar. Called *Il Porcillino*, it is a replica of a 15th-century Florentine sculpture. It is supposed to be lucky to rub the nose (which explains its appearance), but the animal is very ugly and drools (just water fortunately).

The Mint Museum, a colonial building with a big veranda, follows. The Museum and Parliament House were originally wings of the old Rum Hospital, built in 1816 by Governor Macquarie. In 1851, gold was discovered in New South Wales, and the Mint Museum Building became the first branch of the Royal Mint outside of London. Today, the Mint Musuem is open to the public, and the museum is free. Inside there is much to see and learn about early Australian coins and coin-making. Included is an extensive collection of coins from all over the world as well as from early Australia. There are also some fine examples of early Australian furniture and trinkets. Call (02)217-0312 for hours, tours and special exhibitions.

Next is the *Hyde Park Barracks.* The Hyde Park Barracks were designed to house convicts by a fellow convict, Francis Greenway, a friend of Governor Macquarie. Francis Greenway achieved much success in Australia as a convict-architect, perhaps more than he would have if he had not been deported. Today the Hyde Park Barracks is a museum of history. There is an excellent courtyard restaurant where one can lunch in the sun, out of the wind, just inside the barracks and to the left.

At the end of Macquarie Street are two notable churches. To the right is St. James Anglican Church. Built in the late Georgian Period, it is Sydney's (and Australia's) oldest existing church. To the left is St. Mary's Roman Catholic Church, a Gothic church, the largest church in the Southern Hemisphere.

Hyde Park is between these two churches, framed by Elizabeth and College Streets to the west and east, and the Domain and Liverpool Street to the north and south. Established by Governor Macquarie as a town common, it was named for its counterpart in London. Yet another Sydneysider resting place, much spare time is spent here for picnics, reading, or just taking a snooze. Lovers especially appreciate this peaceful setting as a place to be cuddly. Whatever your intention, Hyde Park is a convenient and welcome haven from city traffic and noise. Anyone for a game of chess? If you have the time (from 12–2 on weekdays), join the locals in a game of lifesize chess by the fountain. It may take a while for a turn, and when you finally get the chance, we recommend that you take very little time making your moves. (The regulars get a little restless.)

Nagoya Park is across the street from St. James Church, in the northwest section. This is a quaint Japanese garden. The steps next to Nagoya Park lead downwards to St. James train station. Also in the northern section of Hyde Park is the first of two war memorials: the Archibald Fountain. It was created by Francois Sicard, and it commemorates the French-Australian alliance in World War II. In the southern half of the park is the art deco ANZAC War Memorial. ANZAC is an acronym for the Australia-New Zealand Army Corps, which originated in World War I (see Chapter 3). The ANZAC is remembered yearly on ANZAC Day every April 25.

Across from Hyde Park on College Street is the *Australian Museum*. Admission is free, and this is actually quite interesting. It is not Australia's national museum—that is yet to be built (and may never be as politicians in Canberra cannot agree upon it). But it is Australia's oldest museum of natural history. The museum's attractions are displayed artfully, but it is a dark building, cramped in space. When we visited, the

Dinosaurs Alive exhibit was in full swing, which meant that it dominated the small museum. Don't go during the week, or if you do, peek inside first to make sure there are not hordes of school children. Their noise resonates through the buidling, making one's visit not the calm and unhurried time it should be. We recommended the excellent displays of Australian natural history, particularly the insects. The prehistoric display is also of interest, as are the exhibits of Australian aboriginal artifacts, and many captivating articles from Papua New Guinea. There are some interesting Australian spiders there too. The Discovery Room is particularly enjoyable to children.

Shopping in Sydney

Sydney shopping is a treat, even if it costs money! Although you are bound to find many shopping plazas which resemble the ones at home, we'll bet you haven't shopped anywhere the likes of Pitt Street, Martin Place, Strand Arcade, or the Queen Victoria Building. When planning your shopping adventure, don't forget that this is Australia, and shops generally close at 5:30 weekdays, but may be opened slightly later on Thursdays and Fridays. As a general rule, Aussie shops are closed Saturday afternoons and Sundays, although in metropolitan areas like Sydney, exceptions to this rule are becoming more frequent.

Shopping

Pitt Street. Venture down Pitt Street from Circular Quay. On the right, pass Bond Street, venue of the Sydney Stock Exchange. Step inside just for a minute at the visitors gallery. Take a moment to remember that while you are on vacation, these people are still leading their stressed-out lives! If you are hungering for American news, buy an international newspaper such as *USA Today* at the newstand in the lobby.

The New South Wales Government Travel Centre is back on the corner of Pitt Street and Spring Street to your left. This is an information and help source. Browse through the hundreds of brochures, or ask one of the friendly people there to assist you in any kind of travel arrangement from plane tickets to cruises. Bus maps are for sale here; they are invaluable if you plan on using public transport.

Martin Place is a wide pedestrian walkway on either side of Pitt Street. Explore the stores, examine the buildings, admire the fountain. In the center amphitheater, there is free entertainment from 12 to 2 on weekdays. And at 12:30 on Thursdays, one can catch the Australian army's Mounting of the Ceremonial Guard opposite the general post office.

In *Pitt Street Mall* all cars are banned, and pavement is cobblestone. Whatever time of day or night it is, people in every kind of attire are hurrying every which way. Here the shopping begins (if it hasn't already!). The stores opening directly onto Pitt Street Mall tend to be the bigger chain stores—undoubtedly the rent is very high for such a prime spot. Clothing stores range from very cheap to impossibly expensive.

Perhaps 20 yards into the mall on the right is the famous Strand Arcade. It was built in 1892, and was completely restored in 1976 after a severe fire. Go inside: isn't it just a little more picturesque than your suburban mall at home? The soaring glass ceiling, complete with stained glass decoration, the gold railings and arches, and ornamental lamp posts make this place really special. Browse in the various quaint shops on all three levels, perhaps taking a ride in the old fashioned elevator. It is possible to exit Strand Arcade onto George Street, but for now, return to Pitt Street Mall to continue your shopping adventure.

Catch a video of your favorite pop singer or group as you venture past the ten-foot television screen in the center of the mall. Also on your right is the Mid City Centre Shopping Plaza. Before entering, look up at the people watching you from their meal tables. This is where you may decide to take a rest. Ride an escalator to the next floor, and make a short stop at the Moccha Café. You can select from a menu of crepes, light sandwiches, and exotic fruit juices as you watch Aussies bustling down below in the Pitt Street Mall. Try the ham, cheese and pineapple open sandwich. Afterwards, stop in these shops, which tend to have reasonable prices and good sales.

We've taken you along the righthand side of Pitt Street Mall, but you'll also discover several shopping arcades, such as the Skygarden, Imperial Arcade, and Centrepoint Shopping Plaza on the left side. The Skygarden hosts stores which were too pricey for us, but there is an excellent international food court on the top level. In fact, we've found that Australia has a talent for international food courts. (Shortly we will describe some of these).

The Centrepoint Shopping Plaza is linked to the Sydney Centrepoint Tower and also to Sydney's two major department stores, David Jones and Grace Bros. At this point, you'll discover that Sydney has shopping plazas hiding in every corner. There is an extensive network of underground plazas, which are not shown on any tourist map, and are a good place to get lost. Thus, if you want to explore these shopping tunnels, come up for air every once in a while in order to get your bearings.

Sydney (Centerpoint) Tower. If you are tired of shopping, but still want to make the most of your time, the Centrepoint Tower provides a 360 degree view of Sydney from the observation deck or the revolving restaurant. On a clear day you can see all the way west to the Blue Mountains. The Tower was built in an interesting way: after each section was constructed on the ground, it was hoisted up. But keep in mind that almost everything in Sydney has a pricetag: it costs $5 to see the view from the Tower. We suggest a visit just before sunset, in order to watch Sydney in the daytime and also lit up at night.

Department Stores

David Jones and Grace Bros. are Sydney's premier department stores. They enjoy a friendly rivalry with Melbourne's Myers, although all three stores can be found in both cities.

David Jones is on the corner of Market and Castlereagh Streets. In short, it is vast, decadent, and accordingly very expensive. It comprises two buildings on the same block, with a total of more than 15 floors. Its prices and the types of people who shop there are comparable to those at London's Harrods. But it's an elegant place; it is uncluttered and very shiny, and there is absolutely no offensive music over the speaker system. On one floor when we were there, a lady was playing "Edelweiss" on her harp for our shopping pleasure.

Grace Bros. also carries quality clothes and housewares, but it is not as expensive as David Jones. Probably on a par with Macy's or Filene's in the U.S.; it is certainly above K-Mart, which also exists all over Australia, but only in the suburbs.

Queen Victoria Building. From Pitt Street, turn onto Market Street in the direction of the monorail (the humming, space-age vehicle flying overhead). Take a left onto George Street, and the Queen Victoria Building is the one with the round roof. It is another shopping treat equal to if not exceeding the Strand Arcade. One hundred-ninety shops, cafés and restaurants span three levels of this building. Philadelphia's Bourse might be its little sister. Built in 1898, special features of the Queen Victoria Building include patterned tile floors, ornamental railings with gold trim and the Royal Clock, built in the shape of Balmoral Castle. On the hour, animated scenes of the royal family light up for all to see. We will have more to say about this building when we return for a cup of coffee.

Buying Souvenirs and Other Australiana

For most people, a visit to Australia occurs only once, so they purchase a wide selection of souvenirs and memorabilia to act as memory-joggers in years to come. The Australian tourist industry is not one to let a poor tourist down. But the prudent tourist must be able to judge quality and find a reasonably priced Australian souvenir.

Opals are of course famous symbols of Australia. In fact, Oz produces more opals than any other country. If you are going to buy opals, make sure that you are not just buying a sliver of opal magnified under a plastic shell. This is a common trick used to deceive the unknowing tourist. Always ask questions because your hard-earned money is at stake. North of Martin Place, on George Street, on the sixth floor of the Australia Square Tower, is the "cheapest place to buy opals in the world": The Opal Skymine. Opals aren't really mined here, but the lifesize reconstruction of an operating opal mine just might fool you. Here, and at most opal stores in Sydney, you can buy opals tax-free if you present a valid passport. However, opals are probably cheaper in Coober Pedy where they are mined. (See Chapter 9 for some tips on evaluating opals.)

By far the cheapest place to buy souvenirs, novelty Australian gifts, or almost anything else is *Paddy's Market*. If you like U.S. flea markets or shopping markets in France or Italy, Paddy's Market is king of them all. Completely sheltered inside a huge warehouse, Paddy's Market is open all year round. It is similar to Melbourne's Queen Victoria Market, except that its focus is more on clothing, souvenirs, jewelry (including opals), toys, watches, etc. Stall prices are drastically less expensive than even the cheapest stores in Sydney, which often carry the exact same items. Due to the high price of clothes in Sydney stores, we did all of our clothes shopping here, as many Sydneysiders do. The stalls are run by a wide variety of people: every cultural group is represented from lone amateur businessmen to entire families. Even if you don't buy anything (and you'd be crazy not to), Paddy's Market should be visited for the sake of experiencing it. Paddy's Market (not to be confused with the church markets in Paddington) has two locations: Redfern (right next to the Redfern train station) on Saturday and Sunday, and Flemington (next to the Flemington train station) on Friday and Sunday. For more information, call 11-589. There is ample parking space at either place, though it is very convenient to ride the trains.

Other Sydney Markets

There are many other markets in Sydney's suburbs. Here is a sampling of just a few:

Balmain. On the grounds of the St. Andrews Church, every Saturday from 7:30 to 4:30 you can find brick-a-brac, antiques, clothing and junk. Old books too. The food stalls are worth trying, though for a market venue, they tend to be a bit highly priced. Indian, Indonesian, Asian of various kinds, Greek and other ethnic foods are cooked right in front of you. Egyptian also. Because parking is impossible, take a ferry to Darling Street, or bus #441 or #442 from Queen Victorian Building on York Street.

Drummoyne. Located in Brett Park, the Drummoyne Market is on the corner of Sisters Crescent and Day Street. On the second Saturday of the month, it is great for handcrafts, especially handmade jewelry. A sausage sizzle stall ensures authentic Aussie environment. Buskers perform occasionally. To get there, take a #500 bus from the city and get off at Day Street.

Glebe. At Glebe Public School, Glebe Point Road has a market every Sunday from 9:30 to 4:00 p.m. Antiques are everywhere and clothes are a special attraction including costumes from Australian movies and many children's fashions. Buskers and merry-go-rounds. Parking is ample.

Kirribili. A neighborhood center at 16–18 Fitzroy Street, Kirribili is located in a sandstone mansion under shady trees the last Saturday of every month. The usual junk, organic fruit and vegetables are attractions. A little more sedate as far as markets go, it is a place to enjoy jazz music on the lawn. Parking is at the school next door, or take the train to Milson's Point.

Manly Market. We have mentioned Manly Market earlier in this chapter. Art work is especially a good buy, and of high quality.

Paddington Bazaar. For the up and coming fashion designers, and those who would like to be seen with a chic crowd, go to Oxford Street every Saturday to the Paddington Bazaar from 10 to 4. Many up and coming designers hawk their new models and designs. Vegetarian food, jugglers and singers are part of the entertainment. Parking is impossible. Take any bus going up Oxford Street.

Peakhurst. Every Sunday from 10 to 3 at Peakhurst School of Arts on Forest Road is a small market selling traditional (i.e., 1950s type) wares. Homemade cakes like your mother used to bake, baby clothes like your nanny made and some beautiful hand knitted woolen jumpers (sweaters) can be snapped up here. Tea and cakes add that English-Australian flavor to the outing. Call 02-759-2556 for transportation advice.

Sydney Fish Market. At Blackwattle Bay, Pyrmont, on seven days a week from 5 a.m. until all fish are sold. Viewing areas are available for visitors to watch the activity in a truly modern fishmarket—no ambience of little old fishermen and their nets, or salty old sailors hawking their catch! Retail shops do sell fish to the public, or one can sample the catch at small seafood restaurants that overlook the bay. It is a short walk from the monorail or Darling Harbour. For more information call 02-660-1611, the fish marketing authority.

Chinatown

Walk south of the city center into Chinatown. It is hardly a match for its counterparts in New York and San Francisco, but it is a Chinatown that is uniquely Sydney. Look for the large Chinese arches at either entrance on Dixon Street between Hay and Goulbourn Streets. Here you will find endless Chinese restaurants, Chinese grocery stores, and interesting boutiques of designer clothing. Shopping for opals here— carefully but cheaply—is better than in Coober Pedy itself.

Eat well here also. On Sussex Street, look for the small neon sign that says "Food Court" and enter a small arcade there. Up the escalators is a modern food court which features Chinese or Asian cuisine, with the majority of customers Asian as well. Here one can get an excellent main course plus soup for $5 (We had Chinese roast duck, for example, which we can't afford in the U.S.). Food is superior, although the service a little trying, but worth persevering. There are Chinese smorgasbords, as well as a bar to buy beer, tea or cappuccino. It is probably the most outstanding food value for the money anywhere in Sydney.

Darling Harbour

Easily identified by the white, modernistic buildings garnished with glass and high-reaching rooftops, the Darling Harbour complex, renovated from an old and rundown railway-goods yard, just opened in 1988 to commemorate the Bicentennial. There are many easy ways to get to Darling Harbour. It is within easy walking distance from the City Centre; a monorail connects it with the City Centre; ferries travel there from Circular Quay on a frequent basis; and most buses stop close by.

Sharks, tropical fish, octopuses—you can get literally inches away from them at the *Sydney Aquarium*. This unique aquarium features glass tunnels which enable safe viewing of marine life in a setting very close to the natural habitat. There are also some excellent coral displays along with colorful tropical fish. Perhaps the most unexpected display, and the one the kids will enjoy the most, is the hands-on display. They can reach in the water and touch starfish, even pick them up, tickle sea anemones and lots more. The Sydney Aquarium is a rare treat compared to others we've seen (and we've seen quite a few!). Fees for adults are $12; children/pensioner, $6, family, $29.50. Telephone 262-2300.

Walk across the Pyrmont Bridge and directly opposite the aquarium on Darling Harbour, one finds the *National Maritime Museum*. It is no surprise to learn that the designers of Darling Harbour intended it to have a water or seaside theme. Just opened in 1991, the Maritime Museum's ten stories contain many exhibits of merchant, naval, sporting and recreational vessels.

The Harbourside Festival Marketplace is the heart of activity on Darling Harbour, and, to say the least, a strange experience. The two upper levels hold tourist shops, many geared to the wealthier tourists. Clothing shops dominate, as do endless numbers of souvenir shops. Unique designer items such as Ken Done and Weiss Art abound, as do little craft and trinket stalls which are vaguely reminiscent of Quincy Market in Boston.

On the lower level, there is a food court gone mad. Here, every conceivable variety of food for every conceivable ethnic taste abounds. Tables outside by the harbor offer probably the best view from a fast food store in the entire world.

What impresses most about Darling Harbour is that here it is Australians who are the "tourists." They are Sydneysiders from the suburbs. They come, in fact, to be tourists themselves, attracted by this space-age glass and chrome building complex. T-shirts with Australian animals, aboriginal motifs and Australian slang overwhelm. More Australians wear these shirts than do foreign tourists. The noise level is high, and there are plenty of places to sit and sip a frothy cappuccinno, and indulge in our favorite sport of people watching.

Go on a weekend, if you can, when the place is jammed with families from the suburbs. Or the many bars feature live music, and one can enjoy a beer (for $3) and gaze out across the harbor beyond the yachts to dream of a Sydney that used to be—of convicts, tyrant jailers, and military men who cornered the rum trade. It may take quite a few beers to bring on such a fantasy. One cannot imagine anything more different from the Sydney of old, than Darling harbor today.

The Convention and Exhibition Centres make up the bulk of the Darling harbor area. They are so big, even airplanes have been exhibited here. Check inside to see what shows are on display at the moment. Marvel at the strange spiral fountain along the walkway. Kids love to walk along the dry peripheries into the center. (It is impossible to understand the above description without actually seeing it.) There is also a playground nearby in circular Tumbalong Park, another outlet for the kids to expend energy if they are a little wired up from shopping.

The *Chinese Garden* is the largest and only authentic garden of its type outside mainland China. It features a two story pavilion looking out on a system of interconnecting ponds, streams and waterfalls. Adults are $2; children/pensioners, $.50; families $4. Telephone: 262-2300.

The Powerhouse Museum is a huge warehouse, formerly the venue of Sydney train repair. Follow the signs to it from Darling harbor, or take the monorail. Free to the public, there are exhibits of both history and science with a unique Australian twist. Visit the old Australian chemist for a remedy for traditional ailments, or learn about UPC symbols in the science center. Use the computer to calculate how many immigrants entered Australia in any given year, or see a special exhibit on Aborigines in early Sydney. You'll be surprised to learn what common appliances were actually invented by Australians.

The Sydney Entertainment Centre, on Harbour Street, about ten minutes walk from the harbor area, is the location of all the big performances and productions which tour Australia. When we visited, Elton John, Phil Collins, Fleetwood Mac, Motley Crue, B-52s, and "Carmen" (yes, the opera) were all scheduled for performances. The Centre seats 12,000, and tickets sell out fast. Definitely get them well ahead. A restaurant occupies the premises of the Entertainment Centre (in addition to a McDonald's if that's more your style) and is open before and after performances.

Paddington and Kings Cross

A decade or so ago, Oxford Street was run down and crime ridden. But recently Darlinghurst and Paddington have undergone perhaps the most drastic rejuvenation of any of the Sydney inner suburbs. The area boasts the highest concentration of terraced, wrought-iron-laced houses in Sydney, in wonderful, renovated condition. It is also, along with Kings Cross, the center of Sydney's nightlife (See nightlife section below).

Oxford Street begins at the southeast end of Hyde Park, off College Street, and leads into Kings Cross. A more bohemian crowd hangs out here, and this influence is hard to miss in the appearance of the establishments as well as the people. A walk down this street will take one past numerous unconventional cafés (like *Café Flicks* or the *Hot Gossip Café*), uppity clothing boutiques, shops specializing in everything (from aboriginal art to cowboy ware), discount book and record stores, and even a few adult-only shops (a little influence from neighboring Kings Cross). Restaurants cover the ethnic spectrum. Some cut across traditional lines, such as Afrilanka, summed up as "a Trip to Africa via Sri Lanka." Although interesting to look in to, many of the shops, especially the clothing boutiques, have an air of the untouchable about them. Many are small, and their wares are folded on shelves or chairs. We felt somewhat intimidated by the salespeople, who we imagined were staring at us. It took courage to handle the items for fear of not being able to refold them properly.

The same held true for some of the cafés—many had only one or two tables in them, and we felt as though our conversations at these places would be heard by everyone (if only one person) there. One lively café that does not seem to have this problem is *Café Giovanni*. Easily more popular than any of the others, it offers a wide variety of sandwiches and bagels, and plays cool 30s music. The service is very friendly and open to special requests (One of us got an American-style B.L.T. after giving careful instructions).

Towards the Paddington end of Oxford Street is the *Victoria Barracks*. Two soldiers guard the gateway and salute cars which drive through. The Victoria Barracks is considered to be one of the most historically and architecturally outstanding miltiary barracks in the Commonwealth. It was designed in 1841 by Colonel George Barney (who also designed Circular Quay and Fort Denison), and took seven years for 800 convicts to complete. Military planning staffs from both world wars were housed here. Today, the public is invited to visit the changing of the guard ceremony every Tuesday from 10 to 10:30 a.m. with a guided tour of the barracks conducted afterwards. The Army Museum (thought to be haunted) is also open Tuesday after the ceremony and the first Sunday of every month from 1:30 p.m. to 4:30 p.m. Admission is free. The barracks are closed from mid-December to January. For more information, telephone 339-3543.

Kings Cross. Chintzy, seedy, trashy, sleazy—all might describe Kings Cross. But this is all relative, of course, because if you're from New York, or L.A., you might think this place harmless enough for a picnic. Nevertheless, Kings Cross is trying its hardest to offer the quintessence of XXX-rated movies, peep shows, all-night clubs, prostitutes, etc. European-style café bars look out on the El Alamein Fountain, which should help one feel that here one could sip cappuccino or a gin and tonic with a touch of class. That is, until one is informed by a smirking Aussie that the beautiful fountain, its water sprayed out in the shape of a dandelion, is locally nicknamed "the elephant douche."

There are a few restaurants and shops worth visiting here, such as the *Astoria,* famous for Australian home cooked food, and *Johnnie's Fish Café of New York,* both offering straightforward food at reasonable prices. The classic *Oz Rock Café* and *Hard Rock Café* are also well within reach of the Kings Cross train station.

Sydney's Beaches
There are many beaches around Sydney. Some are prettier

than others, but to the frequent beachgoer, each is a separate form of heaven. Other Aussies, particularly Melbournians, tend to snicker at the mention of Sydney's beaches. While there is no disagreement about the beauty of the beaches, it's a question of the cleanliness of the water. Recent reports by scientific experts and the media contend that the water is dangerous to humans. Public concern has been even more aggravated by the "How I Was Sick With an Unknown Disease for Three Months After Swimming at a Sydney Beach" stories. However, as can be seen by the numerous bathers and surfers today at any of the beaches, many Sydneysiders consider the beaches to be completely safe, and they swim almost every day and claim no adverse effects. The local authorities do, however, publish bacteria levels for all major beaches, and these are reported in the daily papers. So, it's your decision.

Manly and Bondi. Although located in quite separate locations, Manly and Bondi beach resorts are grouped together because they offer a somewhat similar experience. Both offer gorgeous sea views, a rolling surf, long stretches of sandy beach, and a shopping promenade complete with cafés and souvenir shops.

Manly is easily reached by ferry, hydrofoil, or car. See our earlier section on Manly for details. The beach borders open ocean, so waves can get quite big and rough. If you opt to take a swim, be sure to stay between the lifesaving flags, because the undertow is very strong (see Chapter 7 about going to the beach).

While Manly is located on the north shore, Bondi is located on the south. Bondi Beach can easily be reached by taking bus #380 from Circular Quay, or taking a train to Bondi Junction and catching bus #380 from there. Bondi has perhaps a more picturesque shore than Manly, but we're comparing one degree of perfection with another at this point! There is not as good a selection of shops and restaurants directly on the shore as in Manly (although Bondi Junction's shopping plaza more than makes up for this). However, if you're looking for surfers, Bondi is more popular for wave-riding, and virtually every wave carries one or more adept surfers. This is fun to watch, particularly if one is not from California or Hawaii.

Australian sunbathers are unlike the sunbathers one will see in the U.S. Why? Some women sunbathe topless and Australian men wear very skimpy bathing suits. Neither seems to realize that modest Americans consider them very risque! If you want to fit in, follow their example. But if you're a little too modest, at least *don't stare.* They'll know you're a foreigner for sure.

The University Of Sydney

Though half a world away, it is astounding to see how some things remain constant. The University of Sydney, Australia's oldest university, could easily be located in Oxford, Cambridge, Boston or Philadelphia. Of course, we are speaking of campus appearance, the Gothic buildings complete with arches and gargoyles. Such striking similarity is, in fact, not so striking when one realizes that Oxford and Cambridge came first, and the American and Australian colonies were simply copying them.

The University of Sydney is very easy to get to either by train or bus. Alight at Redfern Station if you ride the train, or take any bus that goes down Parramatta Road or City Road. The campus spans a very large area and is within easy walking distance from the station or bus stops. Walk into any building to get a campus map, or ask a friendly student for an idea of where things are. The Main Quadrangle is the best place to encounter a cross section of students and architecture. Students are everywhere, and though the university offers graduate study, there are very few graduate students about. The university is a world of 18- to 24-year-olds, bustling with activity within the student union and other popular hangouts.

Nightlife in Sydney

No matter how you define "fun at night," Sydney can offer it. Here are a few of our favorites, but please discover your own as well:

Kings Cross. Ultimately, Kings Cross is where most of the action is. And we mean all types of action. Girls, please be very careful. Guys too, actually. There are plenty of clubs in this area as well as many forms of entertainment we'd rather not discuss or endorse.

One cute place that is relatively safe is *La Roma Café* on Kellet Street. Italians will wait on you here as you watch the other customers. This place is always packed and sometimes it is hard to get a table even though most people only order cappuccino. Another attraction is the paper tablecloth which you can doodle on with the provided crayons. A very fun place!

The *Oz Rock Café* is located on the main drag of Kings Cross. It is glitzy on weekend nights, often hosting celebrities and musicians who happen to be in Sydney. There are three floors and a roof for dancing to your choice of a DJ or live music. Expensive, but definitely awake until the early hours of morning.

Paddington. Except for Balmain (to which we have devoted a separate section), there are more pubs in Paddington area than anywhere else in Sydney. Classy ones too. Take your pick. We recommend *The Royal Pub* on Oxford Street, which is beautifully decorated and plays hip music. There is also an incredible crepe restaurant across the road, decorated in Victorian style. Plan a whole night: have a drink at the Royal, then crepes for dinner. Live in style.

City Centre. Few actually live in the heart of the city, so any noise you hear late at night is most likely the sound of a pub or club. If you're looking for a place to have a drink before a satisfying dinner, try the *Forbes Hotel* on the corner of King and York Streets. The first two floors are a classy pub, and the third floor is a restaurant. This pub definitely has some character: the curtains and everything else on the third floor are wooden! Mondays and Tuesdays are pasta nights here, and meals are in general reasonably priced.

Across the street from The Forbes on King Street is the *Real Ale Café*. If you're into jazz, this is the place to be. All the best local and visiting jazz musicians perform here. Not only does the Real Ale Café have the best jazz in Sydney, but it also carries the widest selection of both local and international beers—over two hundred. (You can even get Budweiser and Heineken if you're desperate.)

If dressing up is in order, try cocktails at the top of the Treasury/Intercontinental Building on Phillip Street Thursday or Friday night. Be warned, however, that opera and orchestra goers often come here for a drink before and after performances, so sometimes it is very crowded.

Glebe Point Road is the hangout for university students. Definitely the place to see and be seen if you're of college age. Try *BJ's* or *Café Troppa*.

You might like a dinner dance cruise aboard the *John Cadman*. It is expensive, but a once in a lifetime experience. Go to Circular Quay to make reservations, or call 02-922-1922. Available seven days a week.

Sydney's Coffee Shops

Sydney is a city of coffee shops. While the city seems entirely composed of huge bank buildings, we can thank God that beneath all of the heavy structures are scores of coffee shops where one may find refuge from the city traffic, and relax and pretend one is in some small European café. One can enjoy a cappuccino, which Australians seem to have adopted as their very own, almost everywhere. There is nothing more pleasant than to take a few minutes in the early morning to stop in one of these relaxing coffee shops, which vary remarkably in atmosphere and ambience. One will surely find a place to suit any taste. We recommend the following:

Le Chifley Café Bar-Restaurant. Go down the escalator at 7 Elizabeth Street to Chifley Arcade. Named after the famous Labor prime minister of 1945–1949, this rather dark coffee shop doubles as a bar and cheap but good lunchtime eatery. The attraction here is the smokiness of the place. If one is a smoker, one will find a safe haven here. The varnished wooden seats and benches suffer a certain greasiness from the smoke and drink of this café shop's other identity as a bar in the evenings. But the breakfast is probably hard to beat for the price. Try a coffee (bottomless cup) and croissants (made on the premises we are told) for only $3.50. Or cappuccino made with fresh tasty coffee for only $1. Pay at the bar, serve yourself, and join the other breakfast goers who have sneaked in here for a quiet coffee and to read the paper before starting the hurly burly of work. And if you're homesick, this is the place to pick up any foreign newspaper to read while taking your cappuccino; papers from the U.S., Paris or London are available on a rack just inside the door.

If a hankering for bacon, English style, lingers in the primitive recesses of an awakening morning brain, try the takeout outside the Café Chifley; piles of deliciously lean bacon are on display. The place is warm and a bit stuffy. Recommended for those days that are overcast, cool and rainy.

Rossini. On a beautifully sunny day, it is hard to beat the ambience of the Circular Quay with bustling ferries in the serene harbor against the breathtaking backdrop of the Opera House and the Harbour Bridge. Sit outside at the bar Rossini, as close as one can get in Australia to an Italian café, except for the massive high rises towering behind. *Rossini* and its sister *City Extra* (a little more pricy, and not often open in the early morning hours) emulate the service of a bar in Via Veneto. The waiters hover at a respectable distance and are closely attentive to the point of scrutinizing their clientele. The prices are a little higher here: $2 for a cappuccino, for example, but one can dally here for as long as one likes, browsing through the morning paper, watching the commuters emptying forth from the ferries. The big oceanliners also dock just across the cove from here. The best buy is probably a cappuccino and croissant. The cappuccino varies here, however, suffering from the mass production of success. There are just too many customers. We also tried the house specialty, torte torrentino, which is supposed to be a cheesecake. However, it was a little watery, and tasted something like a cross between a cheesecake and custard tart. An interesting taste experience, but for the price, one could go elsewhere and buy a true cheesecake. A small selection of standard Italian dinners can also be ordered; but for a price; it's probably best to look elsewhere for a proper meal.

Just across the walk beside ferry terminal #4, *Sorrentinos* provides pizza and a small selection of pastas. The tables are pleasant on a warm day. The prices are slightly less than Rossini, but again, if one wants a real Italian meal, these places are probably not good quality for the money. If one wishes to take something on board the ferry to sip or munch, we strongly recommend any of the small bistros along the Circular Quay. There are takeaways to suit every taste, though the style is definitely Italian.

Café Creme. A delightful place to find solitude and peace and quiet from the morning traffic is Café Creme. If the weather will not make up its mind what it wants to do (which is not unusual in Sydney) this is the place to go, for there is a choice of seating under umbrellas close to the noise of Macquarie Street, where one can look at the strange Sydney Conservatorium (a heavy, castle-like structure) or under a veranda, away from the noise and cool breezes. If it's too cold, move inside to the warm and hospitable café, where regulars congregate to partake of early morning coffee. Take raisin toast and cappuccino here. The coffee is excellent, the hostess pleasantly informal, a contrast to the European formality of the waiters at Rossinis.

The MLC Centre. There are many food courts in Sydney, but MLC probably is the best. One can obtain a variety of national dishes here, ranging from Australian traditional Yuppie vegetarian to Indian, Malay, Chinese, Japanese and Lebanese. However, our favorite for the morning is the small sit down café called *Sunriser* where one can obtain a traditional English (Australian) breakfast of bacon, eggs and toast for a reasonable price, and in interesting surroundings. In the early mornings, the host prattles on in a constant banter with his customers and staff, a dialog about the meaning of life, what he's doing there, why some people ask him to do things and not others . . . all in all an amusing interlude. The cappuccino is reasonably priced at $1.50, $1 takeout.

The Terrace Cafe. Nestled under the AMP Building just southeast of Circular Quay backing on to Phillip Street, one can sit on the covered terrace, sip cappuccino and gaze out at the bay, the bridge and the traffic trying to cross the bridge. The trains zip by above the quay—a sense of relief is felt that one is not part of this bustle. The local radio station plays constantly in the background, the DJ making amusing commentaries on news items of the day. Try the open grilled cheese.

At the Other End of Town. The majority of the better coffee
shops are situated under or around the huge bank buildings.
Towards the southern end of downtown, one finds coffee
shops geared towards shoppers. The better ones cater to the
weary shopper who would like to pause and enjoy relaxed,
slightly posh surroundings. We have already mentioned one
of these in the Strand Arcade which runs between Pitt and
George Streets. Opened on April 1, 1892, and recently renovated, this arcade offers a taste of the grandeur and elegance
of the Victorian era. (In certain ways there's no doubt that the
colonies flourished under Queen Victoria's rule!) Here you
can enjoy a quiet, if cramped, cappuccino at the *Strand Coffee
Shop,* shop #24, while reading the handwritten sayings of the
day. On the top floor of the Strand Arcade (take the stairs
rather than the antique elevator, as the stained glass decorations all the way up are enough to take one's mind off the
physical exertion involved), one finds *Noonan's Tea Shop,* a
noisy place, if one chooses to sit out on the balcony. It is
worth it to see the highly polished handrails and bannisters
and the beautifully carved wooden facades of the shops. The
cappuccino is OK, but let's face it, you go there for the
surroundings and the view. As the glossy brochure for the
arcade says, "There is almost a left bank feeling of chic among
the people." They do enjoy themselves, perhaps more so
because the arcade is said to be the mecca for fashion shops.
And Australian women (and younger men) dote on high
fashion.

Walk out of the arcade back to Pitt Street towards the giant
TV screen. The food conscious shopper would be well advised to enter David Jones (go via the Centrepoint, taking the
escalators to the lowest level possible). Follow the path right
around the food court, past the tempting takeaways (there's
better ahead), through to the basement gourmet food section.

The aromas are enough to make anyone homesick; there
are foods here from all over the world, and if they have not
been imported, they have been made in Australia (even in
David Jones kitchens, one suspects) to carefully replicate their
European counterparts.

We counted some 20 different patés and pies of unusual

Sydney Harbour Bridge and Opera House (courtesy of Australian Tourist Commission)

Sydney Harbour (courtesy of Australian Tourist Commission)

A convict receives the lash at Old Sydney Town.

Tiny specks begin the long climb up Ayers Rock (Uluru).

Ayers Rock, 280 miles from Alice Springs, rises 1143 feet above the flat desert country and stretches 5 1/2 miles in circumference. Climatic and light conditions cause an ever-changing spectrum of colors to play upon it. (courtesy of Australian Tourist Commission)

The Olgas, Northern Territory. (courtesy of Australian Tourist Commission)

Great Barrier Reef (courtesy of Australian Tourist Commission)

King's Park in Perth, Western Australia, is 405 ha. (1000 acres) of bushland, most of it in its natural state, offering a panoramic view of the city. The display of wildflowers in the spring months of September to November is superb. (courtesy of Australian Tourist Commission)

Calcium leached from the upper layers of a sand dune and deposited in seepage channels deeper inside the dunes formed these calcium -cemented pillars, later uncovered by wind erosion of the surrounding sand.

This array stands in the Nambung National Park approximately 100 miles (160kms.) north of Perth, capital of Western Australia. (courtesy of Australia Tourist Commission)

One of the authors risks playing with the Devil's Marbles.

Melbourne. (courtesy of Australia Tourist Commission)

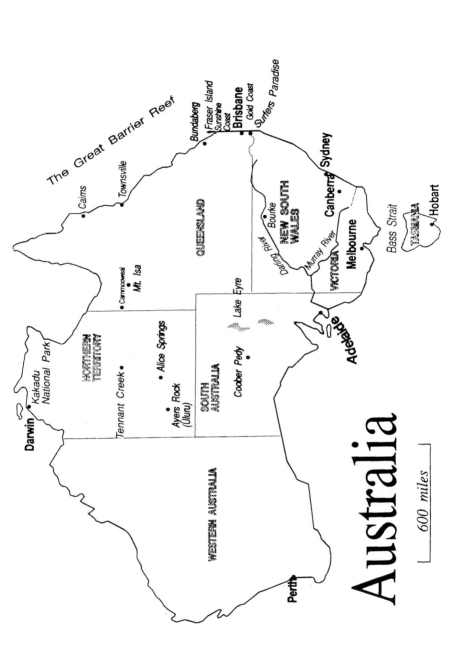

Australia

The Great Barrier Reef

Cairns

Townsville

Bundaberg

Fraser Island

Sunshine
Coast

Brisbane

Gold Coast

Surfers Paradise

Sydney

QUEENSLAND

Camooweal

Mt. Isa

Bourke

Darling River

NEW SOUTH
WALES

Canberra

Murray River

Bass Strait

Hobart

TASMANIA

Lake Eyre

VICTORIA

Melbourne

NORTHERN
TERRITORY

Alice Springs

Tennant Creek

Ayers Rock
(Uluru)

SOUTH
AUSTRALIA

Coober Pedy

Adelaide

Kakadu
National Park

Darwin

WESTERN AUSTRALIA

Perth

600 miles

Western Australia

Kimberley

Ranges

Bungle
Bungle
National
Park

Great Sandy

Desert

Great Victoria

Monkey Mia

Desert

Launceston

Hobart
Port Arthur

Tasmania

Nullarbor
Plain

● *Kalgoorlie*

Perth ●
Rottnest Ils. ▽
Fremantle ●

● *Albany*

Northern Territory

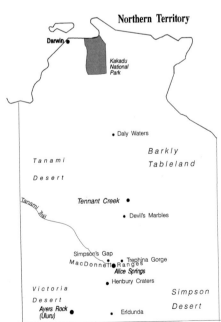

Darwin ●

Kakadu
National
Park

● Daly Waters

Barkly

Tableland

Tanami

Desert

Tanami Trail

Tennant Creek ●

● Devil's Marbles

Simpson's Gap

MacDonnell ● *Trephina Gorge*
Ranges
Alice Springs

● Henbury Craters

Victoria

Desert

Simpson

Ayers Rock
(Uluru) ●

● Erldunda

Desert

Victoria Desert

Oodnadatta Track

Lake Eyre

Oodnadatta

Coober Pedy

Birdsville Track

Marree

Nullarbor Plain

Lake Torrens

Woomera

Flinders Rangers

South Australia

Port Augusta

Kangaroo Isl.

Adelaide

Mount Gambier

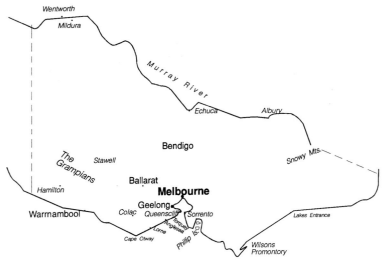

Wentworth

Mildura

Murray River

Echuca

Albury

Bendigo

The Grampians

Stawell

Snowy Mts.

Ballarat

Melbourne

Hamilton

Geelong

Colac

Queenscliff

Sorrento

Warrnambool

Lorne

Torquay

Anglesea

Phillip Isl.

Lakes Entrance

Cape Otway

Wilsons Promontory

Victoria

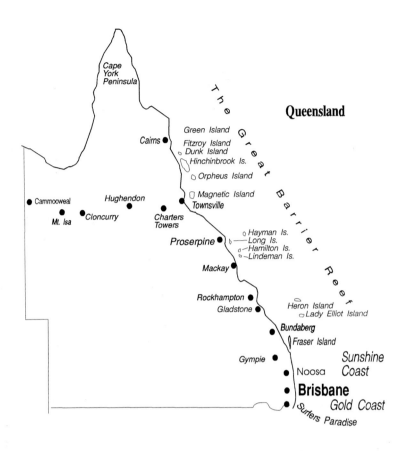

Cape
York
Peninsula

The Great Barrier Reef

Queensland

Cairns

Green Island
Fitzroy Island
Dunk Island
Hinchinbrook Is.

Orpheus Island

Magnetic Island
Townsville

Cammooweal

Hughendon

Mt. Isa   Cloncurry

Charters
Towers

Proserpine

Hayman Is.
Long Is.
Hamilton Is.
Lindeman Is.

Mackay

Rockhampton
Gladstone

Heron Island
Lady Elliot Island

Bundaberg
Fraser Island

Gympie

Noosa

*Sunshine
Coast*

Brisbane

Gold Coast
Surfers Paradise

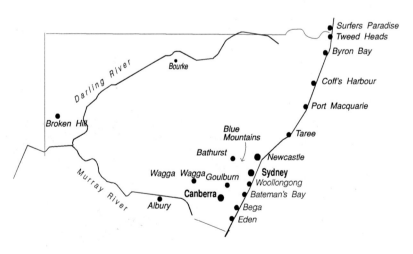

Darling River

Bourke

Surfers Paradise
Tweed Heads

Byron Bay

Coff's Harbour

Port Macquarie

Broken Hill

*Blue
Mountains*

Taree

Bathurst

Wagga Wagga

Goulburn

Newcastle

Sydney

Woollongong

Murray River

Canberra

Albury

Bateman's Bay

Bega

Eden

New South Wales

variety: pork, chicken, leek ($2.25 each), and of course the good old steak and kidney. There are quiches of an amazing variety of taste combinations: salmon and dill, broccoli and camembert and zuctom, salmon.

For a price ranging from $12 to $15 one can sit at an elegant bar and partake of a *pris fix* meal of three courses, glass of wine included. Not a bad deal for the gourmet quality of this food.

If you want something a little cheaper—and with less "side," as Aussies say—continue through David Jones on to Market street. Walk down the hill (away from Hyde Park) towards the Grace Brothers department store. Enter the escalator at the corner (outside the building) and follow the throng. This route leads to *Eats Street* underneath the road, and across to Sydney's most elegant and tastefully restored building, the Queen Victoria. Though the ballistrades are black plastic mouldings, the rest of the building is truly a sumptuous feast for the eyes. There are open balconies on three levels, and from the center one can gaze up at the huge dome. It is not quite the grandeur of St. Pauls in London, but actually the colors and hues are quite special. The dome is of stained glasses in greens, mauves and yellows; the floors are tiled in geometric designs of browns and cobalt blues or carpeted in deep maroon. On the stairs going up to each level (they are called "walks"), are massive stained windows in greens and mauves. This is a building of fantastic colored light. It seems overdone when we describe it, but the many hues and shapes seem to fit together well. Perhaps it is because the colors are quiet pastels, the tone of late 20th-century Australia.

Eats Street is a must. There are the usual takeouts, and tucked in to the right as you approach is plenty of seating where one may relax and enjoy the delights of Aussie's fast food. One place deserves special mention because it sells a rare type of french fries . . . or are they potato chips?—which are thinly sliced and deep fried. They are not quite thin enough to call them "potato crisps" (or potato chips in the U.S.), yet they are not thick enough to fall under the general heading of french fries. Buy a huge bag—only $1.50. It will fill you up for lunch. The unusual name of the concession is the *Lucky Duck,* and the address is 4 Eats Street.

Two other coffee shops in the grand Queen Victoria Building deserve mention. Try the *Old Vienna Coffee House* on Albert Walk for a quiet, traditional lunch, or the *biscopt* (crackers and cheese) and coffee for only $4. You get a coffee of your choice along with a serving of a variety of Australian cookies.

At the opposite end of the walk, on the top level, one finds the *G'Day Café.* This is a cafeteria-style coffee shop which means that the prices are a little lower. Order the special Devonshire tea (scones with jam and cream and cappuccino) for the bargain price of $3. Take it out onto the open balcony and enjoy watching the tourists shopping in the expensive duty free shops.

If it's a sweet tooth that drives you, take the stairs or escalators down to the lowest level, and follow the signs to "Central" (the central railway station). On the right is the *Deli France,* offering French pastries and glazed fruit pies better than one will see on the streets of Paris. Or, sneak into the *Chocolate Box,* just before leaving the Queen Victoria Building for a quick cappuccino and a selection of homemade chocolates and marzipan specialties.

For the person whose life is totally dominated by chocolate, hurry out of the Queen Victoria building onto York Street, and catch a #442 bus to Balmain/Darling Street wharf ($2.20). Or, return to Circular Quay and take the ferry to Darling Street (leaves from #5 jetty). We prefer the latter method to approach Balmain.

Chocolate Extravagances at Reasonable Prices. To prepare for this experience one needs an empty stomach and taste buds that have been recently bathed in something bitter, or at least not sweet. Avoid milk drinks too (no cappuccino for a change). The ferry usually makes its first stop at Balmain's Darling Street on this relaxed, serene journey across the bay, which provides gorgeous views of the bridge, opera house, Dawes Point. Both sides of the harbor are visible. Step from the ferry and walk up the right side of the hill, past the Green Peace regional office, about three-quarters of the way to the top. This is quite a walk, so take it easy if you are not used to it. (Alternatively, one could take a bus at the jetty, either #441 or #445 and alight near the Commercial Pub on the left.)

The place to visit is the *East End Café* at 79 Darling Street. As one catches one's breath from the steep climb, the rich heavy aroma of chocolate engulfs the lungs. But press on and enter this quaintly furnished shop. We usually order a cappuccino, but there are other exotic drinks available. By far the greatest attraction is the chocolate cake with hazel nuts. The servings are small, but don't be put off. This is the richest, most delicious chocolate cake we have ever tasted. The pungent aroma of baking chocolate is an important part of the flavor of this heavy, moist cake, or more accurately a cross between a cake and a pie. The first mouthful quickly signals it will be difficult to finish off every last morsel. The bitter sweetness makes the head almost giddy with delight.

If chocolate must be shunned, there are other rather unusual dishes on the menu. Try the avocado, bacon and tomato sandwich, or Loggers' Revenge (appropriately addressed to the Green Peace compatriots perhaps). The strawberries hand dipped in melted chocolate are not easy to refuse. In spite of the sense of extravagance and overpowering gastronomic delight, the prices here are very reasonable. We paid just $5 for a cappuccino and cake. Try it! It is well worth the ferry trip and walk up the hill.

Should all of this be just too much, and more healthy fare is desired, walk on (or take any bus—it's about a mile or more) through Balmain to Rozelle and *The Coffee Bean* at 612 Darling Street, which is "mostly vegetarian." Cappuccinos are prepared with diligence, and even eccocino (a type of decaffeinated cappuccino) can be obtained. This is an excellent simulation of coffee except that it isn't coffee at all, but a blend of grains. Try it, we liked it! Otherwise the usual vegetarian fare is available, along with bean sprouts, raw vegetables, etc. The place is reasonably priced and frequented by a variety of interesting Hemingway-type characters.

Sydney Pub Tour

Aussies call a tour of pubs a "pub crawl." It is surprising to find that in Sydney proper (that is, downtown) there are no pubs to speak of. Most have been transformed into bistros and "tart bars," as one disconsolate Aussie described them. The transformation of pubs in Australia is probably the most drastic change that has occurred in Australia in the past five years. Once places where women feared to tread, where children were frowned upon, and their parents considered evil for taking them there, these distinctly Australian gathering places have blossomed into an amazing variety of drinking houses, restaurants and bars.

We could not hope to cover even a tiny portion of the pubs in Sydney, so we have chosen one area that is undergoing an interesting gentrification where the pubs are emerging as distinctive institutions of late 20th-century Australia. We make our way once again to Balmain, our favorite place in Sydney's inner suburbs. Just take the ferry from jetty #5, and get off at the first stop, Darling Street. Walk up the hill to the top, or, take any bus at the ferry wharf. Look for the *Commercial Hotel* on the left at the top of the first hill. What surprises the visitor who has been away from Australia for more than five years are the "Family Hotel" and "Family Entrance" and even "Children Welcome." The familiar fare of pub lunches can be had here: they're cheap, and about OK as far as those lunches go. But on this tour, we are there to try the beer and look at the locals. This is a small local pub, rather traditional, in spite of its family orientation. The bar is full of local residents, rowdy, exchanging good-natured, if a little coarse, banter. Ask for a middy. (This is the smallest size of beer. A warning: Australian beer is very strong and has been known to make fools of unwary foreigners! If a large beer is a must, ask for a schooner.) Try a Resch's Old, a tasty brown ale.

Sit by the door to watch the passers by, but be careful not to sit in a local's seat. This is a typical Australian pub, pretty much how local pubs have been in Australia for some 100 years or so. Take one drink only though, please! We have a long way to go. When you are ready, walk up the next hill right to the top, almost in Balmain proper. You will have noticed the interesting mixture of slums, dilapidated structures, and beautifully renovated old buildings which, according to the current real estate market, are worth something like half a million dollars. On the left at the top of the hill is the *London Hotel*. Now this hotel is really different. On Friday nights and Saturday nights, the young drinkers who are out for a night on the town, sit in a row of seats on a balcony overlooking Darling Street. As it gets late, the revelers overflow onto the street itself. These are all very well dressed, up-and-coming yuppies, flush with money and belief in a prosperous future. The inside of the pub is pretentious to say the least, renovated with redwood architraves and a polished wood bar. There is even no familiar yeasty smell of stale beer. The young businesslike girls serve quickly and wear rather 21st-century dress; the bright hair colors and earrings in strange places should not mislead—they are there to collect money! One can order almost any kind of beer except local, as the regular clientele spend big money to try fancy beers from all round the world. One cannot help feeling bouyed with the materialistic optimism of this place, yet the hovels awaiting restoration that still surround the pub are a reminder that decay is never that far away! This is a good place to try a Tasmanian Stout.

Afterwards we walk up the street past the chic (or would-be-chic) shops full of antiques. One announces "We will not be opening until our container of French furniture arrives next month," while another invites one to browse new-age books, and yet others beckon into the *Courtyard Cafe* for "Thursday's roast." Pass the park on the left, the Balmain Church across the road on the right (site of a pleasant market every Saturday morning), and cross at the pedestrian crossing (cars are required to stop, even if you have but one foot on the crossing) to the *Cricketer's Arms Hotel*. This is a small corner hotel which boasts one snooker table, a few "pokies" (poker machines) and lots of older gentlemen, chatting in small groups. This is the local pensioners' hangout. Study their faces, watch their gesticulations as they complain that Australia's no bloody good anymore. We won't say why. . . . ask if you dare. This is another old, traditional pub. The bar lady is older and friendly. Money doesn't preoccupy her as it does the ladies down at the London. Not a lot to choose from here. We suggest a Tooheys New middy, of course. The TV is on here incessantly, mostly on sporting events, many televised from the United States.

Then cross the road and continue up Darling Street to the pub on the corner of Beattie and Darling Streets. Here is a pub with good old Aussie atmosphere! An older woman runs this pub, her daughter (we think) does much of the bar tending. There is good natured bantering between these people and their customers, who clearly love the place. It's noisy and busy. The pokies are hard at work, as is the snooker table out back. It's a bit of a grimy pub, but there are plenty of tables and chairs—unusual for a traditional Aussie pub. If you're lucky, you'll also be able to partake of some cheese and crackers with your beer. Make it a middy of Tooheys 2.2 with a somewhat lighter alcohol content. Then out the door and up Darling Street again. A rather long walk to the top of the hill, then at the corner of Mullens and Darling, find the *Town Hall Hotel* that dominates the intersection, its big double doors open wide all round the corner most of the year.

Now this is a pub that is frequented by gay men of all ages, both as customers and as bartenders. But as well, there are old locals who sit at the end of the bar, staring out at the traffic, drinking their schooner of beer, just as they must have done for some 30 years or more. The clients understand each other well. There is much good-natured banter. This pub has an excellent bottle department. If hunger has caught up with you, especially after the long walk and beer, purchase a bottle of wine from the bottle shop, then cross the road to the other side of Darling Street. Walk a little way down and try the Balmain Pizzeria. Their pizza is delicious, made fresh while you wait. BYO, of course.

Now for our last two pubs. We must retrace our steps back to the *Town Hall Hotel*, then on down Mullens Street to the next intersection, a small roundabout. There are two pubs on corners across from each other, and how different they are! *Dick's Hotel* should be the first experience. This is what would have been called a "bloodhouse" in the old days, and why not, with a name like Dick's? In spite of its signs encouraging parents to bring their children into the beer garden for lunch or dinner, this pub is very much in the old tradition, which means rowdy, aggressive, tough. There is a simple break with tradition: there are a lot of women in the public bar; unusual in such a rowdy pub.

Across the road, it's another world. The *Exchange Hotel* has been transformed into a mature yuppie bar. Here the beer costs a little more, and the aroma of gourmet cooking wafts through the air. Young professional–looking men and women serve behind the bar. Ask for a Coopers or even a local brew, a Balmain Dry. There are quaint prints and artifacts around the bar walls. Sometimes quiet music plays in the background. On Fridays and Saturdays, this pub jumps with energy and youthful success. One can join the group upstairs on the old veranda overlooking the intersection. Dinner with ample wine is the order of the day. Linger here to get your breath, then step out on the Mullens Street side, cross the road and go down the hill 20 yards or so to catch a bus back downtown to the Town Hall (York Street).

CHAPTER 6

Melbourne: A Bridge to Gardens

Melbourne (pronounced "Melbn," not "Melbooorne") is thought of by Australians as the artistic and intellectual center of Australia, in contrast to Sydney which is the banking and business center, a little crass and showy. There is a long time rivalry between these two cities, so that their differences are often exaggerated. What Melbourne does not have—and must struggle constantly to make up for—is the magnificent harbor that simply sets Sydney apart. On the other hand, Melbourne was not settled as a convict colony, so its downtown streets are not narrow and confused, as are Sydney's. Melbourne is well planned, with broad tree-lined streets, and even something that almost resembles a freeway system. And the freeway approach to Melbourne from the south and west over the Westgate Bridge is stunning. The bridge, site of a disaster some years ago when part of it collapsed as it was being built, rises up over the Port of Melbourne like a huge ribbon. Views of the city are startling, and even the industrial suburbs to the west present a kind of stark beauty. The bridge is not exceptional in design as modern bridges go, but does convey a feeling of being in flight. It is a pity that Melbourne does not have a fantastic harbor to go with it!

As for Melbourne's being more intellectual and artistic: well, this is a hot topic. The local wisdom is that Sydney has its theater; Melbourne has its ballet and music. The galleries and museums of each have their strong and weak points, as we will see. There is no doubt, however, that Melbourne's main daily newspaper *The Age* is the best paper in Australia. Its depth of coverage, and particularly its restraint from sensational reporting and general accuracy are shining lights compared to the dismal array of tabloid dailies produced elsewhere. A possible exception is the national daily, *The Australian,* a Murdoch paper, only grudgingly approved of by Aussies. The coverage in this paper is more America oriented compared to most other Australian dailies which are still oriented towards England and Europe.

Downtown

The shopping area of Melbourne is quite small, about a square mile (roughly the same size as New York's Central Park or Rome's Old Rome). Aussies like to shop. Every day thousands pour into this dense shopping area from the imposing (if still a little dilapidated looking) Flinders Street Station. The crowds in the shopping streets are representative of all Australian city centers. The streets are always crammed. Until 5 p.m., that is, when everything shuts down and the city dies. So, plan wisely, and get your shopping done between 9 and 5.

Our guide for downtown Melbourne was a little book called *Walking Around Melbourne* by de Lacy Lowe, (Leisure Press, 1989). However, this book is only for those who have an eye for detail, and a compulsive need to know everything about all buildings. Lowe describes 20 walks. We accomplished them in four days' outings. We didn't hurry, but we did walk quite a bit.

Melbourne is famous for its trams. The clanging of bells, the rattling of metal wheels on tracks are sounds that stay with the visitor for years. But a little warning: they're bloody confusing (as the locals will say). Unlike the Sydney public transport which has a well integrated system of ticketing that's easy to understand, Melbourne does not have a system that everyone likes or can understand. During our visit, a new ticketing system was introduced (January 1990), which few Melbournians could figure out. Here's how the system works: you can buy three hour or daily scratch tickets at most newsagents. You validate the ticket by scratching off the month, day, and hour of your first tram, bus, or train ride. Depending on the type of ticket, you have an unlimited number of rides within either a three-hour or day-long period. So why scratch it at all? Why not use the same ticket over and over? The catch is that there is usually someone aboard to check your ticket. The scratch ticket is also transferable to trains and buses. Our guess is that by the time this book goes to print, Melbourne will have given up on this system and will be trying yet another. Schedules and maps are available at any tourist center.

There is a small loop subway, and all suburban trains from Melbourne's vast, sprawling suburbs converge on Flinders Street station. Don't be surprised if a Melbournian apologizes for the filthy trains. He obviously hasn't been to New York or Philadelphia. Even Boston and London trains are dirtier than these. Melbourne's trains are a definite luxury.

Day One: Downtown

We have planned a long walk for this day. If you are a shopper or perfer to walk slowly, we recommend taking two days, leaving the walk through the Botanical Gardens for the second day. A good beginning is to stop in at the tourist information booth on Bourke Street, just down a little from Swanston Street. Ask for a free map of Melbourne, as well as a guide to transit systems, particularly the tramways system, and the train and subways. Pick up a copy of *This Week in*

Melbourne (also free) which lists restaurants, shows and other entertainments. From our experience, it is best to get shopping urges out of one's veins first. The blocks bounded by Lonsdale, Elizabeth, Flinders and Russell Streets provide some of the greatest shopping challenges. Begin with the huge *Myer Complex* on Bourke Street, which extends for five stories all the way back across Little Lonsdale to Lonsdale Street itself. This is the largest department store in the Southern Hemisphere, and one of the five largest in the world. Sidney Myer arrived from Russia in 1878 to work in his nephew's clothing business. In 1911, Myer bought an old drapery store on Bourke Street and in 1914 the block of land next to it. It was here that he built the eight-story building, which stands today. One can buy just about anything in Myers. Look for the excellent souvenir department for quality souvenirs, and if it's around Christmastime, visit the entire top floor of the Lonsdale Street store which is devoted to toys and entertainment for children.

The Myers cafeteria is excellent for people watching. For decades tired "mums with their kiddies," having traveled in from the distant suburbs, or even from the country for the day, have preferred to eat here. Take the quaint old elevator to the third floor and the cafeteria. It has always been operated by a smart older woman with an affected English accent. A nice touch. On the same floor there is a huge book shop that is hard to resist, although the price of books in Australia is extraordinarily high. However the range and quality of the books may tempt one to dig further into the pocket.

Don't buy your coffee or dessert at the cafeteria. Instead, stop off at the snack bar around the corner from the cafeteria for one of the best cups of cappuccino in Melbourne, equaled only by those obtained in Italy itself, and in Melbourne's Little Italy in Carlton.

Walk back through Myers and exit at Bourke Street. Turn west towards Bourke Street Mall where boutiques abound. Turn right about half way down the mall into the glass-roofed Royal Arcade, and proceed through to Little Collins Street. Across the street another arcade awaits, the *Block Arcade*, perhaps one of Melbourne's more beautiful pieces of Victorian architecture. This arcade was erected in 1893. Note the beautiful glass dome at the center of the arcade where it turns sharply at a right angle and continues to both Elizabeth and Collins Streets. At the Collins Street entrance, pause for a cup of tea at the *Hopeton,* a traditional Victorian tearoom. The European minded may proceed up the hill on Collins Street to the "Paris end" of Melbourne, so-called because of the trees and elegant outdoor cafés.

For our choice, we would rather proceed only as far as Russell Street then on to Little Bourke Street. Take a left or right on this wonderful little street, for here is the heart of Melbourne's *Chinatown.* There are so many Chinese restaurants here, it's best to walk up and down the street until a restaurant takes one's fancy. Australian Chinese food is distinctive and different from its American-Chinese counterpart. To our taste, the dishes are possibly more authentically Chinese, particularly the Beijing cuisine. Traditions are also a little different. One must ask for water, and tea must be ordered separately and is an additional charge. Chinese noodles which are so much looked forward to by children in American Chinese restaurants are never provided unless requested, and one must pay extra. Nor is steamed rice included in the entree. One must order this separately, and pay for it in addition. The food, however, is delicious.

Now for a brisk walk after a large meal. Walk down Bourke Street to Swanston, then south towards Flinders Street station. Cross Princes Bridge, and prepare for a long and enjoyable walk. There is a small stairway just immediately over the bridge on the left; follow this down to the bottom and suddenly the noise of the city is gone. Here one can rent bicycles for $6 an hour, and tour the 25km of bicycle trails along the Yarra River. Helmets are required. Two person bikes are available.

One can saunter along the Yarra, where the huge plane trees shelter one from the sun. The Yarra flows swiftly, its color the usual muddy red of Australian rivers. (The wags in Oz joke that Melbourne is the only city in the world where a river flows upside down!) In about a mile or so, the *National Tennis Centre* becomes visible on the left. Cross to the right before getting too close to the Tennis Center where fast moving traffic is a problem. Walk on up the hill through Victoria Gardens and Kings Domain until the *Sidney Myer Music Bowl* is visible. This unusual structure, which looks more like a canvas awning (which it isn't) than a solid metal and cement structure, was donated by the Myer Trust and opened in 1962. Free concerts are frequently staged in the bowl; the most popular program is the carols by candlelight when thousands carry lighted candles and sing along with the Melbourne Symphony.

Walk out of the bowl and keep going straight. Follow the sign to the Lynch Gate, where one enters the world famous *Melbourne Botanic Gardens.* Pause to read the inscription on the small sign to the right of the gate: "This garden belongs to the people. . . ." as American a saying as one could get! This garden was established in 1846. It is renowned for its 19th-century landscaping and 10,000 species of cultivated varieties from all over the world. A small box just inside the gate to the right offers free maps. Take one. Getting lost is very easy in these gardens, although there are helpful signposts in many places. While it is a most pleasant place in which to get lost, after a full morning's walk, extra mileage is really not wanted. Wandering and lingering by the lakes is certainly a must. The surprising fact about these gardens is their peace and tranquility, situated as they are right in the middle of a very noisy, bustling city. But perhaps the most striking feature of this park is that one feels completely safe in the many secluded nooks and crannies. There are no joggers or bikes either. Just people walking, enjoying the garden. Follow the signs, or ask the locals, as we did, about the way to the kiosk, a traditional meeting place for older Australians. Make sure you are there before 4 p.m. when it closes. Devonshire teas are a must on the patio where one can watch water birds, swans and sparrows that fly right up to the tables. A very relaxed place . . . but watch for the birds overhead.

Now, ask the way once again, for the shortest route back through the gardens to Princes Bridge. This will take you to St. Kilda Road, quite a long walk. Cross the grand tree-lined street of St. Kilda Road and catch a tram back to Princes Bridge. Be sure to look to the west as the tram crosses the bridge. On a small patch of green wedged in between the National Gallery and the Victorian Performing Arts Centre there is usually free musical entertainment until sundown. One can alight just across the bridge and enter the historic *Young and Jacksons Pub*. Climb the steps at the Swanston Street entrance to the bistro and lounge. Here the food is ordinary, but reasonably priced for an inner city bistro. Young and Jacksons is situated on the site on which John Batman, the founder of Melbourne, bought land for $200 and built a cottage for his family. It later became a school for young ladies and finally a pub in 1861. Two Irishmen took over the pub in 1875, and because of their love of art, filled it with all kinds of outstanding paintings. The pub became famous for the nude painting of *Chloe* (through to the inside section of the bistro), by Jules Lefebre, which shocked Victorian society. Ask any young Aussie if he's heard of *Chloe*, and he will tell you where it hangs. Strangely, during the Victorian period until the 1960s (some would say that the Victorian era lasted in Victoria until that time) the painting hung in the public bar. It has now been shifted to the upstairs bistro, frequented by more tidy and proper types, young women included.

Day Two: A Day at the Zoo

Zoos are zoos, so the saying goes. And to some extent, that's right. But there are zoos and there are zoos. *Melbourne Zoo* (the Royal Zoological Gardens) is exceptional in that it is laid out like a massive garden with cages carefully hidden by shrubs and flowers that seem to grow so well in Victoria. Notable displays are the Australian seals (don't miss feeding time) and the aviary in which a simulation of various ecological systems has been constructed. The visitor walks on an elevated platform amid many colored birds, some even nesting. The cage is enormous, big enough for most birds to fly around.

Also well worth the visit is the platypus exhibit, even if it makes one feel a little guilty, since the platypus seems to have developed a repetitive behavior pattern, all too revealing of its suffering in captivity. However, there is no other way in which one could see this strange but gorgeous creature close up.

The penguin display is disappointing. It is best to see penguins at Philip Island (see the following chapter). But walk by and have a light lunch at the somewhat expensive bistro beside Silver Jubilee Island (opened by Her Majesty the Queen during her Silver Jubilee visit), complete with swinging monkeys and a wide variety of birds, many of which leave their marks on the tables and chairs. But the ambience is most enjoyable.

Save the best till last. The butterfly house is worth the price of entry alone. One enters an incredible world of hundreds, if not thousands, of multi-colored butterflies in a tropical surrounding. It's hot and humid, and one at first wants to turn back on entering. But all care for personal comfort recedes quickly when butterflies of all varieties flutter in front and overhead, often alighting on hats or clothing. The enclosure, when considered in relation to the butterflies' size and flying ability, is enormous, and one doesn't feel the slight regret one has in regard to birds in the great aviary. Here one sees butterflies with huge blue wings (the Ulysses butterfly from Dunk Island), gold and black butterflies, and many others. It's hard to leave—fascination with these frail and beautiful creatures holds one rapt.

This is Australia's oldest zoo, established in 1857, and located next to the Royal Botanical Gardens. It is now located only 4 kilometers from the city center in Royal Park. Reach it by a #55 or #56 tram from the city (downtown), an interesting ride which passes through North Melbourne's inner suburbs and Royal Park.

Friends of the zoo conduct guided tours daily between 10 a.m. and 3 p.m. on weekdays and 11 a.m. and 4 p.m. Saturdays and Sundays and most public holidays. The zoo is open from 9 to 5, but most main attractions are open only from 10 to 4:30. Admission for adults is $5.60; children 4–14, $2.80; under 4 free. Strollers may be hired for $2 with a $5 deposit required. Wheelchairs are available free.

Day Three: Parliament House, Treasury and Fitzroy Gardens, Collins Place

"That great America on the other side of the sphere, Australia," is how the American author Herman Melville thought of Australia. It's almost easy to forget that Australia is a member of the British Commonwealth. A visit to *Parliament House* will remedy this situation. Take a tram or train and get off at Parliament Station, Spring Street. Look for a big cluster of marble columns. Note also the lamp posts complete with red and gold crowns on top. Aim for a free guided tour; they're at 10, 11, 2, and 3 o'clock each day. These tours are conducted by very friendly staff, and are thorough and interesting.

The interior ornamentation was restored to its original state in 1985, complete with 23-karat gold leaf, which explains why Aussies pay so much tax. You'll also see paintings of Queen Victoria and her husband Prince Albert, the House of Commons, and the Legislative Council (Upper House). Note especially the luxurious surroundings, i.e., velvet chairs and seat cushions. Some might say that the allusions to royalty one sees everywhere are a little overdone. Is a seat only to be sat on by a queen or king of England really worth the space it takes up?

The *Princess Theater,* an overly decorated gold building, is across the street from Parliament House. Peek in and proceed down Spring Street towards Parliament Station. Pass the Old Treasury Building on the left (nothing to see here but another regal-looking building) and note the Treasury Gardens. These gardens are nothing special in Melbourne's vast array of parks and gardens, but pleasant nonetheless. There is a quiet little pond here and a memorial to John F. Kennedy. Most importantly, the little red brick building is a toilet.

Cross the street and admire the famous *Fitzroy Gardens.* If one's stay in Melbourne is limited, the Royal Botanical Gardens and Fitzroy Gardens are the two must-sees. The two include all the exotic plants and colorful flowers in Australia. Grab a bite to eat at one of the food trucks parked on the street. This might be a time to try an Aussie pie and sauce, which we recommend that one eats standing up (relax on the bench nearby after you have eaten). Or if a bigger selection is preferred, venture to the kiosk in the center of the gardens. Signs clearly mark the way. By now there are two things present in any direction one looks and in abundance: colorful flowers and Japanese tourists. The beautiful flowers here are the most popular back drop for wedding photos in Melbourne. (And no doubt many Japanese tourists have inadvertently appeared in these pictures too.)

Back to our tour. The long white building with the round roof is the Conservatory for plants and flowers. Adults can enter for $.60, children $.20. The man at the door prefers correct change and takes a dim view of large notes. (The author speaks from experience.) The bright and well tended flowerbeds in front of the Conservatory impress; go inside if you can.

Cook's Cottage is the quaint house next to the Conservatory (just follow the Japanese signs). But this was not Captain Cook's own cottage. It was his parents' house, shipped here from England. Why is it here in Melbourne and not in Sydney, which is the historical birthplace of Australia? It was, after all, Captain Cook who first set foot on Australia at Botany Bay and claimed it for England. Good question. For a small fee, one can tour Cook's Cottage to see it as it presumably looked when Mr. and Mrs. Cook received a letter that said, "Dear Mum and Dad, I discovered Australia today." There is a similarity to the colonial buildings of American New England, not surprisingly when one realizes that these buildings are historically related. Thanks to America's revolution, England turned her attention to Australia. One room of the cottage is converted into a presentation of Cook's life. And quite a life it was! Cook was undoubtedly one of the greatest explorers and navigators of all time. He explored and mapped Australia, New Zealand, a large portion of the Pacific and its islands, and circumnavigated the world from west to east for the first time. He even spent time in North America (in Quebec) fighting in the Seven Years War against the French (1750s). And it was on soil (sand actually) that is now American that he was killed. In 1779 he turned his back on a group of angry Hawaiian islanders, and he was speared to death.

Return to the fast metropolitan life by walking back through Treasury Gardens to Spring Street, then left down Collins Street. Pass the Regent Hotel and next on the left is *Collins Place*, recognizable by the abundance of glass. Collins Place comprises two tall towers occupied by offices and the Regent Hotel, with a shopping center at the base. The tallest of these towers, the *Rialto Tower*, is the largest building in Australia. There is an exclusive restaurant on the 35th floor, and one totally glass wall allows the best view in Melbourne. But if you are a little low on money, time, or snobbery, we suggest using the restrooms only. Take a left out of the elevator and venture confidently to the toilet on the right, pretending not to notice that you're the only person not wearing silk. The bathrooms are cleaner than a kitchen and the view is best of all. Both ladies and mens rooms have a completely glass wall. Soak in the view, and on leaving, don't forget to use one of the personalized cloth hand towels provided.

The view at dusk and early evening is especially recommended. And Collins Street is also enjoyable at night. Each tree branch is carefully lined with thousands of tiny Christmas lights which creates a festive atmosphere any time of the year. There are also horse-drawn carriage rides available at a reasonable price year-round.

Day Four: St. Kilda, preferably on a Sunday.

A trip to Melbourne would not be complete without an excursion to *St. Kilda*, no doubt Melbourne's strangest inner suburb. Take #15 tram to Fitzroy Street, and alight when it reaches the beach. Along this shore and overlooking the bay are old buildings reminiscent of another era. Many are large, clumsy stone or cement structures built to impress in the early 1900s. Now, the years of pollution have placed a grey grime on their surfaces, and dark green moss oozes from the more recessed corners. The baths right on the St. Kilda beach glisten with a particular sliminess, and certainly do not encourage one to venture in (we did not do so). Adjacent to these baths is the old *St. Kilda Palais*, a huge monstrosity built to entertain the young and fun-seeking in days gone by. If ever there was a building that seems to be waiting to be demolished, it is this one. And directly across the road is the kind of fun park most often depicted in American horror movies: old run down, the wooden scaffolding of the roller coaster creaks nervously, and a big garishly painted mouth is the entrance. This is St. Kilda's stamp of identity: Luna Park. It was the center of controversy when we were there: should it be demolished, or is it such a classic that it should be saved and restored? We leave it to the curious traveler to decide.

Higher up on the road that bends round the point, and continues on into *Acton Street*, there are some pleasantly renovated private residences, as well as imposing multistory apartment houses. A walk down Acton Street will convince one that here may be a good place to live, for this street is home to some of the best delicatessens in the Jewish tradition, bakeries, restaurants of many other ethnic cuisines, and a range of very unusual book shops.

Sundays are the best time to visit this area, when there is a market in full swing. On the day we visited, there was also a festival as well, complete with processions of strangely dressed people, children on stilts, and a band. Acton Street was closed off to cars (thank goodness) and rock bands performed at each end. Along the street itself, jugglers went through their tricks while onlookers munched souvlaki, strudel, and satay chicken. You name it, they were eating it.

The crowds, while made up heavily of tourists from other parts of the city, are nevertheless strongly influenced by the locals. These are, of course, the main attraction. Artists, avant garde and risqué (not to mention the drug dealers, though we never saw any ourselves) promenade, displaying gaudy hair styles similar to those of the bush cockatoos, colorful make-up, and clothes that seem to have been dug out of grandma's closet. In this sense, they are quite compatible with the buildings that surround them. "Weird" is how someone in our party described the scene. Definitely worth a visit, both to stare at the locals, and to try the ethnic cuisine.

Swimming at St. Kilda. Melbournians will insist that Port Philip Bay has been cleaned up, but frankly a look at the water along the shore of this beach would suggest that it's best to stay out. The bay has a grey tinge to it. We like clear blue waters. If swimming is the order of the day, we suggest a visit to some place else, preferably along the southern coast of Victoria.

Other Places, Other Alternatives

Queen Victoria Market is perhaps the best place to interact with a cross section of Australians. Located by Flagstaff Gardens along Victoria Street, it is huge, and its sheltering roofs make it an all-weather outing. Saturday morning is the best time to visit, because this is when everyone else goes there. Don't try to drive—take a tram or bus—parking is impossible. At Queen Vicky's Market, one finds fruits and veggies, numerous butchers, fish shops and delicatessens, clothes, shoes, watches, and souvenirs. Let a lady at a family-owned fruit stand give you a sample of her mango, and just try to refuse to buy it. (We did, and couldn't.) Indeed, the fruit and vegetables here were the freshest we'd seen anywhere, and at the lowest prices too. A look around will justify any Melbournian's claim that "We only shop at Queen Victoria's Market." However, make sure your group sticks together or establishes a meeting place—it's very easy to get lost or to lose someone.

Victorian Arts Centre and National Gallery

The *Victorian Arts Centre* is Melbourne's answer to the Sydney Opera House. A rather useless attempt, we might add. It is easily recognizable by the Eiffel-Tower-like structure on its roof, which conveys no artistic message except "Notice me," and somewhat resembles a construction crane. There is ample parking beneath the center, which we highly recommend whenever visiting Melbourne as the cheapest and most convenient. Unique sculptures guard the main entrance on St. Kilda Road. One such sentinel looks like an animal with tattoos, but that's only our interpretation. Just inside the front entrance is an information booth, helpful if you wish to attend a concert or show. The interior is fancy, complete with lush carpeting and wall ornamentation. The only way to see inside the numerous theaters and concert and recital halls is to go to one of the frequent shows or concerts. The *Arts Center Shop* is perhaps the best attraction for the casual visitor, especially to those interested in music. Be warned: items for sale, especially the prints, are beautiful and quite expensive.

Next door to the Victorian Arts Centre is the less imposing *National Gallery*. This is Australia's first gallery, founded in 1861. The present building is, of course, much newer than this. Inside is a splendid collection of Australian art, worth at least an afternoon's visit. The gallery conveys a rather cramped impression, perhaps not surprisingly, since its promotional literature claims that there are holdings of some 70,000 pieces. While excellent works range from the antiquities, classical and renaissance to the aboriginal, the gallery probably has the best display of the historical development of Australian art.

Major works are arranged in chronological order, and captions are most informative. A couple of hours spent here will make one almost an instant expert on the history of Australian art. The process of English migrant artists struggling to find the colors of the Australian landscape, the subtle and difficult-to-find hues of greens and browns, makes fascinating viewing. The English artists had to fight against reproducing the style and colors of Constable, thus early works misrepresented the light and character of the Australian bush to an amazing degree. The misty light of the bush, the dull, mysterious hues of the rain forest, the juxtaposition of colors in small dots in the undergrowth . . . all these and more had to be comprehended and reproduced by artists who were used to the rich, though overcast greens of England. Also apparent is the early preoccupation with the bush and enormity of the land that seemed to dominate the early painters. Humans, the settling Australians, were rarely, at least by this display, portrayed. There is not one painting of convicts or the misery of early settlements. The people seemed to take second place to the fauna and flora of Australia. In Australian books and art this perhaps remains a profound theme of much of Australian writing today.

The tidy development of artistic expression was disturbed somewhat by the new breed of Australian painters, such as Pugh and Boyd, who exerted an influence just after World

War II. Their anguish and cynicism about human nature screeches out through the garish, often distorted paintings, almost always set in an Australian landscape of some kind, portrayed as black and brutal. The outback, of course, has remained a strong theme of Australian painters. Look at the Drysdales and Heysens. There is much to enjoy here in this excellently laid out gallery.

If hunger sets in, we don't recommend the gallery cafeteria, unless you like having your choice limited to chicken salad or potato salad and sandwiches. Pay a little extra for the restaurant. The gift shop is also worth a look: there is an extensive collection of art books, prints, cards, and other artsy paraphernalia. Credit cards accepted!

National Trust Houses

There are historical homes in the Melbourne metropolitan area. Here are a few of the more interesting ones:

Como is a colonial version of Victorian opulence and a beautiful example of a town residence of some comfort. Take tram #8 and get off at #30, Toorak Road; walk to Como Avenue. Open daily 10–5. Telephone: 03-241-2500.

First Government House. This is Latrobe's Cottage, a prefabricated home which Governor LaTrobe transported to Australia in 1839. The house is well preserved along with many of its original furnishings. Situated in the Domain, next to the Botanical Gardens, between the Shrine of Remembrance and the Herbarium. Open daily 11 to 4:30. Telephone 03-654-5528.

Government House, also on the Domain. One of Melbourne's most significant landmarks, an imposing, whitewashed building erected in a prosperous time in Victoria, and inhabited by the queen's vice regal representative since 1876. If the flag is flying, the Governor is in residence. Bookings for tours are essential, as Government House is often closed for state functions. Telephone: 03-650-1855.

Old Melbourne Gaol (that's "jail" in America). Six years after becoming a city, Melbourne fell victim to the social problem of all cities: crime. She began construction of the gaol in 1841, and it was completed as it stands now in 1851. Some 104 hangings, including that of Ned Kelly, notorious bushranger, were conducted here before the gaol was closed in 1923.

Located on Russell Street, opposite the Police Station, it is open daily 9:30 to 4:30.

Rippon Lea, a fantastic 33-room Romanesque mansion was completed in 1887. For a touch of exotic architecture surrounded by magnificent baroque gardens, this is well worth a "captain's cook." Take a train to Rippon Lea Station, and proceed to 192 Hotham Street, Elsternwick. Open 10 to 5 daily. Telephone: 03-5239150. Wheelchair access is provided here, along with delicious afternoon and morning teas.

A Visit to the Footy

From March to October, Melbourne and Victoria generally become obsessed with football. This is not any old football, but Aussie Rules football, the game that stays hunkered down in Melbourne. Though other capital cities such as Perth, Hobart, Adelaide and Sydney sport their own Aussie Rules sides, Melbourne is the true home of Aussie Rules.

To experience the authentic atmosphere of a game, it is best to choose the one that will be most crowded, which would normally be the game between the two top sides on the "ladder." We saw Collingwood and St. Kilda play at Collingwood. Collingwood is an inner suburb of Melbourne, distinctly working class. St. Kilda has a broader spectrum of supporters, probably the most "one-eyed" and fanatical. Collingwood is known for "being dirty." One could go on. Each team has its own special reputation. Most games are played on Saturday afternoons around 2 p.m. and continue for some two hours, with breaks at each quarter. Large amounts of beer used to be consumed at these games, but violence has led to clamping down on this very Australian way of having a good time. It is now possible to buy tickets and stand (yes, stand) in "dry areas." Highly recommended. The fans are fanatical enough without having their enthusiasm boosted by a couple of tubes of Fosters.

It's a bit hard to explain this game. One is amazed upon emerging from the depths of the stand entrance at the intense green of the oval (because it's an oval), and at its size. But more overwhelming is the dense crowd that waits with anticipation, until the teams come jogging onto the ground, all showered, clean, taut muscular legs freshly rubbed down, without padding or protective clothing. These young men emanate strength and vigor and, more than anything else, a kind of cocky youthfulness. They prance around the ground like young stallions.

The siren sounds (a little like the old air raid sirens of World War II), and the crowd bursts into a deafening roar. The players run up and down the enormous field, punching the ball to each other and kicking it for long distances—even while they are still running. Bunches of players leap high into the air to catch the footy. One seems to remain suspended in mid air (he's not, he's climbing up the back of an opponent) and falls gymnastically to the ground. He "marked" the ball! (caught it on the full).

There are two tall goal posts at each end of the oval, each flanked by a shorter post. The ball kicked between the tall posts earns a goal (worth 6 points) and through the smaller posts, 1 point (called a behind).

Our advice is to watch quietly, and don't ask questions, unless you are with a good friend who is very patient. Arguments start very easily, usually over decisions made by the umpire (referee). No one seems to like them—there are two on the field, plus boundary umpires. Apart from politicians, footy umpires probably are subject to more verbal abuse than any other group in Australia.

Half time (about a twenty minutes break) brings with it Australia's own special rituals. Boys walk around calling out "drinks, peanuts, lollies." There is a huge long line at what passes for toilets, depending on where one is, under the stands. Many buy hot dogs, and the ubiquitous pie 'n sauce is consumed everywhere by people standing at an angle of some 45 degrees, to avoid having the brown gravy drip in their laps. All in all this is a great sight for the tourist. It is real Australia out for an afternoon and for a good time. Enjoy it!

Gustatory Delights

Melbourne's greatest gift is its restaurants. There are so many, we cannot even begin to list them here. But there is one part of Melbourne that we love to visit every time we pass through, and that is *Carlton*, the home of Melbourne's Little Italy. Take a cab to Carlton, and ask the driver to drop you off at Lygon Street. Here streets are lined with Italian deli-catessens, bars, restaurants, gelaterias, trattorias, pasticcerias, pizza houses. We have tried as many as we could, and all seemed great to us. The prices are very reasonable, and when one considers that BYO (Bring Your Own) wine or beer is the order of the day, a long evening in a restaurant can be most satisfying, and reasonably priced. The quality of the Italian food is far superior to anything we have experienced any-where in the U.S., except for a few special places in Manhat-tan's Little Italy.

The ambience is also amazingly Italian. One hears Italian spoken more than English. Close your eyes while lounging on the sidewalk sipping a *granita di limone,* and you can almost believe this is Rome. Even the Italian men congregate in certain bars and discuss the events of the day, just as in Italy. As if this were not enough, there are also many special book shops, with titles one would find nowhere else, cer-tainly nowhere in the U.S.A. There is much to do here, with relaxed sipping of gelati in the cafes, shopping the book stores, people watching. This is Australia too!

CHAPTER 7

On Country Roads: Victoria

Victoria is known as Australia's Garden State (though there is little in it that resembles New Jersey!). After Tasmania, Victoria is the smallest state. Unlike its sister states on the mainland, however, only about a quarter or less of the state could be termed desert. Its population, while centered on Melbourne, is nevertheless dispersed throughout the countryside, and congregated in several large towns or small cities. The geography of the state is also quite varied, given its range of climate from cool (even snow on the alps for a few weeks of the year) to desert hot in the Mallee and Mildura citrus growing areas. The distances are also not as enormous as in other states, so one can visit the main tourist attractions usually within a half day's drive from Melbourne. We crisscrossed Victoria a lot, but did not manage to see it all. (To be honest, we kept away from the cold mountains.)

Victoria's Great Outdoors

Camping. Victoria's cooler climate (relatively speaking that is) makes it a popular outdoors arena for camping, bush-walking and cliff climbing, to name just a few activities. The Department of Conservation, Forests and Lands is a gold mine of information on camping facilities, tracks, walks, and how to see the natural wonders of Victoria. The department itself manages some 50 camping sites, specializing somewhat in bush camping. By bush camping we mean pretty rough. There may be a pit toilet, if you're lucky. There will most certainly be properly built fireplaces, because these are safer than bush–made fires. Only in the cooler wetter months are fires allowed out in the open, however. The fines are very severe for lighting fires on days of fire danger. One can even receive prison terms. Pick up a copy of the department's "Where to Camp in Victoria's Great Outdoors" at the Victorian Government Information Victoria Center, 318 Little Bourke Street, Melbourne. Or call them at 03-663-3483. Information abounds! And it's mostly free!

The Beach. In summer, Victorians turn into beach bums for as much time as their work permits (which is quite a lot), especially over the Christmas and New Year holidays when kids enjoy a long summer vacation. Perhaps the best kept secrets in the world are the incredible beaches along Australia's shores. All the major cities are poised on the edge of great expansive beaches, rarely more than an hour's drive away. Be warned, though. If you are tempted to join the sun-loving Australians on the beach, prepare carefully. The sand can be so baked that it's too hot to walk on. The sun can burn even dark skin to a bright red in less than 15 minutes. So use plenty of sun screen, especially on the face. Don't be tricked by the cool, sometimes cold, breezes that blow off the ocean on the southern coast. The sun burns just as harshly, even though one does not feel it. You will have a miserable, painful night, unless proper protection against the sun has been taken. Australians have the highest skin cancer rate of any country in the world.

Join the beach culture. Decorate the face with the multicolored zinc sun screens. Wear an Aussie large brimmed hat with shelter for the back of the neck as well, or a 3-flapped cap made famous by tennis player Ivan Lendl. Then, enjoy the beach with the following extra precaution: bathe only between the yellow and red flags. These mark the part of the beach that the surf lifesavers patrol. The beaches can be treacherous to the inexperienced surfer. Sharks are sighted very rarely, but undertows can drag the overconfident swimmer who has ventured out of his or her depth.

Excellent beaches lie either to the southeast of Melbourne leading to the Great Ocean Road or to the southwest, leading to the more developed resort areas such as Rosebud, Sorrento and Portsea.

About surf lifesavers. The Australian Surf Lifesaving Society links together a huge number of lifesaving clubs all around Australia. They provide excellent training for young boys and girls, men and women, and expert patrols for the beaches. If there is a surf carnival, we recommend a visit to watch the unusual sport, and the exciting events in which the surfers tackle the waves on boards and surf boats. For surf carnivals in Victoria, a call to the Geelong Information Center (052-614202) will usually be enough to find out when and where they are to be conducted. Or look in the windows of the local shops—takeaways, hot bread or milk bars—for notices of forthcoming surf carnival events. If you're lucky enough to be at Bell's Beach, usually in January, the world class "Wimbledon" of surfing carnivals in staged here each year.

Philip Island and the Penguin Parade

For an initial taste of Australia's great coastal scenery, take a conducted tour or drive down to Philip Island (southwest of Melbourne) to see, among other things, koalas and the penguin parade. An organized tour to this attraction is probably easier, as the traffic is heavy all the way down to this resort area. The drive out of Melbourne passes through endless suburbs, demonstrating just what an enormous city Melbourne is—it stretches for miles around Port Philip Bay, down the Mornington Peninsula, and is now almost linked to the resort towns of Sorrento. Contact the information booths located in the main streets of downtown Melbourne for tour information. There are several one day tours.

It is also possible to avoid some subruban driving by taking the Southeastern Freeway out of Melbourne and following signs to the South Gippsland Highway. The road passes through the characteristic round hills of Gippsland before coming down to a rather plain, flat expanse, turning into the windswept shoreline drive to San Remo, then across the bridge to Philip Island. Along the way, some one to two hours out of Melbourne, one can take small side trips to a number of well known National Trust Homes. Those worth seeing are *The Briars,* an old pastoral sheep station: open the first Sunday of each month, telephone: 059-74-1240; *McCrae Homestead,* one of the first houses to be built in this area, acquired by Andrew McCrae in 1844: open weekends and holidays, telephone 059-862156; and *Mulberry Hill,* frequented by a number of Australia's artists, writers and politicians (a strange mixture if ever there was one); here Joan Lindsay wrote *Picnic at Hanging Rock.* Telephone 03-654-4562.

Penguins, koalas, seals . . . all are visible in natural environments at *Philip Island.* Named for Captain Arthur Philip of the first convict ship in 1798, this incredible wildlife haven is only several kilometers across at its widest point.

One popular stop is *Point Grant.* The Nobbies (the two islands just beyond the Point) have been "Home Sweet Home" for Australian fur seals since before the first white settlers. A raised boardwalk built in 1985 extends from the point, providing a pleasant and safe walk along the rock face. Steps lead to the bottom of the cliff, where the authors found the best and most beautiful variety of shells during low tide. There is also a lookout tower, from which seals can be seen sunbathing on Seal Rock. Also from this tower one can see the Blow Hole, a great hole bored into the cliff by the waves crashing into the shore. It gives a sense of the massive oceans that lie off Australia's shores, and the shear beauty of her thousands of miles of coast.

Koalas are in all the zoos, but nothing tops seeing these cuddly creatures chewing their gum leaves in nature. This opportunity can be almost guaranteed with a stop at the *Koala Sanctuary* along San Remo Road (Route 186). There are toilets and a spacious parking lot here, but nothing else that might disturb the wild environment. Look for koalas high up in the eucalyptus trees—they're almost always asleep in the daytime, sometimes cuddled up against each other for warmth.

Penguin Parade. No one visits Philip Island without seeing the Penguin Parade. Hundreds of these little birds return from a hard day's fishing every dusk, every day of the year. A newly built boardwalk weaves through the penguin nests, and risers along the beach front provide a perfect close-up view of the parade without disturbing it. It is best to get tickets early in the day in order to know the time of parading beforehand. The penguins emerge from the surf at sundown like clockwork, after a day's feeding. They bring home a catch to feed their young, who wait patiently in burrows dug in among the sand dunes. This is definitely an unusual sight, made even more unusual, perhaps even bizarre, by the hordes of tourists from all over the world, especially Japan, who come to view these ungainly little birds. They waddle to and fro across the sand, stopping occasionally to peer through the dim light at the sea of onlookers who vie with each other for a better view and occasionally succumb to the temptation to use a flash even though it's strictly against the rules.

There is also a fantastic penguin museum at the Visitor Center, which provides creative displays for seeing, hearing and feeling. Allow at least an hour (maybe more if you have kids) to enjoy this wonderfully comprehensive exhibit. Learn how penguins talk to each other, how far they swim in a day, what happens when they molt, how they mate. Penguin leaflets, offering information about penguins and Philip Island, are available in virtually every language, and are free.

There is a variety of accommodations available in the towns of Cowes, Rhye, New Haven, and San Remo. Foodstops range from pancake parlors to Chinese. For further information about what is available on Philip Island, contact the Philip Island Information Center at (059)56-7447, The Depart-

ment of Conservation Forests and Lands at (03)651-4011, the
Penguin Reserve at (059)56-8300, or the Victorian Tourist
Commission (03)619-9444.

Princes Highway to New South Wales

Drive north and back towards Melbourne, away from Philip
Island and through the strangely conical and regular hills of
South Gippsland close to the Strzelecki (pronounced
"Strezlecky") Ranges to rejoin the Princes Highway and proceed easterly on Highway 1 along the Pacific route to Sydney.
The highway is busy, but there are enough places with passing lanes to make it a reasonable drive. You go through the
thriving towns of Gippsland that are developing and growing
at a pace set by the discovery and exploitation of offshore oil
in the 1970s.

Pass through historic and pretty *Sale*, with a population
growing quickly as the center for the administration of the
offshore oil wells. It boasts some of Australia's oldest private
schools and a strong local arts and crafts tradition. Call Ian
Robertson, the local expert in wood turning, at 051-43-1544, or
take a tour of local attractions, by calling Darryl King at
051-445–223. A vast system of lakes begins at Sale. One can
sail from here via a series of lakes and canals to Lakes Entrance, which is our next major destination some 60 miles
ahead.

Lakes Entrance claims itself to be the Victorian Riviera, and
the tripling of its population in summer vacation season at
least supports this idea! The township stretches along a 1.5
mile narrow peninsula, sheltered from the ocean surf by the
90-mile beach, merely a tiny strip of sand running parallel to
the shore. All in all, this makes for a beautiful seaside resort
with calm water boating, surfing, fishing and every other
water sport one can imagine. There is a large fishing fleet
moored here, along with vessels from the nearby offshore oil
rigs. The Department of Conservation conducts activities during the holiday periods, such as tours of some of Australia's
best eucalyptus forests, river tours and night walks (Possum
prowls are a real possibility; see below when we take one!).
For details contact the Bairnsdale regional office at 51-526–

211. For fishing cruises or scenic boat tours, call 51-551–966. Everything is supplied for an exciting fishing excursion, or on the scenic trip, a gourmet dinner.

There is a large aboriginal art display, which claims to be "the only one of its kind in Australia." These artifacts and modern renditions of aboriginal artifacts (made by Aborigines nonetheless) are displayed in a natural Dreamtime setting. We have found much of the aboriginal artifacts sold in Australia to be somewhat, shall we say, pretentious, if that is possible. The art reeks of an over zealous attempt to recover lost art and skills. The commercialization of the art has been absorbed by the aboriginal craftsmen and women, with the result that the products are often garish and struggling for character. Perhaps a new art form will emerge from this courageous attempt to recreate a lost culture. Care should be taken, therefore, in purchasing aboriginal crafts. However, by all means stop by the *Big Boomerang*, and enjoy the Dreamtime setting at 191 Princes Highway, Lakes Entrance. Telephone: (051)55–1505. There is a reasonable chance that some of the wares sold are authentic in the sense that aborigines may have crafted them while maintaining a bush lifestyle. There is an aboriginal reserve nearby at Lake Tyres.

The Princes Highway continues now away from the coast a little, up through Nowa Nowa to Orbost and Cann River through some of the most beautiful rain forest in southern Victoria. If time allows, take a small side track off the main road to Mallacoota, a sleepy seaside village, nestled between estuaries, lakes and hilly forest. This is the last town of any size before crossing the border into New South Wales.

Southeastern Victoria

Wilson's Promontory. If we retrace our journey northward from Philip Island and rejoin the South Gippsland Highway traveling east, we begin the slow but steady pace towards some of Victoria's quietly beautiful green areas. Far south is Wilson's Promontory, possibly southern Australia's favorite national park. This is the Australian mainland's most southerly point. The park offers everything for the bush enthusiast:

superb beaches, some 200 bush walks, secluded caves and a wide range of flora and fauna. These are some of Australia's best preserved yet easily accessible wilderness areas.

Ferry to the Bellarine Peninsula. Had you driven west rather than east from Philip Island, you would have arrived at Sorrento, a developed resort town right on the eastern heads which overlook the narrow and treacherous entrance to Port Philip Bay. A quick way to southwestern Victoria is to take the car ferry. This is a one-hour ride across the "rip" as it is called by locals, a narrow dangerous passage that forms the gateway into Port Philip Bay. Here one alights with car ($35 per car, passengers included, Telephone: 523171) into the old world of Queenscliff.

The Bellarine Peninsula

Queenscliff is the jewel of the Bellarine Peninsula, as the local tourist brochures describe it. This is a town that has steadfastly resisted any change for the last 100 years or so, due to colorful local residents who are active in preserving the quaint Victorian town. The coastal villages along this peninsula—Ocean Grove, Barwon Heads, Portarlington, Point Lonsdale—still retain their early 20th century charm, and many older buildings are well restored. One sees the strong English influence on the Australian natural surroundings, with huge cypresses planted along the coastal main streets (particularly in Queenscliff) imposing a somber tone over all—as if inviting the rain of England to descend. Appropriately, Queenscliff was named after Queen Victoria by Governor Latrobe in 1853. There are several high quality art galleries here, if acquisition of Australian art is one's interest.

For old world charm, try a stay at the *Seaview House,* which provides bed and breakfast accommodations, tea rooms and an art gallery as well at 86 Hesse Street, Queenscliff. Telephone 052-521763. A beer on the patio of the old and delightful Queenscliff pub looking out over the harbor and small fishing wharf aids one's relaxation. There are other pubs of opulent (in their day) architecture, well worth a visit and a couple of beers: try the *Ozone* and the *Vue Grand.* They are such imposing structures that addresses are not needed to find them.

Besides the usual pub fare and the delicious fish and chip shops in this area, for something unusual try *Early Settlers Restaurant,* where one can enjoy damper, traditional Aussie meals, from a reasonable fixed price menu. It is at Hitchcock Street, Barwon Heads, open Fridays and Saturdays only, telephone: 052-542369. Barwon Heads is a small village twenty minutes drive from Queenscliff, at the head of the Barwon River, where it empties into the ocean (having wound its way from Geelong, Victoria's second largest city). Lunch at the *Barwon Heads Hotel* overlooking the river is also recommended, telephone: 052-542201.

A different way to take lunch is on the old steam train of the *Bellarine Peninsula Railway.* Take a picnic lunch and enjoy a journey on the vintage restored steam train that leaves frequently from Queenscliff Station four or five times a day in summer. (During prolonged dry seasons when total fire bans are necessary, a diesel replaces the steam engine.) Individual fare is $4, family, $12. Telephone: 052-522–069 for the latest information.

There is an interesting National Trust building in this area also: *Portarlington Mill* was built 1857. Telephone: 052-21-3510.

Geelong

One can approach Geelong either through its back door from the Bellarine Peninsula, or by an easy freeway drive, just 40 miles from Melbourne. Geelong is a necessary stopping off point on the way to one of the greatest stretches of coastal scenery in the world: *The Great Ocean Road.*

From Melbourne, drive over Westgate Bridge on the freeway out of the city and follow the signs to *Geelong.* It is well signed. Geelong (pop. 180,000) is a bustling industrial city and gateway to the Western District of Victoria and some of the state's richest wool growing farms.

Geelong was established in 1836 and once rivaled Melbourne for the status of state capital. Tourist information is available at West Coast Tourism, 83 Ryrie Street Geelong; telephone (052) 97220. One need not spend too long in Geelong, although there are many good pubs at which to eat lunch. A quick stop at the *Market Square* or *Bay City Plaza* (car parking free for the first two hours) will take one to a shopping mall and food court where one can sample an incredible variety of foods from Indonesian, Chinese, Greek, Italian, American to traditional Australian menus (see section on Australian foods and places to eat). The variety of takeout food (Aussies call it takeaway food) is amazing, and properly reflects the growing cosmopolitan makeup of Australian society. Across at *Market Square* is a tourist information booth with many brochures, maps and announcements of what's doing in Geelong and along the Great Ocean Road.

If shopping malls remind one too much of home, we recommend a pub on the other side of Geelong along the way to Torquay (pronounced "Tor-kee"), the first beach resort at the start of the fabulous coastal drive. Try the *Grovedale Pub* just after crossing the Barwon Bridge. Here one finds a limited but very reasonably priced menu, and an excellent fare of fresh fish, Australian steak, traditional English roast, along with choice of salad or vegetables. The surroundings are tastefully arranged including a salad bar, and one can even order cappuccino or tea, something unheard of in Australian pubs just five years ago. We advise beer for the passengers only, as sleepiness is certainly to be avoided on the road ahead.

If the economy of the area and its way of life is of interest, then by all means see the *Wool Musuem* in Geelong at the corner of Moorabool and Broughm Streets, which is open every day, 10 to 5 p.m.; telephone: 052-264660. Wool, for most of Australia's economic life, has been a mainstay. It continues to be an important export and the major product of the surrounding area of Geelong, especially the Western District. At the museum you can see how wool is removed from the sheep's back and the process of refinement. Follow this up with a visit to the genuine shearing shed. It is remarkable that all wool that ends up in our garments must still be first shorn from a sheep by hand. No wonder that many of Australia's folk songs revolve about the sheep shearer's life. ("Click Go the Shears, Boys, Click Click Click. . . .")

National Trust Houses to see in the Geelong and District area are: *Barwon Grange*, built for a ship owner in 1856; telephone: 052-213510; *Barwon Park at Winchelsea*, a 42-room mansion with stables, built in 1869; telephone: 052-213510.

Then follow the road to *Torquay*, one of Victoria's older surf beaches—its age is marked quite clearly by the massive cypress trees planted along the front beach by settlers who just could not give up their idea of an English country town. The row of cypress is typical of the older Australian southern country towns, but they do not fit into the parched and brown Australian landscape. The colors are wrong and the shape ungainly. Here there is a savagery about them, not the feeling of shelter and warmth they convey in their Northern Hemisphere home.

Follow the sign to *Anglesea*. All along this road there are turn-offs to great surf beaches, *Bell's Beach* being the most famous for waves. In fact a drive along this beach is a good introduction to what lies ahead. The road to the car park winds through an old ironbark forest along the top of a high cliff for some 10 kilometers. The view of the ocean and huge swells from above is truly awesome. The chances are that there will not be as many swimmers on this beach—the surf is very challenging—in fact not to be ventured into by the inexperienced surfer. The slope into the water is some 35 degrees, causing massive undertow and waves that rise suddenly to 10 or 20 feet, then crash down almost vertically. One can hear the large boulders that lie on the floor of parts of this beach rumble together as the waves intermittently thunder ashore then recede rapidly back into the swell, dragging everything with them. Adventurous board riders enjoy this surf and benefit from the huge swell beyond the shoreline breakers. There is a lot of seaweed. Huge mounds of it are washed ashore daily—there seem to be hundreds of varieties, from huge slippery kelp to small dainty lace-like weeds, colored from pure white to dark reds, purples and deep pinks.

The road winds down to Anglesea through scrub bush, then in a final turn, the township lies nestled in a hollow, with the ocean in the background, as though an artist planned it that way. There are thankfully few cypress trees in Anglesea (though a couple still remain in the car park of the surf beach). The township is nestled into scrub bush and stunted gum trees. It is a dreamy little town that beckons the traveler to dally. Ocean Road winds past a small set of shops, then over the Anglesea River. An expanse of lawn unfolds on the left along the river as it makes its way to the ocean. Electric barbecues, the ubiquitous public toilets and a green lawn invite travelers to stop and picnic.

On the right, one finds *The Diana Riverfront Restaurant*, somewhat high priced, but providing an interesting variety of foods, and a slight German influence in the sauces. One can sit under the veranda of this classic Australian house and sip afternoon tea, while gazing out over the Anglesea River and its characteristic scrub bush. The *Mallealuca Gallery* (the name refers to the large mallealuca gum tree outside the building) just across the gravel road and facing the Ocean Road is worth a visit if one wishes to acquire top quality Australian paintings.

There are three motels in Anglesea, all somewhat nondescript, and one hotel which caters to a large number of beer drinkers, with some attention to lodgings. For color and charm and a beautiful view of the ocean with its famous surf, stay instead at the *Debonair Guest House*, which boasts a restaurant as well that is open to the public. It is located just past the Anglesea Surf Beach, as one rounds the sharp corner near the surf shops. To dally longer, and for a big splurge, drive back towards Torquay to *Bells Beach*, and spend an evening at the *Rose Garden Restaurant*. It is somewhat expensive, but well worth it for the delightful surroundings.

A wonderful surprise is *Diggers Pizza*, hidden behind the Shell Service station next to the veterinarian's office. The pizzas here are not only edible but a delightful surprise. They are different from those in America, less crusty and saucy, and more like those in Rome. The owner speaks with a noticeable Italian-Australian accent. Pasta is also on the menu, with all the most popular Italian variations. The only non-Italian variation in the pizzas is one with pineapple, a Hawaiian variation. Best to avoid it, unless ordered with ham and cheese only. Ham and pineapple are a traditional favorite of Australians of several generations.

Stop at the small row of shops just before the bridge. Look for the hot bread shop and buy rolls and other takeouts for the remainder of the trip. A picnic lunch will be most pleasant in Lorne which lies ahead. Or, if there are young children in the party, plan to drive through Anglesea up the big hill, and follow the signs to *Point Roadnight*, a sheltered beach with little or no surf and popular with families with small children. Wind surfing and sailing are common pastimes here, and the children will enjoy exploring the rock pools at the point.

But before you leave the bread shop, check the notices on the window. There are many tourist attractions available in the height of the season—usually December through January, and Easter. We were lucky enough to find a notice by the Victorian State Parks announcing a possum prowl in a small park just a few miles from Anglesea. Reservations are usually necessary.

The Possum Prowl. There are a number of different kinds of possums in Australia, the most common in the Anglesea area being the ring-tailed possum and the silver-tailed possum. They can be quite large creatures, some as big as a raccoon. They are nocturnal animals, hence for the prowl we were asked to assemble at the park at 7 p.m.—and to bring a mug. (This was to be more than a possum prowl!) The park ranger presented an amusing commentary about the park and the habits of possums, then treated us to a lesson on how to bake damper (the traditional dough of Australian bushmen) and make billy tea (tea made in a billy or pannikin without a teapot). There were some thirty people in the party—all Australians—mostly families with young children. Since there was some time until sundown, one of the kids produced a cricket bat and ball, and a game of cricket developed spontaneously. Before long, all the children had joined in, while we grown-ups sipped billy tea.

Gradually the sun sank beneath the eucalyptus trees, and their aroma hung on the night breeze. Even though this was the middle of summer, the night turned out to be quite chilly. In the southern coastal towns, always be prepared for cool evenings with a sweater or sweat shirt of some kind. However, it can also be so darned hot that you can hardly breathe. As night approached, we formed a single file behind the ranger who took us on a half hour walk through a winding track in the bush. He used a powerful flashlight, searching the trees and hollow logs as we went. We saw no possums, though the ranger insisted that he smelled them. The most important thing is that we met Australians and were impressed by their friendly and gregarious nature. We learned how to make damper and billy tea as well. That was certainly worth the time of the excursion. Oh yes, the price for all this: None!

And if it's free entertainment that the traveler wants, as well as to imbibe something of the Australian spirit, the Anglesea wood chop is just the thing.

The Anglesea Wood Chop. At about the middle of January each year, the woodchoppers of Australia descend on Anglesea for an annual competition. The events occur on the river front, amidst a carnival atmosphere. One can stroll down a long line of arts and crafts stalls, buy a cup of tea and scones from the lady working for the local Lions Club, then sit on bales of straw and watch the beefy woodchoppers compete in one of the most spectacular sports one could ever see. These men, dressed often in white singlet (the uniform of the real Australian man) and white pants, along with white sneakers, stand on logs and chop them apart with amazing speed. The razor sharp blades of their axes come within fractions of an inch of their toes. We looked for some without their big toes, but found none!

By far the most spectacular is the tree felling event, in which the contestants must make their way 20 feet or more up a tree, then chop off the top. The men accomplish this seemingly impossible task with utmost ease, the champions often in less than ten minutes. The crowd cheers them on, and one hears words of encouragement, "Good on yer, mate," all around.

It is beyond Anglesea that the scenery becomes more and more stunning. Each bend in the road takes one's breath away: the wild rugged coast, deep blues of the ocean, burn-scarred bushland on the right rising steeply up from the road. Yet each curve brings new scenes unfolding more beautiful than before. There are miles and miles of extravagant beauty. With the road curved into the sides of precipices, passengers are able to look down to the crashing surf seemingly directly below the car. Rich sandy beaches nestle into the cliffs, secluded beaches are plentiful for the traveler prepared to climb down the rough trails. This Great Ocean Road continues on to Lorne and thence further to Apollo Bay. We suggest a lunch stop at Lorne just past the center of town. Here the road rises steeply above the surf beach where one can park and have a picnic lunch, watching the surf riders on waves that roll frighteningly close to the reefs.

Lorne, a mecca for the young on New Years Eve, is best avoided then. At other times, though, this is a pleasant seaside village, only recently marred by glitzy development, bordering on vandalism. However, there is much to do in this beautiful place. On very hot days, bushwalking back into the hills along the creek beds that are cool and shaded by ancient tree ferns dripping with water is an invigorating exercise. Some of these walks can be strenuous, but are well worth the effort to gain a feeling for the exotic, isolated environment of the Australian rain forest, just minutes away from the village center. A few walks worth considering:

1. Teddy's lookout via George Street and return (1 hour).

2. Upstream through the Caravan Park along the Erskine Valley to the Rapids and Sanctuary (1 hour).

3. The walking track from the She-Oak picnic area to Castle Rock for a longer walk and magnificent views of bush and ocean; return to picnic area or continue to Ocean Road via Swallows Cave and She-Oak Falls (1½ hours).

4. From Erskine River bridge follow the track through Caravan Park for some 6 km.; for massive tree ferns and rain forest take the short turnoff to Splitters Falls, and go for another 3 km to Straw Falls, then continue 1 km along the magnificent tree ferns of Erskine Falls. (a tough walk, allow 3 hours one way.)

After reaching Apollo Bay, Great Ocean Road leaves the coast briefly to cut across a small peninsula to Port Campbell. Here you will see one of Australia's coastal treasures: the *Twelve Apostles*. The spectacular Twelve Apostles, are twelve islands of uncompressed rock, carved out of the tall cliffs by the strong current of Bass Strait. The huge swell of the Antarctic waters lumbers up the cliffs, stroking their faces, lash-ing their rocky edges. The wild surf here sculpted the once famous *London Bridge*, a classic, primitive arch. Unfortunately, on the very day we visited it in January of 1990, the bridge collapsed into the sea, and is no more.

Port Campbell itself is a sleepy fishing village, with a few motels catering to tourists who come to see the Twelve Apostles. Take a quick bite to eat here—the one restaurant in town is over priced, and the takeout fare quaint to say the least. We tried a pizza and found most of its ingredients unrecognizable.

Warrnambool. Next stop is Warrnambool (pop. 23,500) with well developed foreshores offering many features of interest. There is a beautiful park, *Pertobe* adventure playground, where water birds abound, and mothers both human and bird, tend their young. Children play all over. A walk around the lake to observe the nesting water fowl is a must. Up and over the hill is *The Flagstaff Hill Maritime Village*, a re-creation of the Port of Warrnambool in the 1870s, complete with persons in period dress, horses, carts, old fishermen's cottages, relics of shipwrecks and much more. In the winter (May to October), at Logan's beach one can view the growing herd of rare Southern Right Whales, when they come to calve and stay for several weeks. (Killer whales are found on the eastern coast; humpbacks on the northeastern and northwestern coasts. For an excellent portrait of whales in Australian waters, see the *Australian Geographic* article and poster, October/December, 1989.)

If time allows, a side trip to *Port Fairy* further along the coast road to the west is rewarding. This small fishing village is perhaps one of the most isolated towns of Victoria, although it was one of the first towns to be established in Victoria. It was a whaling station in the 19th century, used as a shelter by sealers and whalers from Van Diemen's Land (now Tasmania). There are over fifty buildings listed by the National Trust and an excellent historical walk. Bed and breakfast cottages abound here where coastal scenery is always a pleasure. This is a place of old-fashioned hospitality. Thousands flock to Port Fairy every Labor Day weekend in March to attend

Australia's largest folk music festival. For more information telephone: (055)68-1002.

National Trust Houses at Port Fairy and beyond include: *Motts Cottage*, built 1845 for a couple of whalers; telephone: 03-654-4711. *Mooramong*, Skipton, restored in authentic art deco style of 1970s; telephone: 03-654-4711. *Steam Packet Inn*, Portland, built in 1842, one of the oldest buildings in Victoria, displays a hipped roof and dormer windows, most unusual for Australian architecture, thought to have been prefabricated in Tasmania; telephone: 055-23-1685.

Country Cities

The American vision of Australia consists of the big cities like Sydney and Melbourne, and the wild, basic bush. However, many Australians live comfortably between these two extremes, in what may be called the country cities.

Bendigo, located some 90 miles northeast of Melbourne via the Calder Highway, is an elegant, well kept example of an old Aussie gold mining town. Although it has progressed with the times, historical buildings and landmarks remain in good condition, and tourist information is readily available.

Along the main street, one can pick up a tourist tram, the only one left of the once noisy clanging service in Bendigo. For $6.50 each, the tram will take you around the historical route of Bendigo, providing a commentary on buildings and including a visit to a gold mine among other points of interest. If one has never been on a tram before, it is worth the fare. (But if it's trams one really enjoys, Melbourne is the best place for that. The *Talking Tram* runs regular narrated tours, leaving from Violet Street frequently every day. Bookings are essential; telephone: 054-438070.)

Although gold mining ceased long ago, the shafts remain intact, as does the old *Shamrock Hotel*, with its wrought iron decoration, which struggles to preserve the charm of Victorian England, surrounded as it is by noisy streets and people bustling to the modern shopping plaza just around the corner. At noon, one can look up at the Shamrock's balcony, and spy through the wrought iron waiters dressed elegantly in black pants and white shirts with black bow ties, as they tend guests. The tables are draped in starched tablecloths. The balcony has sagged somewhat, the tables not quite level. The decadence seems pleasing enough.

Hargreaves Street (named after the discoverer of gold in Australia, John Hargreaves) is still a main street in Bendigo, but not in mining. It is now *Hargreaves Shopping Mall.* There are other stately buildings in Bendigo, particularly the large heavy stone building on the main highway, at the entrance to the park. This is the *Town Hall.* Heavy stone block buildings were once the order of the day here. One senses that the settlers who built this town had come to stay. In summer, the gardens behind the town hall are a pleasant relief from the hot sun.

National Trust Houses worth seeing in the area are: *Bendigo Joss House* at Emu Point, the only surviving house of prayer from the 1850s period of Chinese influx into the gold fields, beautifully restored; telephone: 054-421685. *Welsh Congregational Church,* Maldon, built in 1863; telephone 03-654-4711. *Denominational School,* Maldon, one of the first buildings in Maldon, and certainly the first permanent school, built in 1850s; telephone: 054-75-2470. *Castlemaine Market,* built in 1862 on one of the richest alluvial gold fields in the world; now converted into a regional museum.

Out and About Bendigo

"Yabbies could be worth a go, mate." Most Australian kids who live in the country know about yabbies. They are crayfish-like creatures that grow to four of five inches in length and forage for food in the muddy bottoms of Australia's southern rivers, streams, and watering holes. Find a muddy watering hole or small reservoir or stream, tie a piece of meat scrap to a long string, weigh down the bait a little, then throw it into the water. Wait. Watch the string, and soon if you have found a good place, the string will begin to be dragged. The yabbie has begun to suck at the meat. Slowly, very slowly, pull in the line, just fast enough for the yabbie to follow the bait to the edge of the water. Be ready to grab him (or her) as soon as the surface breaks. A net helps, of course, but they can be caught without one if you are quick enough.

All of this has been made much easier, however, by the establishment of a yabbie farm at *Baringhap Tourist Farm,* near the historic township of Maldon. One can relax among the farm animals of a genuine functioning sheep station here, and as well have a go at yabbying in the stocked pools and bill-abongs. Telephone the tourist farm at 054-75-2700.

Gold mines to visit are the main mine, which is still a working and productive gold mine, *The Central Deborah Gold Mine.* Wear sturdy footwear and prepare to see gold in the unrefined state. This is an exciting trip: one enters a lift cage (elevator) and descends 60 meters underground for a close-up view of mining operations. For conducted tours, call *Bendigo Tours,* 054-412390, or call the mine itself at 054-438070. If you'd like hands on experience, call *Barry Maggs,* 054-470559, or *Goldseeker* tours, 054-479559, to arrange for a personal guided tour and how-to-do-it gold mining experience. One day tours are standard. You'll have to ask the price—we had trouble getting a clear answer.

The gold mining aura, so to speak, has perhaps inscribed an indelible trait into the Australian character: inveterate gambling. Just 48 km west of Bendigo, the largest nugget of gold in the world was found: the *Welcome Stranger Nugget* weighed 6.5 kg. Sandhurst Town (12 km from Bendigo, Loddon Valley Highway, telephone: 054-469033) revives the good old days with the presentation of early Bendigo. It is fun to ride the Red Rattler through Whipstick Forest to Goldwash Gully diggings. Visit the Hartlands Eucalyptus Farm and Distillery (Whipstick Forest, tel: 054-48 8270) and buy some eucalyptus oil, which is powerful stuff, guaranteed to overpower the strongest odor.

Vineyards. Some 16 vineyards were open to the public in this area last time we counted. Gold was discovered in the Bendigo area in 1851, and the first planting of vineyards was in 1856, appropriately encouraged by German cleric Dr. Henry Backhaus. Stop at the Bendigo tourist information center and obtain a brochure listing all wineries, their specialties and hours.

A Brewery. The uncouth would prefer beer, so some would say. While in Bendigo visit the "boutique" brewery (if that is not a contradiction in terms) to see the inner workings of a restored brewery and sample local brews (Koala Beer, not too original, but the taste is certainly different). Called the *Rifle Brigade Pub Brewery,* it is on View Street, Bendigo, telephone: 054-43092.

We suggest something a little different here; you might try staying in the home of real Aussies. Call *Host Home Reservations,* The Goldfields Host Home Connection, 054-437891. Or, try a bed and breakfast at Albert-on-McRae, 131 McRae Street, just 250 yards north of the post office, tel: 054-437588. It is a small place with eight rooms and a restaurant—guaranteed to be an experience far different from an American motel!

An antiques and gallery guide listing some 14 dealers for Bendigo is available in the tourist information center. Or if gardening is your cup of tea, pick up a brochure on gardens of the goldfields, which lists the locality and type of many beautiful gardens that are open to the public. These include gardens with such great names as Badher's Keep, Bleak House, the Garden of St. Erth, Tumblers Greem, and Yuulong Lavender Estate. Don't miss the Bendigo Easter fair held each year in April.

Echuca and Moama

Echuca and Moama are popular for two reasons: the historical setting along the Murray River and the gambling. These two towns are essentially the same place, but because they sit right on the border between Victoria and New South Wales, they have a double identity. Back in the mid-1800s, Echuca (Victoria) and Moama (New South Wales) were frequent stops for paddlewheelers. Because roads were unsafe (or didn't exist), the best way to travel was by means of paddlewheelers along the Murray and Campaspe Rivers. The glossy tourist brochures of this region boast that two convicts were responsible for the development of Echuca-Moama some 130 years ago. Before them, the area was inhabited by an estimated 4,000 aboriginals, mainly from the Yorta Yorta and Wemba Wemba people. They had lived in the area for some 40,000 years. Wilderness areas nearby can be visited, especially the *Dharnya Center,* located in Barmah Forest, just north of Barmah township. An interesting exhibition of the red gum forest and aboriginal communities is worth a visit.

The Port of Echuca has been restored and preserved. Though in keeping with the rest of Echuca, it is relatively undeveloped by American standards. A peaceful sense of the 19th century remains. The Australian image of parched land, muddy-brown water and the muted green of the ubiquitous gum trees reaches its ideal here. Except for the occasional houseboat, everything seems to fit the historical setting, and allows for the unusual impression that the Australian wilderness is just around the corner. This is one of the few places left where one can pick any section of the riverbank for a leisurely picnic and swim! A ride in an authentic paddlewheeler is an inexpensive and rewarding way to listen to historic commentary while in air-conditioned comfort. Three-course or smorgasbord meals are available on some days (Call M. V. *Echuca Princess* for times and rates: 054-825244 or-835210). Along the old port, there are interesting handcraft shops, where prices are surprisingly reasonable. *The Redgum Works*, Murray Esplanade offers articles carved from redgum, and one can watch the huge redgums being processed in an old style sawmill. For other things to see and do in the Echuca area, contact the tourist information centers at 054-824525 in Echuca, and 054-826001 in Moama.

Since gambling is legal in New South Wales and not Victoria, many Victorians drive to Moama for their gambling fun. The most "pokies" (poker machines, slot machines) in Moama can be found at the bowling club, but you must be 21 to participate.

If one drives from Echuca down through Bendigo on to Melbourne via the small Victorian towns, a strong sense of the changing patterns inland use emerges. The Echuca area takes in prosperous towns like Shepparton, where land is well irrigated with rich farming lands, dairy herds or, more likely, fruit orchards. These are large enterprises, usually centered by well kept houses. In the summer, the landscape is dominated by the dry straw-yellow of long thick grass, waiting to be cut and bailed. Even in the eucalyptus forests, the grass still grows strong, making the bush in this area quite different compared to other places in Victoria. The great gums have large twisted trunks and huge swathes of bark hanging, for gum trees generally do not lose their leaves in winter, but do shed their bark throughout the year.

As one leaves Bendigo and approaches the out-of-the-way towns of Daylesford and Maryborough the landscape changes to long, low undulating hills, dotted with bushy gums. The farmhouses in these areas are very small—some even the original humble cottages built by early settlers over 150 years ago—a single room with a chimney and galvanized roof. If time permits, visit the famous *Hepburn Springs*, just a few miles out of Daylesford. Here thousands of Australians converge every year to sip the mineral water, renowned for its healing and health qualities. The area has been tastefully developed. A picnic lunch of tomato sandwiches washed down by spa water is the Aussie meal to enjoy here.

There is not much to do in *Daylesford*, but the historical atmosphere is well worth a drive-through. Except for the Mastercard and Visa stickers on the shop windows, and the occasional Honda on the street, Daylesford looks and functions as it did more than a century ago, when it was a gold mining town. Most of the original houses, shops, hotels, and pubs are still standing and in use. The *Daylesford Hotel* (formerly the *Commercial Hotel*) sits on a corner overlooking the entrance to the town. Its veranda and old brick construction make it easy to visualize the old days, with horses and buggies hitched to the posts. The bar is noisy . . . if you're not driving, drop in for a pot. Otherwise, stop for a Devonshire tea at the *Regency Tearooms,* a recently renovated house, with a beautiful Victorian setting. All of the sweets are authentic and homemade, and classical music adds to the quaint atmosphere. Strike up a conversation with the owner who also waits table and prepares all meals, and she will enthusiastically recount the history of the area (telephone: Kay Scott, 053-483948). Open every day. That's where we found out about Wedderburn.

Wedderburn, located northwest of Bendigo, was once a gold mining town. People continue to own mining rights to sections of land, while they may not necessarily own the land itself. In the early 1980s, during a flood gold nuggets washed up along the streets. Consequently, people dug up other's gardens and the main street. The gold reef in fact extends beneath the local schoolyard, so there still may be undiscovered gold there which cannot be dug up. Today, although no one seems any richer from this gold mania, few people still have beautiful gardens. Instead, there are mounds of dirt and rock all over, as if some strange burrowing insect had invaded the town.

The areas south of Bendigo are also pleasant drives, and around every corner there appears a small sign directing the way to pottery makers (Bendigo pottery is well known), quaint tea rooms, or galleries. These are roads for the unhurried traveler. One needs time to stop and sample the teas or sip the wines. The pottery is distinctive and reasonably priced, but very heavy to carry home. Tour the *Bendigo Pottery* (established in 1858, they say) on Midland Highway, Epsom, to watch pots being made. Here, indulge once more in a Devonshire tea, while children experiment in the free clay room for kids.

From here one can take the road to Melbourne through Ballarat, or continue down the Brisbane Ranges to Geelong. The *Brisbane Ranges National* Park boasts a wide range of flora and fauna, including grey kangaroos, wallabies, echidnas, possums and gliders. In spring there is a magnificent display of wattles, bush peas and bush orchids. Original aboriginal inhabitants of the *Watheuang Tribe* have left many artifacts, however, much remains to be learned about these ancient inhabitants. The major significance of these ranges lies, however, in the discovery of gold in the Anakie Hills in 1851. Gold reefs were quickly mined near the town of Steiglitz, but when gold was no more, Steiglitz became a ghost town and remains so today.

Ballarat

Center of the major gold rushes of the 1850s and 60s was Ballarat. One can visit the popular *Sovereign Hill* in Ballarat, which is a reconstruction of a mining town, complete with gold mine, characters in period costume, shops, streets and many other artifacts. This is a nonprofit community organization, run by the Ballarat Historical Park Association. Well worth a visit, even if a little on the expensive side! Sovereign Hill is laid out as accurately as possible on the sight of an actual 1850s gold mining town, complete with shops, main street, government barracks and camp, tents and so on. In fact, one can stay overnight in some of these accommodations, ranging from tents in the Government Camp to dormitory-style government military barracks of the period. These accommodations are, of course, priced to suit the youthful, backpacking market. The tents have wooden floors and cost about $6 a night. Could be fun in the summer!

The city of Ballarat itself is one of the largest provincial towns of Victoria, somewhat cooler than other cities because of its slight elevation. It probably has more pubs than any other town as well. Excellent tours are available to soak up the cultural history of this part of Victoria. *Designer Travel* conducts goldfields cultural tours; telephone: 008-034-238 (toll free) for an excellent range of tours and information on Australian old gold mining attractions, as well the great sheep shearing traditions.

You can also rent a horse-drawn wagon and go off prospecting for gold. One can learn a great deal about the bush, the sounds, its mystery, and learn to pan for gold as well, telephone: 054-38-7201 in Newbridge; cost about $180 a weekend.

The Wimmera District

The Wimmera is an area of Victoria largely defined by its land use, predominantly wheat and sheep farms, roughly in the mid-western section of Victoria. The area also boasts important wineries, especially those around the *Great Western* Area. There are signs to wineries, both small and large, at many places. Tour *Best's Concongella Vineyard,* first established in 1866 by Henry Best. There is a picnic area and tastings from 9 a.m. to 4 p.m. Red and white table wines a specialty. For information on tours of wineries at appointed times, usually beginning at 9:30 a.m., telephone: 053-562250. Best's is located off the Western Highway (Melbourne-Ararat Highway). Visit the *Montara Wines Vineyards* of the McCrae family, just two minutes south of Ararat, just off the Melbourne-Ararat highway (Western Highway). Sample Shiraz port and various white wines in this old colonial celler. There are spectacular views as well.

While the distances are vast, the landscape incredibly flat, driving though this district can be pleasant. The farms are huge, the fields straw colored in summer and stretch into the horizon of bright blue. In winter, they are green and heavy. Here one experiences the vast openness of Australia without the desert-like qualities in the red center. Flocks of gang-gangs and galahs (the former white cockatoos with yellow crests, the latter grey with deep pink breasts) hunt in packs making the noise of a thousand yodelers. The enormity of the country along with its riches lulls the traveler into a kind of reverie. Here the land has been conquered. The fields are fenced and farmed as far as the eye can see. The gum trees, where they have been left, dot the landscape only here and there. The wind drives against windbreaks of cypresses and pines, the dark European colors clashing with the Australian light. The pines and cypresses add their distinctive black green coloring to the straw colors of the grass. The trees have grown in thick strange shapes, as though they did not want to be in this forbidding dry climate, like monsters chained to the earth.

Horsham, the capital of the Wimmera district, is the commercial center of the Wimmera, and boasts the usual attributes of a commercial center—particularly American fast food restaurants! The tourist office at city hall provides ample information for the entire region. Horsham can be used as a starting point for a number of day trips.

Go to *Naracoorte,* founded 1845. Or visit *Bool Lagoon,* a wetlands game reserve. Guided tours over a tea-tree boardwalk provide access to observation of water birds in their natural habitat.

See the *Little Desert National Park.* This is an ecologically unique desert, with an abundance of rare plant life, and is home of the mallee fowl, an elusive bird most known for the large mounds it builds in the scrub. Probably, the best way to see this unusual area is through an organized tour. Try

Whimpey's Little Desert Tours, 26 Brougham St., Nhill; telephone: 053-915232 or-911714. The independent tourist may wish to drive to *Kaniva* for a number of well marked bush walks. The time to do this is spring or early summer. Between April and December, 20 different species of orchids have been identified in this area. Among other species are Flame Heath, Desert Banksia and Scarlet Bottlebrush.

Mt. Arapiles is rock climber's heaven. Situated seven miles west of *Natimuk,* this rocky outcrop is Victoria's answer to Ayer's Rock. The world's top rock climbers have mapped some 2,000 climbs on its sheer cliffs. From the lookout atop the 370-meter Mount one sees "truly a vast vista" of the Wimmera Plains, according to the tourist brochure.

Horsham's sister city, *Stawell,* famous in Australia for its annual foot race the *Stawell Gift* with prize money of $75,000, boasts an unusual chiming clock tower. Gold is mined in the Stawell area even today, approxmately 80% of Victoria's gold. If there is time, take a tour of Overdale sheep station. This is a conducted tour of an operating sheep station, which is very educational, telephone: 053-581075 or ask at the tourist information center.

However, by far the greatest attraction of the area is nearby *Grampians National Park,* where tours can be obtained. We suggest *Buandik Grampian Tours Pty. Ltd;* telephone: 053-566221 for 4-wheel drive day tours on Sundays, Tuesdays, Thursdays. Book at Halls Gap Newsagency; telephone: 053-564247. One can also experience the Grampians in other ways by hot air ballooning, telephone: 053-584020; scenic flights over lakes, mountains and waterfalls, telephone: A. G. Airwork, Stawell Airport, 053-582855; horseback riding at *Hall's Gap Ranch,* Rose Gap Road, Halls Gap, telephone: 053-564327; or rockclimbing from *Base Camp and Beyond,* telephone David Witham: 053-564300. However, we prefer to do it the typical Australian way: pack a modest picnic lunch and drive there.

The Grampians

While local Australians think that the Grampians have been very commercialized and developed to cope with the major influx of tourists in recent years, by American standards the development has been limited and restrained. The best way to visit this park is to drive, taking one's time, stopping for a picnic lunch (tomato sandwiches and a cup of tea, of course) at one of the many roadside stops where picnic tables have been provided.

Zumsteins, on the banks of the *MacKenzie River,* is a beautiful spot deep in the heart of the bush. Kangaroos are plentiful, and they are very used to posing for photographs. A barbecue lunch would be in order here—one will see many Australians doing it, though this should be in a season when there is no fire danger. Kookaburras are also plentiful. They wait in the trees for something that looks like a snake (they feed on these creatures), then swoop down and deftly pluck it up. We have seen kookaburras pluck a sausage out from between pieces of sandwich bread!

Drive slowly around the sharp curves and stop to see *MacKenzie falls,* and the many grand views of unusual rock formations and distinctive skylines of the Grampians peaks. These are precipitous sandstone ranges whose sandstone sediments were tilted, sometimes perpendicular, then worn away by millions of years erosion. Wildflowers are the outstanding feature of the Grampians and include some 900 native plant species. They range from stunted heaths on the Major Mitchell Plateau (Major Mitchell discovered the area in 1836) to stringy bark forests, redgum woodlands and luxuriant fern gullies. Watch out for the many species of fauna: possums, gliders, echidnas and koalas.

Continue to *Hall's Gap,* the center of Grampians tourism. There are a small number of motels, a campground and some small restaurants, offering the usual Aussie fare. We liked the *Kookaburra Lodge and Restaurant* largely because of its name, 13-14 Heath Street; telephone: 053-564395. Rich and Vonne Heinrich have been serving spinach pie, duckling, and chocolate truffle cake to appreciative customers for some ten years. One can choose from a wide range of local wines as well. Or, for a light feast, try *Jallukar Arts and Craft,* Halls Gap Road, Pomonal; telephone: 053-566300. One can sample 16 varieties of scones (biscuits) with strawberry jam and other Aussie snacks. Browse the handcrafts as well. Open Friday and Saturdays, 10 a.m.

There is an excellent tourist information center just 1.5 miles through the town on the Dunkeld Road, where one can view a display about the history and life of the area, as well as an audio-visual presentation. Soon to open is a cultural center in a strange building whose architect seems to have tried to emulate the shape of the Grampians peaks. This building will house a display on aboriginal life in the Grampians—there are aboriginal rock art sites dotted throughout the area.

Drive South to Dunkeld along a valley between the two great ridges of the Grampians Mountains. The bush here takes on an unusual eerie quality—reminds one of the reconstructions in museums of the scenery of the dinosaur age. There is a distinct feeling of primeval bush here.

For the energetic, there are walks aplenty in these ranges. These are well marked trails, some very hard, others less so. Walks are easily the best way to absorb the beauty of the Australian bush. Some of the best walks are:

Mt. William Summit, the highest point in the park (1168 m). It is a steep walk up the road from the car parking to panoramic views. Access via Mt. William Road from Dunkeld Road, 9 miles south of Halls Gap. (1½ hours)

The Pinnacle, access from Wonderland car park and Mt. Victory Road. Fascinating rock formations and magnificent views. (2½ hours)

The Balconies from Reid lookout car park, for fine views. (1 hour)

MacKenzie Falls, from Zumsteins; this is one of the most spectacular waterfalls in Victoria. (2 to 3 hours)

If the yearning to see still more wildlife won't go away, visit the *Wallaroo Wildlife Park* in Hall's Gap, Halls Gap-Ararat Main Road, telephone: 053-564346. This park caters especially to children who would like to pet some of the animals (one can hand feed wallabies, kangaroos, emus, possums, waterfowl), and the farm boasts many types of birds often not seen in other parks. But it may be worth the visit if only to see the legendary dingo, the villain suspected of carrying off the baby Azaria (see Chapters 4 and 9). Open daily from 10 a.m.

As we descend from the mountains to Dunkeld, the rolling plains of the *Western District* begin to unfold. In the summer, these are plains of parched yellow grass, with stripes of gum green. In winter, the fields are a heavy green, the skies often grey, providing a foreboding, somber tone. If we continue south, we reach Warrnambool once again, a thriving coastal town at the western reaches of Australia's premium wool growing area, the Western District. Here the farms are a little smaller, but definitely more productive. Some of the best established and oldest Victorian families reside in this area. The land and climate are ideal for raising sheep for wool. Take the inland route through *Hamilton* (pop. 10,250), center of the wool growing district (telephone: 055-730498 for information on the many local attractions), *Camperdown* and *Colac*, the rich farming district, with its volcanic soil. Here the cypress and pine wind breaks are more common and closer together, although some farmers grow wind breaks of gums, which have been lopped off about five feet from the ground, so that they grow into a bushy shape. The European influence on the countryside is never more telling than here. The small towns are also distinctive, each with its familiar square-towered clock, painted white, of course; each with its pubs and lacy wrought iron balconies and verandas. The countryside is a very old volcanic area, and the remains of volcanoes can be seen everywhere. Stop briefly at the *Stony Rises*, strange stony rocks and billabongs full of bright irridescent green algae. There are snakes here, so stay on the path and watch where you tread. Look up in the heights of the manna gums to see koalas blissfully chewing eucalyptus leaves.

One can continue along the road to Geelong, through *Colac*, or turn off at Colac for *Beech Forest*, and follow the winding road all the way to *Otway National Park*, and join up again with the *Great Ocean Road*. It is said that it rains every day in the Otway Ranges. The road winds through some of the most beautiful southern bushland, with shaded lush valleys. Leave plenty of time for this drive. Swamp wallabies and ring-tailed possums abound here, as do comparatively rare birds such as the grey goshawk and king parrot. For further information, tel: 052-315799. After particularly heavy rains roads may sometimes be blocked by landslides (telephone: 052-373243 for an update.)

Taking the other fork directly to Geelong transports one across lakes and crater country. The streams are well stocked for fishermen. Try your luck at rainbow trout or redfin perch in the lakes, eels and native blackfish in the streams. Recommended bait is mudeye, whitebait, worms. Or, you may wish to return to the coast around Apollo Bay and Port Campbell and have a go at catching salmon, snapper, shark or whiting in the surf, or bream, mullet and perch in the estuaries. Recommended baits are shrimp, sand yabbies, podworm, sand worms or crabs. Tel: 052-632007 for more information.

CHAPTER 8

Beyond Sydney

Away from Canberra

On a bus trip we once took from Canberra to Sydney, as is the custom, our driver addressed the passengers as he drove the bus out onto the main street and away from Canberra. Australian inter-city and inter-state bus drivers have an amusing habit of addressing the passengers through the speaker system in much the same way as captains do on airplanes. Bus drivers always have jokes to tell, or some amusing anecdote. They try their best to keep up the leg pulling humor of Henry Lawson or Banjo Patterson. Ours observed that he couldn't tell us anything about Canberra because he was from the Northwest himself (meaning Darwin) and he'd just as soon spend as little time in Canberra as possible. In his opinion, the best view of Canberra was of it receding in the rear view mirror.

The bus driver's opinion is shared by many Australians, and understandably, because Canberra, although the capital of Australia, is not by appearance or atmosphere a true representative of the rest of Australia. Indeed, any visitor gets the feeling of having entered a sort of New England country club. The roads are flawless, and carefully planned and groomed gardens and lawns grace every street (there even used to be a law that street corners could not be built upon). In the fall maple trees display brilliant foliage almost rivaling that of the New England Catskills.

Canberra's history began in 1901, when Melbourne and Sydney could not agree on which was the more important city, worthy of capital status. It was decided that a completely new city would be planned and built. "Canberra" would be the name it was decided, and a competition was held to determine the city's design. But much to everyone's disdain, the competition was won by an American, Walter Burley-Griffin, and there were even some rumors that "Canberra" was actually the aboriginal word meaning "a woman's breasts," and not "a meeting place," as was previously thought.

Canberra is completely and exactly symmetrical, with all roads radiating from the Parliament House center (which is exactly aligned with Mount Ainslie). And because all Australian cities seem to be attached to bodies of water, Lake Burley-Griffin was created, complete with the quaint islands necessary for a beautiful lake. The lake is deep and very popular for sailing.

Many residents of Canberra are employed by the government, and enjoy a peaceful living atmosphere blessed by extraordinarily low housing costs. This is not the place for energetic nightlife, but for cozy dinner parties and the pick of some of the best restaurants in Australia. Bike paths are as common as roads, and many Canberrans especially enjoy hiking and fishing, oftentimes just a five minute walk from their house. Wilderness has been preserved in the form of Mount Ainslie, where one can still enjoy the challenge of climbing a mountain, and as a reward, see kangaroos, rabbits, or wombats, and a spectacular view of the city from above.

There are a number of important sights worthy of a tourist's eye. The first, of course, at the center of the city is *Parliament House*. There are actually two of these; a new one was just built and opened in 1988 directly behind the old one. The new

Parliament House is about as modern a building as one will find in any country. Built into a mountain (well, a small hill), the building is huge, and much of it extends underground. The approach is reminiscent of the Vietnam War Memorial in Washington D.C., in the sense that it is an understated design, not a construction that protrudes into the air. It expresses something of the Australian character and the slightly belligerent dislike of the garish trappings of authority. As one Aussie mentioned to us, "It's there that ordinary Aussies can just walk all over their members of Parliament." (It's possible to literally walk over Parliament House, and in fact walk to the top of it over grassy rises.)

The front foyer is decked with columns of blue and brown marble (Australian marble, of course), and each corresponding room has a separate unique Aussie design which is very different from anything anywhere else. The ballroom, used for dinners and rented out, boasts a wall with a giant tapestry of gum trees. Portraits of the prime ministers and other distinguished persons line another lobby amidst various historical memorabilia. Both the House and Senate assembly rooms create quite an impression with design features such as a multi-hued green color scheme. Also please note the beautiful tennis courts intended for members only (members of Parliament, that is).

One can also take an elevator to the roof, where views of Mount Ainslie and the city are at their best. The sky above is framed by a huge triangular steel structure with an Australian flag at the peak.

Also visible from the lookout are: the *American Embassy* (a colonial-like village with many tall chimneys), the *War Memorial* (the building resembling the Parthenon directly in front of Mount Ainslie), *The Lodge* where the Prime Minister lives (white picket fence), the *Telecom Tower* for tourists (looks like a UFO sticking unnaturally out of the mountain), *Civic* (downtown, identifiable by relatively large buildings), and the *Defense Buildings* (at the front of which is a tall tower with an eagle at the top), and *The American War Memorial*, given to Australia by the U.S. and which many Canberrans think gives the place a bad image.

If there's time, we recommend climbing Mount Ainslie. It isn't too difficult (even for those who do not jog regularly), and the views and wildlife enjoyed on the way up are worth the toil. However, one can also drive up to the look-out, which is what most tourists do.

The National Science and Technology Centre, "a joint Australia-Japan Bicentennial Project," is also a must. Here are magnificent hands-on exhibits of various scientific phenomena. One can experiment with exhibits in physics, math, biology, and have just plain fun.

Civic (the city center) has at last begun to prosper, having for some years fallen into the ignominious position of having its very existence denied. "Canberra doesn't have a city center," people used to say. Rather, Canberra was an orderly group of villages placed carefully in several valleys. But with the opening of new office buildings and government offices, the city center has flourished, and provides an attractive area for the tourist in search of—well, dare we say it—Europe, especially France and the Riviera. Large portions of the city center are closed to traffic, so there are many walks for just pedestrians. These are bedecked with sidewalk cafés and restaurants with colorful umbrellas. The food is probably as good or better than anywhere in Australia, and caters to an enormous variety of international tastes. On a sunny day, winter or summer, this is a quiet, colorful place to relax over a fine meal and lots of Australian wine (which Australians drink copiously, as if it were beer). It is very much a place for the homesick European, we would say. Try the *Dante Italian Coffee and Spaghetti Bar,* 106 Alinga Street, Civic. BYO, of course. The focaccia is especially tasty, and the servings generous.

Approaching Sydney

From Canberra. Canberra lies nearly an hour's drive off the Hume Highway which connects Sydney to Melbourne. Before we turn to Sydney, we should make a brief side trip south, towards Golburn, to view a typical New South Wales town. A small detour will take us through Wagga Wagga (the name itself beckons), nestled on the banks of the Murrumbidgee River. The road transports us through green grassy hills interspersed with graceful gums and occasional patches of eucalyptus forests. Wagga Wagga was settled in 1829, and proclaimed a town in 1849. It now has a population of 52,000. Wagga Wagga is a typical New South Wales (N.S.W.) town: the cars park at 45 degree angles, tail in. The shops line very wide streets, their awnings jutting out over the sidewalks for protection from the summer sun. There are many historical buildings in this area. Call the tourist information center at 069-23-5402 to see what's happening.

Turning north again to Sydney, the Hume Highway gently winds through some of the most beautiful grazing and farm lands in all of Australia. There are rolling hills, rich pastures, eucalyptus forests and great grey gums (eucalyptus trees) dotting the farmlands. This is the kind of countryside Australian city dwellers think of when they are homesick for Australia. Unfortunately, when one nears the outer fringes of Sydney civilization the beauty of the farming country changes dramatically to Australian deserts of a different kind: Miles and miles of suburbs. Expect to take at least an hour to pass through these western suburbs into the center of Sydney.

From the Southern Coast. When you cross the border just after Mallacoota, driving up the coast to Sydney, the scenery and seaside towns become more and more gorgeous. Contrary to what one sees on North American television, the colors are anything but red, brown and bare. Here, rainfall is plentiful, and even the eucalyptus forests have a deeper brighter green than forests elsewhere (even more than in the tropical Queensland).

Roads in New South Wales. It is a shame to say so, but the difference in the conditions of roads between Victoria and New South Wales is indeed striking. Victoria's roads, by and large, are well kept, and generally safe. Not so in New South Wales, as one finds almost immediately on crossing the border. The road surface is uniformly poorer, potholes quite common, and generally there are fewer passing lanes. So, we urge the driver to be patient, and slow down when necessary. Serious accidents do occur on these roads more often than they should, often involving large busses which end up on the wrong side of the road too often (for reasons that are quite obvious to anyone using the roads).

One passes through *Eden*, fishing port and tourist resort, its old pubs full of geezers from the sea and from the logging camps. These pubs are rough places, avoided by tourists. But there are restaurants and motels a plenty for tourists.

Eden is an old whaling town, with the result that it does, of course, have a Killer Whale Museum. Today, Eden has one of the biggest fishing fleets in N.S.W., and their regular unloading in the afternoons is never short of fascinated onlookers. Picnickers in the many state parks nearby may catch sight of yellow-bellied gliders or swamp wallabies. For fishing trips and other tourist information call 064-961953.

"The sapphire sea and sapphire coast"—those are the words tourist brochures use to describe this coastal area. The beaches are unsurpassed here, possibly with more character and longer stretches of sand than most other places. The water still retains the slight chill of southern waters, which does not disappear until the beaches beyond Sydney. We pass through Pambula, Merimbula, Narooma, Bateman's Bay, Nowra, all progressively more developed and places of a happy lifestyle for the well-off bureaucrats of Canberra which is some three hours drive inland. We pass through Bermagui, where the great fisherman Zane Grey fitted out his blue water fishing craft for his great deep sea fishing adventures. It is best to dawdle along this highway. Perhaps the most entrancing stretch is the inland stretch before Bega through the historic town of Bodalla (Moruya), a town preserved just as it was in the 1800s. The countryside is a dairying area, rich in green pastures, almost Swiss in its contours and hues (though there are no towering mountains to form the background). Deep valleys and hills abound. This is a memorable drive, one thoroughly unexpected in an otherwise parched and red land.

Too quickly, the route enters *Wollongong*, New South Wales' third largest city (after Newcastle), with its sister city *Port Kembla*, a huge iron smelting and heavy industrial complex. Climb the steep rise to *Bulli Pass* just north of Wollongong, and take a side trip of a couple miles to the lookout. The Pass is actually at the top of an enormous cliff face that extends for miles parallel to the shore front, offering for the first time physical proof of the elevated tableland of much of central and western Australia, which sharply drops down to sea level at Wollongong. Colorful hang gliders spring out into the wind tunnels and updrafts from this point, often rising high above the lookout itself.

The road becomes a freeway. Sydney is upon us. We should not be misled, though. Sydney has no freeways to speak of.

From the Northern Coast

The Gold Coast to Sydney is a most scenic drive, slightly longer than if traveled on the inland route. Tropical forests and ocean views are the highlight of this trip. And due to the pineapple, banana and avocado farms all around, there are plenty of roadside fruit stands from which to buy delicious farm-fresh fruits for farm prices. However, because the road is not the best of quality, there have been many accidents on this road. So drive carefully.

Woolgoolga, "a hard name to say, but a great place to stay," as the sign points out. A very quiet, undeveloped, country town, Woolgoolga has some wonderful beaches. There are also several campgrounds offering on-site vans, as well as a few motels. In Australia, camping trailers of the hard top variety are called caravans. There are many campgrounds throughout Australia that have caravans installed permanently on camp sites, and these are called "on-site vans." They are excellent value for a large family, providing convenience that is somewhere between a basic motel room and camping. Their greatest advantage is that they often sleep as many as six people, so that a large family can take one and pay much less than it would cost either for a suite or two motel rooms. Prices vary depending on locality, but we rarely paid more than $30 a night. Conveniences include TV, refrigerator, hot water, etc., and some even had their own toilets and showers. The auto clubs listed in Chapter 4 publish detailed listings of campgrounds with on-site vans, and will also make reservations.

We mention this place because we were particularly struck

by the giant Taj Mahal-like building in the center of the town.
No, Donald Trump has not made his mark here. In fact this
place is a kind of Indian community center for the large
Indian population living in Woolgoolga. It is complete with
Indian shops and a restaurant (which we recommend highly).
There is even a train ride for the kiddies along the perimeter
of the building and a giant pool of balls into which they may
dive and jump. Not at all what one would expect in a town
called Woolgoolga.

A visit to *Byron Bay* is like a trip back to the 60s. Nothing has
changed, except that the hippies are now middle aged, and
they have hippie kids and grandkids too. The shops and
restaurants here all have a bohemian atmosphere. Cafés post
little quotes or mottos on the walls, and shops still sell Indian
cotton clothing. Indeed, one could come to Byron Bay just to
watch the people (be on the lookout for Paul Hogan; he has a
mansion near Byron Bay). The easternmost point in Australia,
Byron Bay has no shortage of beaches or surf. There is a
popular youth hostel here, so there are always university
students to add that extra cultural spice during holiday periods. Byron Bay is seemingly unchanged by the outside world,
and is much fun and comfort to anyone who has felt that
those wild and crazy 60s are gone forever.

From here the road winds down into Coffs Harbour, tourist
resort and heart of banana country. The inevitable Big Banana
is passed along the way, at the entrance to a banana plantation
that offers rides, entertainment, and everything that can be
made to look or taste like a banana (telephone: 066-525160).
Try the chocolate-coated frozen bananas. In this same area is
river rafting from Bigfoot Safaris (telephone: 066-523924).

Slowly the countryside changes; leaving banana plantations behind, there are groves of avocados, then dairy farms.
The road is narrow and crowded. Care in driving is needed,
and night driving not recommended. Any number of these
gorgeous coastal towns could be the place for a delightful
vacation. The beaches are clean, hardly used, scenic. We pass
through Nambucca Heads, Port Macquarie (home of the Big
Bull and Big Oyster), Taree, center of a rich agricultural
district on the Manning River. From Taree, a brief detour to

Tuncurry and Forster reveals yet more secluded and quiet coastal resort towns poised between inland lakes and inlets, protected from the ocean surf by high sand dunes. The road winds it way through O'Sullivan's Gap to Bulahdelah, center of a logging industry, then becomes busier as we near Newcastle, second largest city in New South Wales. But it can be bypassed. The freeway takes us by Lake Macquarie on to Gosford and through the spectacular Hawksbury River district, with its steep sided mountains, dropping down to the river far below. The road stays way above the river in many places, offering a stunning view of the Hawkesbury and its tributaries. The traffic, though, can be thick. By the time we get to Gosford, we are very close to Sydney, although the traffic and lack of freeway will make it still an hour until we reach downtown Sydney. There are plenty of places to see outside of Sydney, however, including right here, near Gosford. This is the reconstruction of Old Sydney Town.

Old Sydney Town. Old Sydney Town is a historically authentic reconstruction of Old Sydney as it was in the early convict period from 1788 to 1800. It tells much of Australia, both then and now. Robert Hughes in his classic *The Fatal Shore* complained bitterly that there is not the slightest commemoration in Sydney of the poor souls, sick and ravaged by disease, who were dragged to the inhospitable shores, shackled so heavily that they could barely stand. Their plight is brought to life in this village, which gives character and life to the dry historical accounts of Australian history that can otherwise be quite easily forgotten.

While there are many interesting exhibits, such as reconstructed old houses, a windmill, and inhabitants in period costume, by far the best attraction—and the most revealing of the Australian character—is the street theater. Actors simulate convict escapes, a Botany Bay wedding, settlement law and punishments, a pistol duel, and give demonstrations on everything from how to use a windmill to making candles and leather. All is completely in character, and in addition to relating historical circumstances, the actors are very entertaining, though the humor accordingly crude. Visitors are often asked (or should we say made) to participate in demonstrations, and this adds significantly to the fun of the place. One will even discover the origin of such terms as "underdog" and "top notch." The belligerent attitude to authority and generally ribald way Australians have of relating to each other is evident in the street theater shows. Be sure to obtain a program as you enter. Don't miss the convict escape and saber duel put on at the gaol (jail to Americans, but pronounced the same anyway), the various convict task works in timber, sawing, etc., and most amusing of all—probably should be rated "X"—the demonstration of law and punishment.

Tourists are able to view a mock trial which is long on blue humor and rather short on history. Afterwards the convict receives twenty lashes on the bare back, complete with pretend blood. This demonstration elicits laughter and cries of approval from the crowd. Funny indeed, though we ought to hesitate a moment and reflect on the incredible damage done to individuals who received hundreds of lashes, enough to remove the flesh completely from their shoulders and back so that the bones could be seen. The actors relate this to the crowd. Allow about three hours to see this attraction. Open 10 to 5 Wednesdays through Sundays; telephone: 043-40-1104.

Also near Gosford is the *Forest of Tranquility*, a rain forest and bird sanctuary, open 10 to 5; telephone 043 621855. *Australian Reptile Park* is a wildlife sanctuary with platypusary, noctarium, and feeding of reptile demonstrations daily. Open 9 to 5; telephone: 43-284311. The drive into Sydney from Gosford takes one on the freeway south, a stunning journey through deep valleys and orange cliffs along the beautiful estuaries that make up the Hawkesbury River area. Allow a good hour, however, as the traffic can be thick and slow.

The Blue Mountains

Only 65 kilometers west of Sydney, the Blue Mountains are easily seen in one day by car, train or bus leaving from Sydney. The road is narrow, winding and crowded, such that the drive to the Blue Mountains is best left to the buses, or better yet, the train. The classic train ride over the tops of the mountains, up the Switchback track (the railway actually zigzags up the side of a steep mountain) is an experience probably unequaled anywhere else in the world.

Between 1789 and 1804, seven attempts were made to cross the forbidding mountains, but each time, the explorers were forced back. All had tried to find a pass through the mountains following various river valleys and gorges. Then Gregory Blaxland with his colleagues Wentworth and Lawson and four servants set off on May 11, 1813. They decided to take a route along the tops of the mountains. Upon his return 26 days later Blaxland pronounced that they "accomplished what no other white man had done." His hunch had proved right.

A road was begun in 1814 by 30 convicts and a guard of eight soldiers. They had to hack through heavy timber to a height of 4,000 feet. It was not until 1823 that a truly navigable road was properly forged. Forty years later the railway had reached Penrith. In order to cross the Blue Mountains, especially Mount Victoria, it was necessary to construct a switchback railway up the mountain and down it. This became known as the ZigZag naturally enough, and was in use until 1910. It is now preserved as a tourist experience. (Modern trains tunnel through the mountains). The ZigZag may be boarded at Lithgow. A genuine steam train is preserved and hooked up to vintage carriages, which operate every half hour on Saturdays, Sundays and public holidays, 11 a.m. to 4:30 p.m. Times do change, though, as it's run by a voluntary group; tel: 047-57-3061.

Today even the regular train journey takes one on a fabulous ride across the ridges of the Blue Mountains, where one can look down on either side of the train to deep valleys or across to high, cliff-like peaks on the same level as the train. This is a journey that needs to be taken in good weather. They are pesky mountains, these Blue Mountains. Visitors are often foiled by their incessant clouds and rainfall (and sometimes snow in winter). It is always a few degrees cooler there as well. Though the mountains are not high, as mountain ranges go, the view from above conveys a scene of forbidding, rugged country. One would not like to be lost here; there are no houses for miles around and very few roads. The darkness of the forests also conveys a sense of mystery and forboding so well captured by the Heidleberg School of Australian painters.

Part of the huge Blue Mountains National Park, the second largest in New South Wales, the wilderness will remain forever untouched. The mountains really are blue, too, there is a mistiness that forms in the valleys and on the sides of the mountains, even on bright clear days (sometimes especially on such days early in the morning) caused by droplets of eucalyptus oil that evaporate from the forests and the light reflecting off them. The sense of awe and beauty of the Australian rainforests is strong, almost overwhelming. Individuals cannot help but feel overshadowed by nature's magnificence and power among these rugged, challenging precipices.

Katoomba is the main commercial center of the Blue Mountains and the town itself offers some interesting attractions. The *Great Western Hotel* built in 1822 is a majestic building of surprisingly American design, but with the unmistakable Australian touch of lattice wrought iron. Large tall pot chimneys are reminiscent of those seen occasionally in New England. To make sure everything is right for your visit, call the Katoomba information center at 047-396266 or for a 24-hour hot line dial 04739177. For those interested in authors and artists of Australia, the *Norman Lindsay Gallery and Museum* is located in Springwood, not far from Katoomba. Lindsay is best known to generations of Australians for his children's book *The Magic Pudding*. A handsome (if rather pretentious) koala called Bunyip Bluegum was the hero of that epic. Rather different from today's Ninja Turtles and superheros, but just as far out.

Katoomba is visited most often because it is the starting off point for the most famous of the natural wonders of the Blue Mountains: the Three Sisters.

The Three Sisters are possibly some of the best known tourist scenery in all of Australia, next only to Ayer's Rock. These precipitous crags of rock jut out from an enormous cliff face. One walks down to them via a narrow trail and a system of ladders and narrow metal bridges. This is not a walk for those with acrophobia or vertigo.

There is an aboriginal legend about these rock formations: Once upon a time there were three sisters . . . . their father, a witch doctor, left them high on a rock as he descended into the valley. They lived an idyllic existence in this beautiful country, except that the Bunyip lived in a deep hole in the valley, and they feared him greatly. As the father left, a centipede appeared and frightened one of the sisters. She threw a stone at it, and started a land slide (for which the area is well known). Their father, fearing that the Bunyip would eat his daughters, turned them into stone. He in turn was chased by the Bunyip and dropped his magic stone (wand). He continues to look for it today. The Bunyip has returned to his hole.

Another version goes like this: Three sisters from the Katoomba tribe were in love with three brothers from the Nepean tribe. However, law forbade them to marry, and the brothers decided to take the sisters by force. A large battle ensued, and the witchdoctor from the Katoomba tribe turned the sisters into stone for safekeeping, intending to revive them when danger had passed. But he was then killed, and to this day, no one has been able to break the spell to bring the three sisters back to life.

There are many wonderful bush walks in the Blue Mountains. Call the information service or national parks for details (047-878877). But, abide by a couple of important rules: don't stray from the marked trails. The themes in Australian paintings and stories of "lost in the bush" are no coincidence. Getting lost in the dense bush is very easy. Even Zane Grey's star cowboy Sterl, in his Australian novel *Wilderness Trek*, got lost for three days! And if there is fire danger, abide by the published rules of fire use. Remember that on total fire ban days, no fires or stoves can be used at all. There are many other trails and self guided tours, some marked as historical and others as geological. Some are simply to enjoy bush tranquillity; still others are for those in wheelchairs.

One of the more challenging and exciting is the Giant Staircase trail. Carved into the rock in the early 20th century, there are some 800 steps which lead from the top of the cliff to the valley. However, realize that there is nothing but wilderness at the bottom of the steps, so whoever climbs down must also climb up! Although the trail rewards the stair-climber with some exhilarating views of the Blue Mountains, no one we spoke to who had completed the trail had enough breath to tell us much about it, except that it took two and a half hours. But isn't all that fresh eucalyptus air and exercise worth it?

We weren't brave enough to descend the entire 800 steps, but went down twenty. This took us to a bridge which actually spans the thin air between the cliff and the first Sister. It is a prime photo opportunity—but don't drop your camera—it's a long way down!

It might appear that Katoomba, although quite isolated from the stresses of city existence, uses glorious views of the mountains to entice one into gambling with one's life. This is precisely the case. Take the Scenic Railway, located off Cliff Drive, for instance. We quite innocently bought tickets to this short ride, thinking we would catch a spectacular view. Our only clue as to what was to come was a rather prominent disclaimer, posted by the entrance. Before we knew it, we literally plunged down a vertical drop of no less than 45 degrees and closer to 90. Gravity's pull shifted, causing us to kneel on the seat in front of us. The eldest of us was scared out of his wits. At the bottom, there are trails extending in all directions to the old coal mines. Here is the history we learned after the fact: the railroad was built in approximately 1888, originally meant to transport coal (it looks and runs like it's that old, too, let us tell you!). Around the turn of the century, requests from hikers and campers to go up the cliff face via the railroad became more and more frequent. As a result, a small compartment was built for carrying passengers. Eventually the coal mining ceased, and the railroad became the popular tourist attraction that it is today. It is reputed to be the steepest railroad in the world. We believe it.

There is also a Scenic Skyway, actually a large gondola, which can carry up to thirty people across the Blue Mountains gorge. We don't know which is worse: hanging on a wire or plunging a steep rockface on a rickety old railroad.

More Places Beyond Sydney

Koala Park. A two-hour drive northwest of Sydney via the Epping Highway, one can find koalas, those cuddly marsupials everybody loves and wants to touch. They are very shy animals, and prove difficult to get close enough to even for a good photograph. At Koala Park, there are koalas aplenty, some even for petting and pictures. There are wombats and kangaroos to pet as well. And a koala hospital. Telephone 02-484-8009 for more information.

City Rail Off-peak Discounts. Inexpensive tours to some of the better known sights around Sydney can be had through city rail off-peak fares. Pick up the brochure at any travel information center in Sydney. The one that attracted us was the Riverboat Postman tour. For $20 one can take the train to the Hawkesbury River Station, then walk to the Hawkesbury ferries wharf (about 200 yards). Here, you can join the riverboat postman as he makes his way up and back the Hawkesbury, stopping at many settlements on the Hawkesbury to deliver mail. Morning tea is included!

Butterfly House. Becoming immensely popular in Australia are butterfly houses. We have already waxed profusely about the butterfly house in the Melbourne Zoo. Sydney has her butterfly house, as well, at 628 Old Northern Road, Dural 2158, about one and half hour's drive west of Sydney (depending on the traffic, of course). Australia's tropical butterflies are hatched and displayed in a simulated Cairns temperature. There are 30 types, and hundreds flying around at any one time. Telephone: 02-651-1868 to check on times. Hours are more or less 9 to 5.

The Road to Bathurst

The road follows the mountains over the ridges to Lithgow,

thence on to Bathurst. It descends slowly to the slopes, as the locals call them—enormous low rolling hills—in winter a deep green and lush pasture, in summer dried to a dull brown, the color burnt out by the sun. Trees, large heavy looking eucalypts with thick trunks, and bushy in shape, dot the landscape. Here are rich farming areas for sheep, although closer to the Blue Mountains, there are also dairy herds. The early colonial influence is less noticeable in this countryside. The scars of cypres, and pine, so much a part of the Victorian farmscape, are less evident here, creating an authentically Australian countryside.

Bathurst itself is a small college town, proudly harboring some historic buildings from the early 19th century. Here the influence of the colonial period is marked. The red brick buildings still stand, some now 150 years old. Their preservation commands the rest of the town and its characteristic main street lined with modest shops and connecting verandas stretching out over the sidewalk. The public buildings were clearly once majestic in their structure. Today, they are surrounded by the new order of shops and cars. One has the impression that times have changed, though not much progress has occurred. Some 20,000 people live here, a few less when the university is not in session. Little old country pubs are all around. The streets are wide and dusty. Time moves slowly here.

The Murray and Darling Rivers

In 1886, Alfred Deakin, then premier of Victoria, invited the Chaffey Brothers to Australia. These Americans had already established irrigation communities in California. They received a grant of crown land in Mildura (now the dominant city on the Victorian side of the border which is defined by the Murray River), and irrigation systems were introduced into Australia. The area was transformed from a dry, sandy desert, to a lush garden of citrus and grape plantations. Almost all Australia's dried fruit production originates here. A labyrinth of irrigation systems and channels now spans many hundreds of square miles, drawing water from the Murray and the Darling Rivers that meet at the twin cities of Mildura and Wentworth. These towns are now the heart of Australia's citrus and grape growing districts, and about 100 years old. Mildura lies on the Victorian side of the Murray River which traces the border between New South Wales and Victoria. Wentworth is on the New South Wales side, some few miles west of Mildura.

The meeting of the two rivers is itself worth seeing: the mixing of waters from two quite different sources, the Murray from the cleaner snowfields of the Victorian Alps and the Darling from far away Queensland, turbid and earthy.

That the Chaffeys were American may explain the layout of Mildura, its broad streets and tree lined avenues. The riverfront has been carefully developed, preserving the historic sites, particularly the customs house and buildings of the steamboat period. The original home of the Chaffey brothers may be viewed. Chaffey is also the stepping off point to the outback, the fascinating mining town of Broken Hill, and 60 miles to the north, the huge sand dunes of The Wall of China.

Armidale and the Trip to Brisbane

Once one manages to shake loose from the tentacles of Sydney's suburban traffic, the trip to Brisbane via Armidale can be taken at one's leisure. This is one of the inland routes, leaving the Great Divide on one's right, and some 200 miles from the coast. The fields (most having been cleared forest) open out into deep green pastures, frequently dotted by single huge gum trees, interspersed with patches of eucalyptus forests. As you approach Armidale, you are immediately invited to compare it to England—"New England" is the name given to this area and the name of the university which forms the center of the town's activities. The town was there before the university, however. It was the chosen area for the establishment of a number of private, fee paying schools, such as the Armidale Anglican School for Boys, established in 1894. The school is resplendent in old style red brick and turreted buildings amid carefully mowed lawns. The boys still wear English-style uniforms, and the visitor could swear it was England all over again.

A National Trust building worth a visit is *Saumarez Homestead*, one of Australia's most elegant properties dating back to 1835. This is a two story building with classic Australian style veranda and wrought iron. The interior is restored to period design, the furniture all authentic. Open September to June only; telephone: 067-72-4486.

CHAPTER 9

Alice: A Journey to the Center of the Earth

To get to Alice, we tried the train. We'd recommend it to others, though one should be prepared for the unexpected. We put our car on the train in Sydney and traveled with it on the India-Pacific to Adelaide, a route that journeys from the Indian Ocean to the Pacific. This is a slow moving train by any standard. However, the way is through some of the most interesting outback farming areas in New South Wales, including Broken Hill, the famous mining town of Western N.S.W.

The train must also traverse the Blue Mountains as it leaves Sydney—a view well worth being on the train for its 26 hours or so. In our case, the trip was a little longer, as the train lost half its carriages at one point, making us five hours late! Select the inexpensive seats, "the sitting up car," as it's called, and enjoy watching how the train staff manages to treat the sitting-up people like a kind of unclean class. Mixing with the First Class passengers who wine and dine themselves and slumber in secluded sleeping cars is kept at a minimum. However, if you feel bad about this, be satisfied to know that the First Class passengers pay some four times more than you did for cramped sleeping conditions. Not worth it!

The food is also a bit limited. There is the usual instant coffee, pies and sausage rolls, passable sandwiches, and beer, of course. One is probably advised to take food, as well as a spare blanket, just in case the heating does not work properly (which happened to us once, not on this trip though).

The rather casual service, and the lack of any feeling of dedication of the staff to the passengers, is more than made up for by their charming sense of humor, that special Aussie mixture of belligerence and self deprecation. Aussies are great at making fun of themselves. And one gets the feeling after a while that they actually believe the terrible things they say about themselves. It's called the Australian inferiority complex. But it might simply be that Aussies are very ordinary people, more in touch with life's banal realities than most of the Western world. Their convict heritage, after all, as we found in Old Sydney Town, runs deep in the Aussie character. They don't stand for any bull dust (they use stronger language than this, though).

The train passes through wild country where there are loads of kangaroos grazing and hopping about, herds of emus too. Farming country begins after leaving Broken Hill. One certainly gains an impression of the comfort or freedom of the rural life on these massive, and probably quite prosperous spreads, with sheep and cattle grazing alongside emus and kangaroos.

One can leave the train in *Adelaide,* or stay on until the train moves on to Port Augusta. (The India-Pacific, as the train is called, also continues on across the vast Nullabor Plains to Australia's western most city, Perth.) We chose to unload our car in Adelaide, as we wanted to see something of that town. And a town it is! One American acquaintance of ours described it as Australia's Utica, New York. There are few skyscrapers (some would say that there are none at all), but there are many wide open parks. The streets are such a contrast to those of Sydney. After all, Adelaide was settled by free settlers, not convicts. The streets are laid out symmetrically, have wide green strips down their centers. There are fountains, landscaped gardens and parks.

Adelaide calls itself the Festival City, promoting its image as the supporter of the arts in Australia. There are many theater events, topped off by the biannual Festival of Arts. The most notable building in this respect is the Adelaide Festival Centre on the banks of the Torrens (the river that flows through downtown Adelaide). This complex boasts a huge auditorium, a drama theater, an experimental theater, and open air amphitheater where some 950 shows a year are staged; tel: 2168600 for information.

The *Adelaide Town Hall* is of interest to the traveler, since its architecture is 16th-century renaissance, though it was built in 1863. But no matter, the Victorian influence remains supreme; the faces of Queen Victoria and Prince Albert are carved into the front.

Eat with the marsupials. We had a fun meal at the *Urimbirra Fauna Park Restaurant* at Victor Harbor (five minutes from town center). Here one can dine in as natural a setting as one can get, and view the native animals as well; open seven days; telephone: 54-6554.

Ayers House (288 North Terrace, telephone: 2231655). The pick of the national trust houses in Adelaide, this magnificent 19th-century mansion was once the home of Sir Henry Ayers, five times premier of South Australia. This is a 19th-century mansion, featuring period furniture, drawing rooms, nursery etc. Politicans have always lived well in Australia!

But the key to fine living in Adelaide is its wineries, for some of Australia's best and famous wineries are within 30 minutes drive of the city. A visit to these is worth considering. Many wines produced in these areas are now readily available in the United States. While there are many grape growing valleys to visit, by far the most famous is the Barossa Valley. Among the many wineries prepared for visitors, are: Redgum Cellars (085-244511), Basedows (085-632060), Hermitage of

Marananga (accommodations also offered presumably if one overdoes it a bit with the tasting: telephone: 085-622722), Peter Lehmann (085-630283) known for a wide range and especially sauternes, Blickinstal (beautiful accommodations affording views of the Barossa Valley; telephone: 085-632716), Penfolds (085-621811) which is Australia's answer to Gallo, Wolf Blass (08-621955) widely available in the United States and best known for its sparkling whites and award winning young reds. And for a delightful family owned and operated winery, visit Rockford Winery, where the owner Robert O'Callaghan has restored and rebuilt ancient machinery of the Barossa, and will discuss the ancient craft of wine making while he serves you one of his fortified red table wines; telephone: 085-632720.

Continue to drive northward to Coober Pedy. Again, one can see emu and kangaroo grazing dreamily in the unfenced fields along the road. The countryside becomes increasingly more desolate, though never entirely barren as the picture postcards portray it. There is always a strong touch of spinifex and brush coverage over the deep red earth. Beyond the horizon lie the famous trails of the outback adventurers. There are the Birdsville and Tanami tracks, the Canning Stock route. Over towards the east are the fabled towns of Marree and Ghantown (the railway from Adelaide to Alice Springs is called *The Ghan*), where the Afghan cameleers passed on their great treks through the desert. (See the excellent article in *Australian Geographic*, October/December, 1990). Some of these tracks can be traversed by those who are prepared. We will note them shortly.

About Driving in the Outback. Our advice is: Do it! We had read guidebooks that advised taking extra water and gas, extra wheels, springs, etc. In fact, we did not purchase any of these things and got along famously. While we would not advise driving much along Australia's southeast corridor because of the volume of traffic (and narrowness of the roads, especially on the coastal road from Sydney to Brisbane), we found driving on the single lane highway from Adelaide to Alice Springs thoroughly enjoyable and very easy. The reason is that there is practically no traffic (and we drove it during a peak holiday season), and very few hills or bends. The result is that the driving is virtually identical to freeway driving. In South Australia we could cruise at 110 kph and in the Northern Territory there is no actual speed limit. The road surface is good bitumen. There are roadside stops at reasonable intervals providing everything one could need. In fact, we blew a tire at one point, but after changing it, drove in to the next roadhouse and had it fixed in less than 20 minutes. However, roadhouses are far enough apart to necessitate use of every one of them. Furthermore, although we did not need additional water, we traveled during winter. In summer, when it becomes unbearably hot, it would be sensible to carry additional water, just in case. Most of the roadhouses have lost their outback character; one has to go north of Alice Springs to Tennant Creek to find the charming, rundown spruced up shacks and garages.

The approach to *Coober Pedy* is announced by the oversized ant hills, which are actually excavations, many of them mines worked by people hoping to strike it rich mining opals, or perhaps simply trying to eke out a living. Coober Pedy is, of course, the opal capital of the world. The entire countryside around the frontier town is scarred by opal mines. Opals have been mined here since 1916, but the town doesn't look much different from the way it must have then. The main road is bitumen, but everywhere else is covered by red dust. There are no sidewalks, all other roads are actually tracks, and because many of the houses and hotels are converted mines, they are underground. It is often difficult to tell if one is walking down a street or over someone's house.

Stay in an underground motel, if you can. Many are simply furnished, without changes to the walls at all. Lights (somewhat meagre) and holes bored through to the surface for ventilation are provided. Their great advantage is that they maintain a constant temperature—air conditioning not needed—and in the summer months, the temperature outside can rise to as high as 120 and sometimes more. And in winter, the mine is a welcome relief from the cold winds that may blow. In fact dust storms can make life pretty miserable here. If you don't believe it, ask the cast and crew of the *Mad Max* movies. This is where the movies were shot.

Coober Pedy represents to us, perhaps the closest one will ever find in real life to the frontier town of the American wild west. The roads are barely there, no sidewalks, and red dust (and after the rare rain, red mud) covers everything. Scruffy looking men with bushy beards and beat up old pickup trucks ride in and out of town to collect supplies. Opal buyers and brokers dot the small main street. One merchant sells mining supplies. Even the new shopping mall is built at the end of town behind a solid brick wall without any windows facing the street. Only tourists walk up and down the street. The locals are too busy scavenging for opals, drinking at the local pub, or purchasing the necessary provisions for their next dig.

Make sure you have your passport and international air ticket when you come here. Opal stores offer valuable "duty free" discounts. There is easily the widest variety of opals available here and the prices are reasonable. The cheapest way to buy them is uncut, or at least unset. Educate yourself before buying though, especially about doublets and triplets.

About Buying Opals. Opals are mined in four areas of Australia, all of them near the center. These are Quilpie in Western Queensland, Lightning Ridge in New South Wales, and Mintabie and Coober Pedy, both in South Australia. The white, milky opals tend to be the most valuable, but not always. These are found at Coober Pedy. The best deal can be obtained at the duty free shops (show your passport and round trip air ticket), but care must be taken. Avoid triplets which are simply a plastic backing, with a thin opal veneer capped with a clear dome of quartz. Buying opals already set in jewelery means that you will pay several times more. If you have a family jeweler back home, it would be much cheaper to buy the opals unset.

The Big Winch sells opals of all types and prices and has the largest opal fossil in the world on display. Valued at $2.5 million, they say.

Old Timers Mine shows how the old timers mined. But the attraction is the good fossicking area; telephone: 086-725555

For an *underground motel*, stay at the *Radeka Dugout*. Very simple and down to earth, if we may pun a little! Rooms are in the actual mine; the walls sparkle with calcite. You're not allowed to chip away at the walls though, but it's hard to resist the temptation to dig for one's own opal while laying back in bed with a good book!

The Opal Factory is a place to see rough opals cut and polished. One can even design jewelery for selected opals; telephone: 086-725300.

There are underground churches, shops and other attractions. A fun tour is with Tom and Pat. Ask about their tour at your motel.

Fancy Digs Desert Cave Resort is also underground, though quite a bit spruced up, and has an international hairdresser available (who would need one in this place is beyond us). There are, however a few good restaurants, but you must search for them. Try camel and buffalo steaks.

To the Center: Ayers Rock (Uluru)

Uluru is the aboriginal name given to Ayers Rock. We turn off to it some 411 km north of Coober Pedy at a place called Kulgera. This is simply an expanded roadhouse with motels and caravan park. If you travel on a budget, we recommend staying here, as the rates are some 35% cheaper than in the Yulara resort complex that has been established especially for the Ayers Rock tourist market. However, bear in mind that it is a good 2 hours drive from Kulgera to Ayers Rock.

Upon entering the Yulara resort, follow the signs to the visitor center. Here you will find an informative display about the history of Uluru and its surrounding area and from a colonial, aborginal and natural science point of view. Guided tours by park rangers are conducted daily, some of which are highly recommended. One can obtain a listing of current tours available and make bookings for them as well. All the tours are included in the park entry fee ($10). If for some reason you can't make it to the visitor center, tel.: 562299 to

make bookings. However, since most of the phones are close
to the visitor center, one might as well go there and do it all at
once.

Yulara Resort

The Yulara Resort was established and opened in 1985
specifically to service the increasing tourist trade in the Ayers
Rock area. The entire region around the rock is an aboriginal
protected area and also a national park. In 1985 the area was
handed back to the aboriginal community (the Mutitjulu)
who own the freehold and lease the land to the national
parks. The Yulara resort was established outside the park,
and is perhaps unique in the world as a community established solely for one purpose: the exploitation of tourists who
have no choice but to stay in one of the several accommodations (ranging from the plush *Sheraton 4 Seasons* to a caravan
park with less than comfortable conditions).

The caravan park is not without its own attraction, however, since it was here that the Chamberlains lost their baby,
and Lindy Chamberlain coined the now famous expression,
"A dingo got my Baby." In fact, we suggest that you rent the
movie that traces this saga of injustice and persecution, but
manages also to convey a certain sense of the outback and the
Australian mentality. In the U.S. the movie is called *A Cry in
the Dark*; in Australia, *Evil Angels*. Meryl Streep plays Lindy
Chamberlain, in a brilliant rendition of an Aussie mum, complete with perfect Aussie accent.

The resort closes at an early hour and banks nearby do not
keep resort hours, but hours geared to the big city, as in Alice
Springs. When we were there it was show day in Alice
Springs, so the bank was shut. No ATMs either. It is very
difficult to find an affordable restaurant. If you plan to go to
the Four Seasons or any of the other restaurants, it would be a
good idea to make reservations the day before.

The resort town is something of a technological accom-
plishment supporting 700 permanent residents and 5,000 visitors a day. All water is drawn from an underground aquifer
and must be desalinated. About 70% of all hot water is solar
heated. If you're into techno-resorts, then by all means take
one of the resort tours; tel: 562-240. But we would suggest

that one spend as little time in the resort as possible. The only place worth a visit is the visitors center (follow the signs upon entry), where one should go first. Here there is a video and other displays that tell about the park and what to see. There are ranger tours conducted daily, including an "edible desert" botanical tour and the base tour of the Rock; others are about aboriginal folklore, the stars (night walk, of course). Some of these need to be booked. It is a good idea to spend some time at the center planning one's stay and making the bookings. There are also daily childrens' activities, ranging from videos, stories, animal tracking, scavenger hunts and so on. Pick up the latest flyer announcing these.

Climb Ayers Rock, of course. Drive to the base, follow the signs. This is a very steep climb, but worth it. It's a long climb too, much longer than it looks from the bottom. The views from the top are tremendous, not to mention the feeling of exhilaration one has upon reaching the top. People struggle going up and stop often for rests. Those coming down are, without exception, elated and lighthearted. They are people who have accomplished something! Quite an achievement. If you stick it out, you too will be one of them. The top seems to move further away the higher one climbs. Fear gives way to wishful thinking. Temptation to turn back constantly descends on one's shoulders. But others smaller or weaker than oneself seem to be returning with that happy smile of having made it. Go on! And when you do, sign the book at the top.

The colors of the surrounding rocky outcrops, especially the *Olgas* in the distance also change with the climb, and no doubt as the time of day moves on. The reds, mauves, purples and greens constantly trade their hues with each other. Pastels dominate. The sky sparkles with emptiness. One gains the first genuine impression of the "Never Never Land" as the aborigines called it. It is vast. It is empty. The huge open sky floods it with light.

The Olgas. By the time this book is in print, the road to the Olgas (18km) will be a sealed bitumen road, thank goodness. These rocks are a wonderful attraction, previously only reachable by a very dusty, heavily corrugated road traversed by uncaring buses that throw up choking dust into one's car.

But as one can see easily from Uluru, the Olgas have a charm of their own, their "many heads" (Kata Tjuta) protruding in different directions as one approaches them, the colors changing constantly. Walks through the gorges here and around the Uluru rock are well worth the effort. However, follow the many precautions issued at the visitors center and on all tourist brochures about walking in the outback. It can be dangerous. Water and a clear idea of where one is going and of one's physical capacity are essential.

A Note on Safety. The climbs and walks are potentially very dangerous. Dress appropriately with excellent sturdy walking shoes (no slippery soles or loose shoes). In winter, wear warm clothing. It can be very cold on top of the rock; hypothermia can result. Similarly, in summer, temperatures can climb to over 110F. Take plenty of water. Stop frequently, drink often. It is best in summer to start the walk early in the morning, 6 a.m. if possible. In winter, start late morning. Stay on marked paths. People have strayed from these paths and become suddenly lost, especially in the Olgas area.

The Uluru Park is supervised by a unique cooperative arrangement of the aboriginal owners (the Anangu) and the government wildlife and conservation departments. The aborigines have the majority vote on the supervising board.

Nestled in against the base of Uluru are two beautiful and secluded gorges. Follow the tracks to them to see the aboriginal rock paintings. View the incredible colors of the gums against the red rock. They offer shades of pastel greens, purples and reds found nowhere else in the world.

At sunset, join the throngs at the appointed time and well signed place along the road to Ayers Rock to view the sunset on the rock. Here, one will see the constantly changing hues and tints as the sun gradually reaches the horizon. One gazes out across the red earth, dotted with mulga bushes and spinifex. This is countryside that has taken millions of years to form. The rock is the small protruding part of an immense sedimentary rock, the surroundings of which have eroded. The shape of the rock is itself formed by the erosion of millions of years of wind and sand. The aboriginal lore has it that Uluru and Kata Tjuta were created by giant animals whose imprint is left on every feature and pattern of the rocks. It was first seen by white man in 1872 and later in 1873 by W. E. Gosse who mapped much of the aboriginal landscape. In 1987 the title of the land was handed over to the Anangu aboriginal people, who immediately leased it to the Australian National Parks.

Aboriginal artifacts can be perused at the small ranger station on the way to Ayers Rock, just before the turn off to the climb. We found these crafted products, mainly wood carvings, to be of excellent quality and most reasonably priced. One can chat with aboriginal craftsmen as well as make purchases. Sets of aboriginal hunting spears and other implements are available.

A note on traveling through officially designated aboriginal lands. In the Northern Territory it is necessary to obtain permission to pass through aboriginal lands. One should apply approximately four weeks before the intended trip. Contact the Central Lands Council, P.O. Box 332, Alice Springs, N.T. 5750, telephone: 089-523800. For visits to the usual tourist sites, these permits are not necessary. They apply only if one wishes to stray away from the established areas. For the top end and tablelands, contact Northern Land Council, 47 Stuart Highway, The Gardens, Darwin, N.T. 5794. Tel: 089-817011.

To Alice

The road to Alice Springs, virtually due north and dead straight, continues without much change. There is little wildlife to be seen by day, though evidence of much during the night, since the road from here all the way to Darwin in the north and Townsville in the east is littered with the carcasses of kangaroos who have collided with cars during the night.

Alice Springs is a welcome sight after so long in the desert. Alice throbs with activity, its roads are rather busy, and its center city nicely laid out. A small mall has been set aside and closed to traffic, and tourists along with aborigines like to parade up and down this walkway. One will find here many souvenir shops, some restaurants and banks (including a couple of ATMs). After the relief of finding a small smattering

of city life quickly wears off, one realizes that there is little to
do in this town.

In the center of the mall is the historic Adelaide House,
Alice Springs' first hospital. Flynn of the inland designed it. A
stone hut at the back was where Flynn used Traeger's historic
pedal radio to send transmissions across the outback. It was
through this radio system and the airplane that the Australian
Flying Doctor service was made possible by Flynn. It was also
what made Australia's famous distance education possible via
the pedal radio. Children at remote stations sit at home and
take lessons via radio telephone, powered by a pedal gener-
ator.

Some of the best selections of aboriginal paintings can be
found in the several galleries of this mall. Prices do not vary
from one shop to the other. But at the time we visited, prices
ranged from $500 to $1,000 for aboriginal paintings of good
quality. The style and technique of these paintings is one of
great fascination, since they have relatively speaking only just
begun to be discovered. We talked to one gallery dealer who
insisted that most of the best paintings were done by the
women who stayed away from the shops and allowed their
men to do the selling, claiming the work as their own artistry.
Whether this is so or not, we did see in one gallery an
aboriginal woman actually creating a painting. The paintings
are authentic, although we see these paintings as an interesting example of a new culture of aboriginal art emerging,
changed and modified by contact with white man's ways, yet
rooted in the ancient traditions of a particular aboriginal tribe.
Or at least of the traditions and stories that have been preserved.

It must be remembered that much of the aboriginal culture
in Australia was destroyed by the white man's arrival,
through persecution, plague, disease, and destruction of the
aboriginal subsistence economy which was finely tuned to
living at one with the land. Furthermore, it was systematically
modified by the Christian beliefs of the missions that were
established throughout Australia in order to "save the sav-
ages." We have little way of knowing the extent that the so-
called legends or stories that go along with the intricate paint-

ings are genuine aboriginal folk lore or not. They may well be invented for the purposes of the white man. The tables are turned, in a sense. The aborigine is now paid to recreate his/her culture.

Restaurants are not well developed in Alice, and the pace of service is definitely outback pace. However, for a bit of a splurge, we suggest the *Overlander Steakhouse* at 72 Hartley Street. This restaurant exists largely (if not solely) for tourists, so it is a bit pricey. However, it has an unusual feature at the back of the restaurant where blue-grass country and Western folk music is performed live. It comes as a surprise to find that the Australian outback seems to have adopted the American country music as its own. But when one reads Zane Grey's only western set in Australia, *Wilderness Trek*, one sees how effortlessly he transported his mythical wild west to the Australian outback. His characters marveled at the strange Australian fauna. But they were right at home in its wide open spaces, the macho outdoors life, and the contradictions and conflicts between solitude and intimacy that followed. The Overlander features some rare (though authentically Australian) dishes: witchety grub soup, camel steak, kangaroo tail soup. Try them all. We found them exciting to the palate, especially the witchety grub soup. It's a little nutty to the taste and is a thick white soup. Very filling. (Witchety grubs are considered a delicacy by the Australian aboriginals, who forage for them under the bark of trees. They are a large fat white grub, about the size of a big thumb.) The camel steak is like a reasonably strong tasting beef, a little on the fatty side. Kangaroo steak, in contrast, is very lean. This is a popular eatery. Telephone: 089-522159 for reservations.

Finally, a must in Alice Springs is to check the local papers and bulletin boards for the Alice Springs Camel Cup race program. Started in the 1890s, this offers a spectacular rough-and-ready camel race, much more exciting than a horse race, we think.

The Macdonnell Ranges

Wonderful pinks, mauves and pastel greens and reds may be savored in the Macdonnell ranges. These mountains are not high as mountain ranges go, but there is something special about them, well worth the time and effort to visit. It is the colors. We spent much of our time in Australian cities admiring and a little curious as to the widespread use of pastel colors in buildings, ranging from modern low rise houses and shopping plazas to fancy huge shopping malls and enormous skyscrapers. (The C & L Building in Sydney, for example, stands out amongst the many skyscrapers because of its pastel hues of blues and pinks.)

The gorges and chasms in the McDonnell ranges faithfully produce these beautiful tones of pastel. Though the landscape of the desert and outback is thought of as harsh and unforgiving, the gorges and chasms are, in contrast, havens of softness and peace. The gorges along the Ross Highway (in the West McDonnell ranges) are secluded, peaceful nooks, with shimmering and sometimes glassy pools of water, perfectly reflecting the cliffs and bush surrounding them. At *Trephina Gorge* (77k west of Alice) along a river bank (a river of sand most of the time) one can take a quiet walk along a well marked path, following the river to its rocky pools. There are quartzite cliffs above, giant rocks rise from the black pools, just beckoning kids to climb on them. The trees are of soft green with a bluish tinge. Birds abound and sing many different songs. In the evenings one may see euros or wallabies.

Towards the east there is *Standley Chasm*, visited by hordes of tourists at 12 midday, in order to see the sun shine directly from above down the middle of the narrow space, thus lighting up the sandstone walls with a red fire. We were disappointed at the large numbers of tourists—these gorges cannot be appreciated with a mob. They are places of solitude and reflection. We suggest that one visit these popular places at times when there are not hordes of tourists spewing forth from busses. (And we mean hordes. When we were at Standley Chasm one Sunday in July there were at least ten tour busses.) It would be well worth walking the chasm at another time, missing the spectacular sun admittedly, but gaining no end of peace and solitude. The same may be said of *Simpsons Gap*, another gorge close to Alice Springs, (24k) and a popular tourist spot.

For further information about access and highlights of these wonderful parks, call the Conservation Commission at 089-508211.

There are a number of tours one can take, if one wants to experience the outback lifestyle, without actually roughing it too much. Call *The Camp Oven Kitchen*, 089-53-1411, or fax them at 089-53-1327 for information and bookings. Their main tours are a colonial tour of homesteads that includes delicious four course meals with wine (the homesteaders probably didn't have it quite this good); a *Ross River Country* visit to the gorges, gaps and scenery of the Eastern MacDonnell ranges, sampling billy tea and damper with a ride on horses and camels if you want; or, for the gustatory courageous, try the tour of aboriginal bush tucker, spending a morning hunting with aboriginals learning how to survive in the outback, how to find witchety grubs and eat them. Aborigines will have the upper hand on you here. For the *bush dinner tour* at $35 per person, tour operators cook dinner in a camp oven. You are encouraged to BYO to this. Maybe that will be the entertainment!

In general, we recommend staying on the bitumen roads. Most sights of interest can be seen from these. Admittedly there would be some excitement in traversing the unpaved roads, but believe us, the sights at the end of these roads, with the exception of the Olgas and one other to be mentioned shortly, do not warrant having the stuffing shaken out of you. A possible exception may be the much tooted *Palm Valley*, a red gorge dotted with ancient and unique species of palm. The road, however, is definitely only for four-wheel drive vehicles. The valley is a kind of dry, tropical oasis.

About 143 km south of Alice along the Stuart Highway, there is a short unpaved road of about 12km which is not too bad, as unpaved roads go. This road leads to the fascinating *Henbury Meteor Site* where a number of meteors rammed into earth some 3 thousand years ago. A brief walk around the craters left by the impact, with informative signs at each point of interest, is well worth it. The walk is flat and easy. The meteors, probably only the size of large petroleum drums, left enormous craters upon impact: 201 meters in diameter and 18 meters deep.

The Ghan. This is a refurbished old Ghan railway, the legendary train that plied between Adelaide and Darwin. It ran its last trip in 1980, when it was replaced by a modern train, and a different route as well. Visiting the old Ghan is much cheaper than the real thing. If one wants the excitement of traveling by train over the desert in a first class sleeper, be prepared to pay a lot of money, about the same as regular air fares. Prices on the old Ghan, including historical displays and narratives, run $10 for adults, $5 kids; with a barbeque lunch, billy tea and damper, $30; telephone: 089-530310.

For the Young, Foolish or Adventurous

As we mentioned above, we were happy to stay on the bitumen roads that are well marked and signed, with service stations every 100 miles or so—enough to make us feel reasonably confident that we could make the trip. If this does not satisfy your ambitions or fantasies, you can take up the challenge by attempting to traverse some of the famous tracks of the Australian outback. Four-wheel drive vehicles are a necessity, as are many other precautionary measures (See Brian Sheedy's book *Outback on a Budget,* for detailed instructions). Try some of these highway adventures:

The *Gunbarrel Highway* that links Alice Springs to Perth, a mere 2750 km over a road that is graded earth, no more. Before attempting this trek, look at Beadell's *Outback Highways.* Beadell built the highway. Best to go only in the cool dry season, April to October. Check on road conditions ahead of time, tell the local police station where you are going. Remember, these areas are deserts, with no one to help you should you run into trouble. The adventurer must be self sufficient! The *Canning Stock Route* can be completed in about three weeks, and follows the route Canning and his crew laid out some 80 years ago to drive cattle from the Kimberley markets to the southern goldfields. It took him two years to do it! (See the detailed article with poster in *Australian Geographic,* July/September, 1989). The *Birdsville and Oodnadatta Tracks* are possibly the most famous in Australia, largely because they have been featured in many folk songs and stories. Sand drifts can cover sections of the Birdsville track to the extent that it may be impossible to find one's way. Bull dust (a fine red dust) may cover huge potholes that the unwary driver can hit traveling too fast; broken springs are not unusual, as well as damage to the sump. On the Oodnadatta track, if rains come, the road may be covered in water, or turned into thick, impassable mud. Check road conditions ahead of departing (we know we already advised this, but it cannot be emphasized enough). If your car breaks down, stay with the car. Again, we advice reading up the books on traveling the outback tracks. Better advice would be to stay on the bitumen. (The *Australian Geographic* offers advice, detailed maps and much more information in its October/December, 1988, issue.)

To Hell and Beyond

The road north from Alice takes one through semidesert. The termite skyscrapers (huge mounds of excavated earth) become more frequent, standing often taller than a person. They stand out like skyscrapers in a bombed out city. The ground is parched and hard. Red dust settles on everything. We keep the red dust on our car as a kind of status symbol. It tells people in the east (presuming we get there) that we've "done it," we've been to the outback. The roadhouses are far apart. And those that do appear out of the misty dust of the desert have not yet been transformed by an oil company into modern roadhouses with well organized gas pumps, digital displays, computerized cash registers, or neat signs to brand new toilets. Rather, these stopping places are still rambling old sheds joined together with corrugated iron. Locals (aborigines and otherwise) hang around the front and back, playing cards, drinking. One wonders where they come from or go to. Stand in the front of these places and look in any direction. There is nothing.

If there is a hell, one imagines that it is something like this. And pretty soon, nearing Tennant Creek, we come upon the devil's idleness itself: the *Devils Marbles*. Take a small detour away from the main road through these amazing conglomerations of boulders, heaped on top of each other, precariously balanced. The boulders are indeed like giant marbles, thus their name. That the devil should own them and not God is not hard to figure out; they are at once strange in their design, a little fearsome in their orientation, but entice you to walk into them, to climb them, as children especially love to do. These are boulders of volcanic origin, which have been left after millions of years of erosion of the sand and rock around them. John Flynn, the founder of the fabled Flying Doctor Service was buried down near Alice Springs (at Mt. Gillen), and has his tombstone made of one of these marbles.

Tennant Creek emerges from the void. It is an old mining town, known for its gold. There are some remnants of this today: a few high mounds of mullock (the Australian word for the refuse left over from mining) and a big iron winch. But generally, this is an established small town, with its typical verandas, shops, takeaways and pubs. We even found a squash court with glass walls, and a posh restaurant to over- look it. A strange mixture, watching sweating lunging play- ers, while quaffing down gourmet meals and expensive Aus- tralian wines. But that's just what the people from Tennant Creek did. It was impossible to get a table, the restaurant was booked even nightly. We managed to eat there by going a little earlier than the locals (about 6 p.m.).

At Tennant Creek, the road branches off to Darwin in the north and its concomitant attractions, such as Kakadu Na- tional Park, and east across the desert to Mt. Isa, outback Queensland and eventually the exotic coast of the Great Bar- rier Reef.

The road north to Katherine, continues with more of the same. Katherine is a well established town, with a commercial air strip. Katherine Gorge offers splendid scenery along the Katherine River with near vertical cliff faces. The gorge is situated 29km upstream. At Katherine, the main road branches to western Australia, via the coastal route and even- tually to Perth.

Darwin

Darwin is in on the edge of nowhere, but in the midst of everything. Located about as far north as one can go, there are no other big settlements for hundreds of miles. There is not even much to see in the city itself. All these factors make

Darwin the perfect home base for exciting safaris into the lush tropical forests surrounding the city.

There are two seasons in Darwin: the dry hot season (April to October) and the wet hot monsoon (November to March). Don't visit in the wet season—it rains all the time and is unbearably hot and humid with an average temperature of 40 degrees Celsius (that's over 100 degrees F). Many roads, or should we say tracks, to Darwin turn into impassable mud pools during the wet season. People have been known to get stuck on an isolated strip of muddy road for days, weeks, and even months, having to wait for the rain to stop to retrieve their car. Tragedy can result.

On the other hand, the dry season, with infrequent rain and average temps of 30C degrees, or 80F degrees, makes Darwin the perfect vacation spot during the rest of Australia's winter. Despite rapid growth, accommodations are very limited in the dry season and fill up quickly.

Today's Darwin, with its combination of ultra modern and semi-original buildings, is a result of an evolution of strange twists and turns. It started in 1839, when Captain J. Stokes sailed *The Beagle* into the magnificent harbor and named it after one of its most famous passengers, Charles Darwin. Three attempts to establish a permanent settlement in the Darwin area occurred between 1824 and 1849, and failed most likely because the settlers were not prepared for the extreme wet season. Then nothing happened until 1869, when a shipful of south Australians successfully settled here, calling their little town Palmerston. A telegraph line finally linked the north with the south in 1872, and rumors of gold enticed thousands to rush in to seek their fortunes. Farmers capitalized on the cheap labor to raise cattle on their million acre properties.

World War II brought the first taste of disaster to Darwin. Closest to the action, Darwin was a crucial military base. Darwin endured 64 Japanese air raids—64 more than any other place in Australia. Many buildings were destroyed and 243 people lost their lives. Darwin was rebuilt and revamped, including tree-lined streets and parks and earned the title of Australia's City of Planning.

"Twas the night before Christmas and all through the house, not a creature was stirring . . . ," except Cyclone Tracy, whose presence created much more than a stir! Gusts of up to 280 kilometers an hour (175 mph) disturbed the sleeping residents of Darwin at midnight, Christmas Eve, 1974. Sixty percent of Darwin's 11,000 homes were destroyed beyond repair, and Tracy claimed 66 lives. Many historical buildings were also flattened.

Darwin's residents decided to make the best of this misfortune, and set about building another new set of buildings, and restored a few of the old historical ones. The result is a surprisingly pleasing combination of imposing mini-skyscrapers and rugged (and we mean rugged) old, original buildings.

Darwin has a population of 50,000 people, almost half that of the whole Northern Territory. Most of the people who live in Darwin are public servants (this accounts for the seeming excess of public buildings) and consider their stay here temporary. Think about it: it's either the weather (it is too hot or wet for any animal or crop) or location (industries would find it too costly to transport their goods from this end-of-the-earth location), or both the weather and the location. It's understandable.

But Darwin is definitely an OK place to visit. The harbor is beautiful, as are the beaches. Try Fannie Bay, Mandorah, Vestey's, and Casuarina. (Watch out for sea wasps on the beaches during the wet season, though.) Darwin is world famous for its annual *Beer Can Regatta,* held every June. Boats, rafts, and unidentifiable flotsam, all made of used beer cans, are sailed in the harbor. There are several points of interest:

The World War II period of Darwin's history is portrayed in the *Artillery Museum* at the East Point Reserve. It is open from 9:30 a.m. to 5 p.m., for a small admission fee. There are also numerous walking tracks in the reserve, where wildlife can be seen, especially at night.

Like every large town in Australia, Darwin also has a *Botanic Gardens.* Darwin's gardens have many interesting flora exclusive to this tropical climate. It is located between the city and Mindil Beach.

Historical buildings, predictably, are quite rare in Darwin. Rugged survivors include the *Old Navy Headquarters*, built in 1884, *Fannie Bay Jail*, 1883, and *Brown's Mart*, 1885.

The *Northern Territory Museum of Arts and Sciences*, built after cyclone Tracy struck, is reputed to be one of the best museums in Oz. Located at Bullocky Point, and completed in 1981, it houses numerous exhibits of scientific and cultural interest. This museum boasts the best collections of Australian aboriginal art and culture anywhere in the world. Admission is free, and the museum is open everyday.

Here's a real wilderness experience: *Doctor's Gully.* Scores of all sorts of tropical fish swarm the gully every hour for their daily meal. They eat bread right from the palm of one's hand. Great fun, the kids will love it, and cheap too—$1 admission covers everything, including the bread.

For more information about what to do in Darwin, or about safaris in adjacent country areas, visit the Northern Territory Government Tourist Bureau. It is located at 31 Smith Street Mall, and open every day except Sunday. The National Trust, located on the corner of Smith and Knuckey Streets, has a useful Darwin walking tour leaflet.

Kakadu

The truth is that tourists visit Darwin on their way to somewhere else. That place (if in Australia) is almost always Kakadu National Park (otherwise it's nearby Bali in Indonesia). This is a huge park in what is known as Arnhem Land. It comprises flood plains, billabongs (small lagoons), paperbark swamps and rivers. There are ferocious looking frill-necked lizards, whistling ducks, and green tree ants with a burning nip. The idea of a crocodile snapping one up at the slightest moment was popularized by the Crocodile Dundee movies. Indeed, there is the danger. The official tourist brochure of the Northern Territory Government states:

> Saltwater crocodiles can and do swim in fresh water. Do not swim in any creeks, rivers or billabongs—it is extremely dangerous. Keep a watchful eye on one's children. . . . Crocodiles not only eat babies, but whole people here.

Large portions of this park have special significance to the aboriginal communities. The variety and range of rock art is inspirational. There are paintings, engravings and stencils giving evidence to aboriginal habitation as far back as 20,000 years. There are thousands of rock art sites scattered along the escarpment and overlying plateau of the Kakadu Park. Most common are the Mimi paintings, portraying the small spirits that are delicate, agile, and often carrying weapons. X-ray art is also common; birds, reptiles and animals are depicted in outline, showing internal organs and skeleton as well as important internal organs. Stencil art is produced when aborigines forcefully eject a mouthful of paint at an object, most often the left hand or a weapon, placed against a rock wall. Colors come from natural ochres found in the surrounding earth. They were sometimes mixed with animal fat and applied with sharp sticks or fine brushes. Pigments of the ochres range from white and deep yellow to reds, pinks and purples.

Aboriginal rock art represents an incredible accumulation of thousands of years, of hundreds of generations, of artists leaving their messages and expressions for posterity, making the heritage of Western Civilization seem a fleeting moment in time. All aboriginal rock art expresses the Dreamtime, that misty period in the dawning of the Australian continent that aborigines relate in their legends and folk stories. Huge spirits, part man part giant, roamed the land, creating it out of their conflicts and torments: the boulders, the cliffs, the lakes, the fauna and flora, the mountains and valleys (see Chapter 2). There are walking tracks that pass several galleries of aboriginal art and provide panoramic views of the plains. Inquire at the information center. This experience should not be missed.

The most popular way of seeing the park is on a motor launch that cruises the South Alligator River. Visitors can eat Barramundi, see crocodiles and dine on buffalo fillets. Two to five hour cruises can be pleasant. Call *Kakadu Holiday Village* at 089-790166. For any reader who has taken the safari tour on a visit to Disneyland and wondered what the real thing would be like, the boat tours in Kakadu will surpass the Disney experience. Fear, however, is real in Kakadu. The crocs aren't mechanical, and it would be difficult to sue the crocs or their owners if one were eaten.

What is mechanical is the Ranger Uranium Mine which forms an enclave within the park. The subject of much controversy, the mine remains in the middle of Australia's greatest wilderness area. Strange neighbors indeed! (The *Australian Geographic*, July/September, 1990, reviews the history of this mine, and its uncertain existence alongside this beautiful wilderness).

One can camp in the park in specified areas or at Kakadu Holiday Village. There is an information center at Park Headquarters, 2.5 k south of the Arnhem Highway near the town of Jabiru. Check road conditions always.

To the East: On Wilderness Trek

At the beginning of the road east, we were faced with an enormous stretch of bitumen, cutting across the heart of Australia, moving gradually through desert and semi-desert, through the strangely green and flat Barkly Tablelands, at last to hilly sparsely treed ridges around Mt. Isa. The distances are vast here. The enormity of Australia surrounds the traveler. One can drive for 200 km without seeing another car, or a living thing. Death looms constantly. The carcasses of strayed cattle, kangaroos, and an occasional camel lie strewn along the side of the road. The cattle are attracted by the warmth of the bitumen. The kangaroos and camels are confused and attracted by the lights of the vehicles at night. They know nothing of their fate.

An air conditioned car insulates one from the barren, threatening landscape. Time stands still here, only sometimes disturbed by the presence of tour buses spewing forth their occupants at one of the rare roadhouses. We stopped at a little town inside the Queensland border called Camooweal (population 350). It had been very warm for July. We asked the gas station attendant whether this was typical of this part of Australia. "No, this is really unusual. It's only been like this for the last ten years; before that it was always cold."

A trivia silliness: Mt. Isa city council took Camooweal

under its umbrella as part of the Mt. Isa City (188 km east). So what's the largest city in the world and where is the longest main street? It's Mount Isa, with a main street (the Barkly Highway) of 188km.

Mount Isa emerges from behind the hills, and you see the enormous mining installations that form the actual center of the town. This is a thriving, bustling town, with new malls and supermarkets. There are more new cars here than we have seen elsewhere. The mine extends some 1,800 meters underground. This is a young, successful town. Mining is an exciting, modern venture at the site of one of the world's greatest mines. Silver lead ore was discovered in 1923. Trips to the mines and other areas are popular. Call 077-43-7966 for tourist information. If fossicking for gemstones and other ores is a preference, talk to Joy Long at the *Cloncurry/Mary Kathleen Memorial Museum*. Permission can be obtained to fossick on other leaseholders' properties.

An hour ahead to Cloncurry transports one back again into outback cattle stations. This is a town for station hands to visit. Wide streets, few pavements, plenty of pubs. And heat. It was here on January 16, 1889, that the highest ever temperature in Australia was recorded: 53.1C (122F). Call 077-467166 for tourist information.

Further east, for a few hundred miles, the country turns increasingly green and grassy. There is, however, a persistent feeling of dryness throughout the country, even right down to Townsville. The road winds into *Charters Towers*, a historic town, with many beautifully preserved Victorian and Edwardian buildings. In its heyday from 1872–1911 the population of Charters Towers was 30,000. It was producing 6,800,000 ounces of gold ore. The population is now 9,500. Stop at the tourist information center at 61 Gill Stret for a guide to these fascinating buildings.

Cross the mountains now, such as they are. Part of the Great Divide, they extend north as far as Cape York. But once you are on the eastern side, the growth becomes more prolific, and you wind down to Townsville. The wonders and excitement of Queensland await.

CHAPTER 10

Queensland:
Laid Back Charm

Queensland is the land of sunshine and pineapples, and its population is growing faster than any other state. Why? Perhaps because it is the ideal place. Like Florida in the U.S., Queensland is the place for retirement. But don't think that Queensland is populated completely by old fogeys. Quite the contrary. Because of the perpetual holiday atmosphere, there is always a party on in Queensland. Home of the Great Barrier Reef, Sunshine Coast and Gold Coast, Queensland is Australia's playground for the young and old.

Everyone has heard of *The Great Barrier Reef.* All that colorful coral (350 species to be exact), fish swimming all around (1,200 species) without a care in the world. These days a trip to the far north may cost an arm and a leg (and basking limbless in the sun doesn't paint a pretty picture, does it?). Nevertheless, if one can find the money, a trip into Australia's world-renowned wonderland will provide pleasures that will

easily blot out the memory of any expense. All kinds of
resorts line the Reef, each appealing to the many island fantasies for which people yearn. One can pursue the great fish
as a Hemingway, dive among the coral reefs as a Cousteau,
watch birds and turtles nest, mingle with the rich and famous
on exotic island resorts, as well as just be oneself, and just-lay-
around-and-do-nothing-without-being-disturbed. All find
their favorite niches in this fantastic northern paradise.

Townsville

A strange town is Townsville. It is a town with a split
personality. One half of the city is clearly industrial, being the
main outlet for the ore and other goods shipped from Mt. Isa
and central Queensland. This is south of Ross Creek which
runs smack through the center of town. On the north side,
most of the central city buildings, many quite handsomely
preserved but a large number modern, surround a new walk-
through mall. A food court follows the banks of Ross Creek,
and glassed-in Victoria Bridge struts across, trying to join the
two sides—the tourist and the industrial—together. It doesn't
work. Few people seem to come across the bridge. The restaurants and shops struggle to keep afloat on the south side. On
the north side, the commercial and tourist side, the town
throbs with activity from around 11 A.M. to 5 P.M. After that
time, the town literally dies. The mall becomes virtually deserted with the exception of the occasional tourist trying to
use the one credit card phone in the mall. A white and blue
police car slowly patrols through the no-cars area. All action
has moved away from the town. . . . guess where? To the
Sheraton Breakwater, of course, Townsville's brand new casino. This small version of Las Vegas permits 18-year-olds to
play. The games are the same as in Vegas, except for one: the
Aussie game, two-up. If you are a gambler, or like to watch
gambling, this is a fun spectator game. Watch the spinner
(who tosses two pennies in the air from a special board), and
the croupier (it stretches the imagination to call him that) who
supervises, complete with a colorful running commentary,
full of Aussie slang. Players bet on whether the two pennies
will turn up heads, tails or uneven. Pretty simple. Very noisy.
Lots of fun.

The Great Barrier Reef

We used Townsville as our base, but one may choose from any of the well established coastal towns of northern Queensland all the way from Cairns to Grafton. Grafton is probably the most southernly point of departure for the Great Barrier Reef, helicopter and boat trips out to Heron island being the most common.

For a total reef experience, it is hard to beat a sojourn of several days on one of the coral cays that are located some two hours by ferry down the coast of Queensland. However, without exception, accommodations on these islands cost a great deal. A cheaper way, and possibly more effective way is to stay at either Townsville, Cairns or Airly Beach, then take a cruise to the outer reef. The cruise costs about $80 per person for a full day's outing, morning and afternoon tea and an excellent lunch included. Also provided are snorkeling gear, flippers, and fishing tackle if one wants to fish.

In Townsville, these launches leave the Great Barrier Reef Wonderland (at the end of Flinders Street East, a big circular turreted building) around 9 A.M. every day. It is best to book the day before, although we saw many buy tickets that morning. A bus pick-up can also be arranged. The vessel is a high speed catamaran, designed specially to cut through the ocean waves. It can get a little choppy out there. One needs to be a good sailor—not recommended for the queasy.

The outer reef is nothing short of stunning. The colors, coral patterns and varieties of fish are much greater and more striking than those of the inner coastal corals, as seen on coral cays, or around the volcanic islands that dot the area. Call *Pure Pleasure Cruises* at 077-213555 to leave from Townsville or *Great Adventures Cruises* at 070-510455, from Cairns. At the time of writing, the fare from Townsville was $85 adult, $45 for kids. Well worth the money. One is transported on a high speed catamaran to Kelso Reef on the outer barrier reef, at the edge of the continental shelf. Imagine the excitement and awe of simply jumping over the side of the ship into the Pacific Ocean. A frightening experience until one realizes on gazing beneath the surface, that the water does not reach miles down to the ocean floor just here, but rather the bottom is raised by the massive and wondrous coral structures.

It's like swimming in a vast aquarium, except one is aware because of the light and the swell that this is an ocean. The reef runs for 1,000 miles or more. On each turn around a coral outcrop, there are new species of fish, strange creatures living out their everyday lives, giant clams with bright purple lips, fish of all shapes, colors and designs. Massive creatures of the deep appear to browse through the feeding grounds of coral life. The light penetrates in geometric patterns from the surface. In the distance, in a haze of sand, luminescent creatures are suspended in the water. Here is a paradise and wonderland.

The time zips by. The ship sounds its siren to call everyone for lunch. The allure of the reef tempts one to skip lunch, but don't. It's a simple and typically Aussie lunch of cold chicken, plenty of salad, desserts and the usual alcoholic attractions. Don't miss it (skip the alcohol). But, after a sensible time, one can hardly wait to splash down in amongst the perch and tuna bigger than one's arm, schools of fish that grudgingly give way when one swims through.

Scuba lessons are also available at a reasonable price; wet suits, for hire ($10). If we were returning for a second trip here, we would definitely take a scuba course before going, then use scuba gear (can be rented) to go further down into the deeper reefs. Though what we saw just snorkeling was enough to leave an everlasting impression. This was a day that will supplant the most exotic of daydreams.

The experience can be continued on shore. Our starting off point, the Great Barrier Reef Wonderland, houses probably the most extensive and authentic recreation of a coral reef in any aquarium. We strongly recommend taking in this aquarium before going to the real thing, because we enjoyed and appreciated the aquarium reef so much better. Everything in the real life reef ecosystem has been simulated: the swell of the ocean, the outer and inner reef, the production of algae, the range of fishes and corals. The aquarium is virtually self perpetuating. The visitor walks by huge glass walls for a kind of cross sectional view of the reef, but then one turns the corner into a massive tube that allows one to walk underneath the fish. It is almost as good as being in the water with them. Worth every penny of the price of admission ($8.00, children, half price).

Islands on the Central Reef

Magnetic Island is just ten minutes ferry ride from Townsville. This is a volcanic island, most of it national park. It is ringed on one side by a small coral coastal reef. But otherwise, it is best known for its delightful mountain scenery, koalas and other natural fauna, and probably most important of all, its secluded beaches. The best way to see the island is by a combined ferry/bus ticket which gives unlimited bus travel on the island. Otherwise, rent a minimoke on the island and drive around to the secluded beaches. There are a number of walking tracks in Magnetic Island National Park ranging from medium to quite difficult. Pick up a leaflet at Queensland Government Wildlife desk in the Great Barrier Reef Wonderland building, which describes the various 22 km of walks, many of them leading to hilltop lookouts, and traveling through forests populated with koalas and other Australian fauna. For information, telephone: 077-785378.

There is a sizable residential population on the island and many holiday shacks. It is a quiet, get-away-from-it-all island. A car ferry is available, but this ferry runs infrequently, and must be booked in advance and is quite expensive. Best to leave the car in Townsville for this trip. Excellent scuba diving courses are available on Magnetic Island, some combining the courses with diving on the outer barrier reef. Call 077-785799 or stop at *Magnetic Diving*, Shop 4, Arcadia Resort, Magnetic Island. The best we saw was a six-day dive course, including three days on the outer reef, all for $335 including accommodations.

Orpheus Island is largely undeveloped, mostly national park. Take a cruise with Perfect Pleasure Cruises to the island for a day, and tie up to the old U.S. wharf which serviced submarines during World War II. One can snorkel over the coastal reef here and sample the wonders of the barrier reef. The colors are not quite as striking as those of the outer reef, but fabulous just the same. The cruise operators are congenial and helpful. Scuba instruction is available (extra charge), snorkeling gear, flippers and an excellent lunch are provided. This is a volcanic island, with beautiful walks and secluded beaches.

The Southern Reef

Heron Island. This resort for wildlife both in and out of the water offers all the adventure one could possibly want without having to work too hard for it. In order to get to the island, one must take either a boat or helicopter. We recommend taking one each way. Heron Island does not offer luxury accommodations, and this is definitely part of its charm. One gets a feeling of camaraderie with other guests, as there are designated mealtimes when friendly conversations take place, and being on an island, everyone takes part in similar activities. A schedule is posted daily, describing various ventures available to the boarders, ranging from the popular scuba lessons to educational beach walks. Porpoises (and sometimes sharks) often swim alongside the boats here, and one gets the reassuring feeling that at least somewhere on earth man and animal can live harmoniously. A true back-to-nature feeling! On the sandy beach at night, turtles dig big holes and lay some 100 eggs at a time, which will hatch in about ten weeks. The heat of the sand will determine the sex of the hatchlings. Between October and April, the tiny turtles make a beeline for the water. Sea birds of every variety swoop down to gorge themselves; big crabs and other sea creatures wait impatiently for their supper. Only a small percentage of these delightful little creatures make it to old age, but those that do may expect a long life—well over a hundred years.

Lady Elliot Island is the most southern of the barrier reef islands. This is the only coral cay with its own airstrip (a doubtful advantage), easily accessible from Bundaberg. Cabins are available in keeping with the casual, more natural environment on this island. There is a coral pool, where swimmers can hand-feed gorgeous tropical fish. The usual snorkeling, reef-walking, diving and observation of a coral wonderland are available. Bird rookeries (some 50 species of birds) and nesting turtles are also an inspiring sight, as on Heron island. To the extent that a budget vacation is possible, one may find something like this here, and enjoy it as well. Call 071-516077 for reservations. Only a limited number of people are allowed on this island at any one time, which means that overcrowding is impossible. It also means that getting reservations must be done far in advance. And it's expensive too.

Green Island and Michaelmas Cay. Green Island is a small, well vegetated cay just a brief ferry ride from Cairns. It is perhaps the most visited of all coral islands in Queensland because of its proximity to Cairns, and also because of its developed underwater viewing area, and the possibility at low tide for reef-walking. At nearby Michaelmas Cay, the tumultuous noise of some 30,000 ground–nesting seabirds can be heard. The birds include terns and noddies, and it is the largest nesting sight in all the reef (the next largest is probably Heron Island).

The Whitsunday Group. These islands are reached from Shute Harbor or Airlie Beach. Many boast fine resort complexes and excellent snorkeling on coastal reefs. *New Lindeman Island* is a luxury resort covered by 500 hectares of national park, complete with lush vegetation, secluded sandy beaches, vibrant lorikeets, and turquoise sea. Resort facilities include child entertainment and day care, bars galore, a pool with swim-up bar, nine hole golf course, diving instruction, para sailing, jet skis and more. This is for the total vacation. Bring plenty of money!

South Molle Island. Nature walks and hilltop lookouts are the attraction here, reached by a calm ferry ride from Shute Harbor. There are extensive walking tracks winding through the beautiful tropical scenery. Combing through the coast coral reefs is a pleasure. Call 008-075-155 Australia wide, or fax *Lindeman Island Resort* at 079-469-598.

Hamilton Island. Probably this island offers Queensland's largest and most luxurious resorts. There is a fauna park and dolphin pool. It is so developed though, one might as well stay on dry land. It can be reached by plane from Proserpine, then ferry to other Whitsunday islands.

Long Island Palm Bay. This is a quiet unspoiled island (just a little different from the Long Island known so well by New

Yorkers!) with 13km of well graded bush walking tracks through a national park. Prices here are a little more afford-able, the services oriented more towards families. Accom-modations are basic, but there are beautiful beaches and safe swimming in the protected lagoon.

Islands on the Northern Reef

Fitzroy Island. A short cruise from Cairns reveals one of the more popular islands in Australia's northern reef, Fitzroy. The island is described as virtually an entire living rainforest, providing a range of butterfly walks, through secret gardens, and diving in the coastal coral seabeds. A range of water-sports is available.

Lizard Island. Lizard is the most northern island of protected Great Barrier Reef Marine Park. There are over 1,000 hectares of national park and miles of unspoiled beaches. Some of the best coastal reefs are available here. Lizard attracts many game fishermen from August through December, who are after its black marlin. Of the 1,000 hectares of national park, eight hectares have been put aside for 30 private suites, two deluxe suites, and Lizard Island Lodge. There are 24 private beaches available for the use of guests. This amounts to a very exclusive experience, at a very exclusive price. If you have the money, this could be close to the idyllic vacation.

Hinchinbrook Island. This is Australia's largest island national park, separated from the mainland by the deep Hinchinbrook Channel. The island rises to an imposing 1242 meters, with sheer escarpments of Mt. Bowen dropping almost straight to sea level. Apart from the wide variety of vegetation, from rain forest to brush box, there is also a sizable mangrove forest. A careful stroll, or should we say excursion, through these mangroves is an experience never to be forgotten. At high tide, there is a silence made eerie by the knowledge of the predation going on underwater. At low tide, slurps, pops and clicks gurgle up from the blue grey mud, as snapping shrimps, crabs and mud skippers go about their business of warning intruders or signaling amorous intentions. But be-ware, there are saltwater crocodiles (the ones that eat you) lurking in these dark waters. But more threatening are the bugs. Take lots of spray. Accommodations are only at one secluded low key resort. The rest must camp, for which one must obtain a permit. Call the Queensland National Parks and Wildlife Service at 070-668601.

Dunk and Bedarra Islands. About half way between Cairns and Townsville, these islands are easily accessible from either town, or from Tully, the closest point from the coast to the islands. In 1770 Captain Cook sailed through these waters and named Dunk Island. There are three levels of accommodations here, with sandy beaches and lush tropical vegetation available to all. Dunk Island is largely a national park, made famous by the writer-beachcomber E. J. Banfield. There are grass covered hills, eucalyptus forests and many rainforest plants, including palms and thick looping coiled lianas. *Bedarra* is privately owned. Bedarra is described as a virtually cashless society. The resort ambience definitely takes over. Great to get away from it all. Just pay up before you go!

The Queensland Coast

Undaunted by our train experience from Sydney to Adelaide, we loaded our car on the train at Townsville, and headed to Brisbane. Again, we bought tickets in the sitting up car, which proved to be seats something like those in an airplane. This was a very long trip on the legendary *Queenslander,* taking some 30 hours and stopping at just about every small town along the way. But as in the trip from Sydney to Adelaide, it revealed views of the Australian landscape that are often not afforded the motorist. And the views can be taken in calmly and with leisure, without worry about traffic and narrow roads.

From Townsville, the train pushes through some 300 km of tropical bushland, interspersed with some of the finest sugar plantations in the world. The plantations seem to crowd against the track, grudgingly allowing passage. The cane grows far above the height of humans, dense and thick. Here and there the sky is smudged by the smoke from sugar refining plants, their single tall chimneys jutting against the horizon. In the evening, reds and oranges radiate into the sky where the cane is being burned off ready for harvesting. The train passes through Proserpine and McKay, gateways to many Barrier Reef islands. Rockhampton marks the southernmost tip. Many people leave the train and new passengers climb on here. The average age of passengers seems rather high to us. Many elderly persons, pensioners, travel by train as there are substantial discounts provided them by the Australian government. But no matter what the monetary reason, this way of traveling avoids the hustle and bustle, slows time down. Grandparents alight at the stations, met by their children and grandchildren. A sense of time moving onward, as it preserves its past pervades this journey. It made us want to be part of this Australia.

If a 30-hour trip all at once is too much, we recommend a brief break at Bundaberg, the center for the sugar industry and not by coincidence the production of rum. Bundaberg was established in 1867, named after the aboriginal Bunda tribe. Its population is now over 30,000, and it produces some 25% of Australia's sugar. Points of interest include trips from here to Lady Elliot and Lady Musgrave Islands, the southernmost islands of the Barrier reef. For bookings call 071-516077.

Isis Central Sugar Mill provides conducted tours July through November, Monday through Friday at 2 P.M. Located 10 km north of Childers on the Isis Highway, tours show all facets of the sugar industry.

Beaches abound, all great, and too numerous to mention. Pick up a free Bundaberg and Coral isles tourist guide for a listing and description of their special delights.

Bundaberg Distillery promises the unusual experience of smelling and touching $1 million of rum in each of the distillery's oak vats. All aspects of rum production are shown, including, it is rumored, a small sampling of the product! Open Mondays through Friday; telephone: 071-524077 for reservations.

Hinkler House offers a glimpse into the life of colorful Australian aviator Bert Hinkler. This rugged individualist watched the magnificent flight patterns of the ibis as a child, and thereupon devoted his life to flying. He began by strapping makeshift wings on his back without success. Hinkler managed to acquire other people's planes to fly, and after a stint in World War I, he set a new long distance record for solo flight from London on February 7, 1928, to Darwin in 15½ days. He was killed flying the same route in 1933. The house is located in Bundaberg Botanic Gardens at the corner of Mount Perry Road and Young Street. Call 520222 for hours and further information.

Turtles on the Mainland. If you missed seeing the turtles hatching and nesting on the Barrier Reef islands, there's still a chance to see them on the mainland. Take a brief drive to Mon Repos Beach to see the turtle rookery. About 400 turtles return each year to lay their eggs in the sand. The National Parks and Wildlife Service has provided a walkway and the lighting necessary to observe the turtles doing their thing. Or call 071-520266 to arrange a guided tour (November through January), including pick-ups from accommodations.

A drive of approximately 120 km south to Hervey Bay takes one to the northerly setting-off point for a most unusual island, *Fraser Island*. This is the world's largest sand island, and the largest island off the coast of Queensland (184,000 hectares). The colored sand cliffs interspersed with rocky headlands make this island unique in its scenic quality. There are numerous freshwater lakes and creeks, and plants ranging from low heathlands to tall thick forests. Window lakes are of particular interest, since they are formed when the ground surface dips below the water table. These are usually crystal clear. Other lakes, called perch lakes, are above the watertable level, usually on saucer-shaped hard pans formed between sand dunes. These are usually a tea colored, some as high as 120 meters above sea level. At Lake Wabby, one finds a massive sandblow that is advancing westward at about three meters annually.

Swimming, fishing, camping and walking are the preferred recreational activities on this peaceful island. In addition, the island is renowned for its indigenous inhabitants, a special breed of dingo. They will approach a car or bicycle, hoping for a handout. There is much talk that they may be dangerous, especially to children. It is probably best to treat them as any other wild animal, with caution. The entire island is controlled by the Queensland National parks and Wildlife Service, and entry to the park, especially by vehicle, is strictly controled. Few vehicles are permited in the park; in fact, only four-wheel drive vehicles are of much use, as roads are limited. Vehicle access fees are $15 for a month, if bought on the mainland; $20 if bought on the island. There are motels, resorts and campgrounds aplenty.

Our train continues its way south, winding through the Many Peaks Range, thence to the Glasshouse Mountains, along the Great Divide beside the Sunshine Coast to Brisbane.

The Sunshine Coast

The Sunshine Coast extends north from Brisbane over some two hours drive. Perhaps one of the most noteworthy resorts on the Sunshine Coast is *Noosa*. Completely undeveloped just fifteen years ago, now Noosa has the reputation as the resort for the rich. Tourist brochures describe Noosa Head's fashionable Hastings Street as "the Riviera of the Sunshine Coast." And we agree. We saw many beautiful people parading up and down this street. Naturally, we kept driving, through to the campground.

The biggest attraction in Noosa is the beach. Noosa is famous for what many have termed the perfect wave: long, cylindrical breakers that the adept can catch and the not-so-experienced can battle against. The sand is also abundant and white, making the perfect setting to "catch some rays." There is one other unusual attribute of the Noosa Beach: it faces North, whereas almost all beaches on the Australian eastern coast face the East. For sun worshipers, a northerly facing beach promises even more sunshine for the day (not that there isn't too much of it already on Australia's beaches, regardless of which way they are facing).

Noosa National Park, established as far back as 1879, fortunately has stood in the way of the rapid urban development of the Sunshine Coast. The park offers rain forests, grasslands, heathlands and many tranquil walks. For further information call 071-473243.

The beach between Noosa and Fraser Island (40-mile beach) culminates in Rainbow Beach and boasts an amazing range of colored sands and cliffs. Aboriginal legend has it that a beautiful black maiden, way back in Dreamtime, was in love with a rainbow that appeared off the banks of the Noosa River. She was, alas, kidnapped by a bad man from a distant tribe. He beat her and made her do all his work. She ran away and he pursued her angrily throwing his killing boomerang. Rainbow heard her cries for help and zoomed down to help, but was attacked by the boomerang. There was an enormous explosion, and the boomerang was destroyed, but the rainbow broke into many pieces. It is these colors that are now strewn throughout the sands and cliffs of Rainbow Beach. The colored sands are about 23,000 years old and over 72 different colors have been identified.

Noosa River and Lakes. The Noosa River rises in Coolola National Park, among 50,000 hectares of mangrove–lined waterways. The lakes and waterways are a boater's paradise. Pelicans feast on plentiful mullet, flathead and prawns (shrimp), and black swans descend on Lake Cootharaba to consume lake weed. Brahminy kites soar overhead. This is the place for a peaceful, away-from-it-all vacation. Call 071-471411 to rent a houseboat on the Noosa River.

Accommodations options range from the fancy, pastel-painted Sheraton to on-site vans. We recommend *Sunrise Holiday Village*, located directly on the beach and offering great ocean views for the small cost of a campsite. The on-site vans are really little cottages (complete with thatched roofs) and much cleaner than a motel one might otherwise stay in without the view. (We would rather save our money on accommodations, and spend it on food.)

Where there is money, one usually finds good restaurants. This rule applies at Noosa. We tried the *Riverside Trattoria* and found the Italian fare authentic and appetizing. The freshly made pasta was especially impressive, and the pizza definitely edible. The prices were reasonable. Call 475366, the Sound Shopping place, Noose Sound. For an unusual (and expensive) dining experience visit the Japanese restaurant *Sanosa*, in the bay village shopping center on Hastings Street. The restaurant has several different dining areas, specializing in tempura, teppan-yaki, sushi and samshimi.

Sunshine Plantation may be a good sidetrip for the children. It specializes in parfaits and sundaes, sugar cane rides, kangaroo petting and a nutmobile (we don't know who for). It is an hour's drive north of Brisbane on the Bruce Highway.

Bribie Island. Further south, almost to Brisbane is Bribie Island, popular weekender for Brisbane city dwellers, and even now for suburban commuters. Connected to the mainland via a small bridge, Bribie offers to the resident and tourist recreational facilities that Queenslanders take for granted: safe still water swimming, surfing, fishing, sailing, power boating. Although there has been much development on this island, there is still bushland of beech trees and birdlife, often accessible by bike trails.

Brisbane

It was not too long ago when Brisbane was thought of as a drab, dull city that, if it had ever had its day, had passed its prime. The tendency to judge Australia's cities by bridges means that Brisbane comes out rather near the bottom because its low slung, architecturally unimaginative Victoria Bridge seems to struggle to span the Brisbane River (the bridge was washed away by the great floods of 1893). But since Brisbane hosted the Worlds Fair in 1988, the city has blossomed. Sparkling new skyscrapers reach into the northern sun, their varied and unusual designs tugging at the eye. The Brisbane River meanders through the city and out to the suburbs, and the Victoria Bridge now seems to blend gracefully with the newer tall structures of the city, just as small vines cohabit with the great trees of the Queensland rain forest. Six major bridges now span the river, the newest being the Gateway Bridge with a center span of 260 meters, the longest concrete box girder in the world, so the tourist brochures claim.

Brisbane received its name from its river in 1823, in honor of the governor of New South Wales, Major General Sir Thomas MacDougall Brisbane (this was when Brisbane was still part of New South Wales). Like its sister city Sydney, Brisbane's sole purpose in being settled was to contain the worst class of Australia's convicts. It was not until 1842 that free settlers began to move in, and along with convicts and ticket-of-leavers (parolees), they began to build the city that has emerged today. There are, however, two convict-built structures remaining in Brisbane: the Commissariat Stores on William Street (now the home of the Royal Historical Society of Queensland) and the infamous Windmill on Wickham Terrace. This mill was built in 1828 to grind flour, and soon became known as the tower of torture because convicts were forced to turn it when there was insufficient wind to power the sails.

Brisbane is perhaps the most interesting city in Australia from an architectural point of view. Her new and unusual glassy skyscrapers mix with a wide range of historic buildings in a display of many different architectural styles and building materials. Of special note are: *Brisbane City Town Hall*, (King George Square) built in 1920–1930 of sandstone, the tallest building in Brisbane until thirty years ago. The hall sports a massive tower and clock and a superb circular concert hall inside.

The People's Palace (corner of Ann and Edward Streets) designed by the Salvation Army for low cost accommodation, opened on June 27, 1911. Features are an elaborate cast iron balustrade of three levels, decorating deep verandas.

The Mansions (corner Margaret and George Streets) is a row of six terrace houses erected in 1890. The striking feature of these buildings is the use of red brickwork contrasted with light limestone, in a design that repeats Venetian arches and bay windows which extend through the roof of the building to become attic windows as well. A catwalk runs along the top. Definitely a unique building.

There are some 40 other historical buildings, all quite fascinating. Stop at Queen Street Mall tourist information center and obtain a brochure for a self-guided walking tour. This is one of the best historic city walking brochures we have seen. Allow about two hours for a leisurely walk. The distance is not great, but one will want to stop and browse often.

For a taste of the modern, both architectural and gustatory, enter the Myer Centre which occupies almost the entire block bounded by Queen Street Mall, Edward Street, Elizabeth

Street and Albert Street. This is a tastefully renovated old building (or should we say several buildings that have been gutted and redesigned) of several levels, with balustrades and catwalks, escalators and elevators. It is a shopping mall the likes of which we have seen nowhere, including in the United States. There are food courts on each level, offering fare of every imaginable ethnic taste. The noise level is rather high, though, because this place is always jammed full of people. Furthermore one hears the high pitched screams of children, as though there were roller coaster rides inside the mall.

Take the elevator to the top level to see a child's dream come true. Legoland has an extensive display, and there is plenty of Lego paraphernalia for all kids. There is an adventure playground where children play hide and seek for hours on end. Lego is free, but there are entry fees for other activities, or one general ticket to admit to all—well worth it. The peak of craziness is reached with the roller coaster that whizzes kids around the upper atmosphere of the mall, clinging close to the roof, swerving high over the heads of shoppers. The concept boggles the mind, but one cannot help admiring the sheer boldness of the creators of this mall. They have taken the concept of the modern shopping mall to its logical extreme. The only trouble is, that we doubt there are many adults who could stand the noise for much longer than half an hour. But there is something about this mall; we returned to it often. The kids in our party did not seem to mind the noise at all.

Brisbane River Cruise. Take the *Kookaburra Queen I* paddlewheeler from the pier at Waterfront Place, Eagle Street. There are a wide variety of cruises to choose from, ranging in price from $9.90 to $19.90, depending on whether one wishes to dine on board or enjoy live entertainment. Night cruises are also popular. Because the river meanders through the city, this cruise is an excellent and relaxed way to learn about Brisbane. Call 07-2211300 for reservations.

Mount Coot-tha Botanic Gardens. Founded by the Brisbane City Council in 1976, these gardens boast some 10,000 plant species. This is possibly one of the more beautiful and natural of Australia's botanical gardens—less influenced by the very English and Victorian layout of Australia's most renowned botanical garden, that of Melbourne. The emphasis here is on Australian fauna. Special attractions are the Central Lagoon, surrounded by agapanthus, harboring a rich waterbird life, and the tropical display dome featuring the giant water lily *Victoria amazonica* (yes, Queen Victoria's influence extends even here!). There are also a planetarium, auditorium, souvenir shops, picnic tables, cafeterias and even a botanical library. Also great views of Brisbane from the top of Mt. Coottha. Take bus 39 from downtown. Open every day; telephone: 07-3778891 for information.

Queensland Museum Science Center. Similar to the science museum in Canberra, though on a smaller scale, this is a delightful hands-on museum for people of all ages (though the designers of the museum obviously had kids, big and little, in mind). The wonders of science are incorporated to entice young minds: children can draw abstract patterns with a pendulum, make frozen shadows, see a cone that rolls up hill, a briefcase that doesn't want to go where you take it, make music with 24 drain pipes and a rubber sandal, listen to your echo, and lots more. A short walk from city center to Stephen's Lane off George or William Streets. Call 07-2246003 for information. Open seven days.

An hour's drive south down the busy freeway, Route 1, leads to Australia's playground, the Gold Coast, sort of the equivalent to Waikiki, except that the beaches are far superior. But the glitz, and glamour are very much the same.

The Gold Coast

Gold Coasters hardly sleep. By day, it's the beach, and by night, it's across the border to N.S.W. to hit the casinos. Perhaps the most famous and pretentious resort along the Gold Coast is *Surfers Paradise* (*Surfers* to the locals). What resort could fail with a name like that? Skyscraping hotels and condos crowd the beach, some brashly encroaching on the beach itself. Yet the enormity of the beach with its broad gradually sloping sands, the shallow waters slowly giving way to gently rolling breakers, manages somehow to resist this over-development. The beach stretches for miles in every direction. One sits with back to the condominiums, the space ahead uncluttered by the accoutrements of civilization. Only in the late afternoon do the condos interpose; their shadows sneak down the beach, beckoning the vacationer to retire and prepare for a night's entertainment and fun.

Restaurants for any taste or pocketbook abound, as do shops ranging from uppity boutiques to budget souvenir shops. Possibly the best deals on T-shirts can be obtained in Surfers. Coffee shops abound and small pub-like restaurants with sidewalk service flourish. Prices are high here, but the surroundings and quality of food are probably worth it. There is no ambivalence in Surfers, either one is out for a good time and hang the expense and the glitz, or one goes somewhere else. There are the usual tourist attractions as well: a Ripley's museum, nightclubs, and large beer gardens.

Of the restaurants we tried, one stood out: the *Mongolian Barbecue Restaurant* in Miami. Rapidly becoming a popular feature in many Australian cities and towns, this cuisine, if it could be called that, provides a fun experience along with a menu that includes foods that are Australian favorites to begin with: beef and lamb. Beef, lamb or chicken are frozen solid, then fine shavings of them are made with a special knife. One makes a selection of these rolls of frozen meat, along with an assortment of vegetables alredy chopped and gives this selection to the Mongolian cook (actually, in our case a very Australian looking teenager), who adds a Mongolian sauce. With great flair, he tosses the mixture onto a huge flaming barbecue hotplate, and swishes it around with chopstocks as long as his arms. (The reason for their length is that the fire is so hot). The extremely hot barbecue singes the frozen slithers of meat, and lightly browns the vegetables, mixing the sauce through the whole thing. In a few minutes it is cooked, and the mixture is deftly whisked off the hotplate and into the bowl, not one piece of it spilled. A delicious meal, though a little expensive. (On the other hand, if one has a large appetite, the price is for all-you-can-eat.)

Other Gold Coast resorts in close proximity to Surfers include Burleigh Heads and Miami. All lie along the Pacific Highway and can be easily reached in a few minutes drive. One of the most recent additions to the Gold Coast glitz is the *Jupiter Casino*. It's easily recognizable; it has enough lights to light up Jupiter and an ostentatious monorail (like the one in Darling Harbour) to carry hotel patrons across the Pacific Highway (only a 5-minute walk). Here you may kiss your money good-bye 24 hours a day if you choose.

There are also the usual tourist attractions: *Dreamworld* fun park (tel: 075-533300), *Seaworld* on the Spit at Main Beach (next to Surfers) complete with water ski show and monorail, dolphin and whale shows.

A visit to the Gold Coast would not be complete without a visit to the *Currumbin Bird Sanctuary*. In 1946, an Aussie, Alex Griffiths, was trying to grow his gladioli (a distinctly English pastime, we might point out). The trouble was that pesky green and red birds kept attacking his flowers, looking for their favorite nectar. Resisting the temptation to shoot them (a daunting task if ever there was one, since they number in the hundreds of thousands), Griffiths began to feed the birds in hopes of saving his gladioli. Today thousands of these beautiful birds, called lorikeets, descend at appointed times (8 A.M. and 4 P.M.) every day, expecting to be fed. Mr. Griffiths donated the sanctuary to the National Trust in 1974, and it has become a major tourist attraction. The sanctuary has since been developed, perhaps explaining the rather hefty admission price. One can take a small train around the sanctuary, viewing other attractions such as koalas, kangaroos, dingos and waterbirds. But the great attraction is to obtain a tin plate full of nectar and seed, hold it up high above one's head, and wait for the birds to descend. The shrieks of delight from children and their mothers fill the air—almost as loud as at the Myer Centre Mall. It is nothing for lorikeets to descend on one's head and shoulders and arms, a dozen at a time. The plate becomes heavy to hold with so many birds clawing at it. Claws can dig into the skin so be sure to wear protective clothing. Located at the Gold Coast Highway, Currumbin, tel: 075-341266. Don't miss it!

The most southerly town of the Gold Coast is Tweed Heads, just across the border into New South Wales. It is less glitzy and the building rash less garish. Many people like to retire here. One sees lawn bowls clubs and rinks everywhere. The relaxed lifestyle of Northern New South Wales beckons.

CHAPTER 11

Tassie and Perth: Two Extremes

It is a regrettable fact that Australia has not until very recently cared much about its early past. In most of the places we have visited in this book, there have been on occasion preserved historic buildings, most of these dating back only to Queen Victoria's time. The old original settlement in Sydney Cove, for example, is virtually unrecognizable today. A historic walk, starting at the Rocks, has to struggle to point out actual original buildings or settlements of the early convict days. What could be saved in recent years has been saved and restored magnificiently—after a fashion. It must be admitted that the restoration has followed a particular line of development: the commercialization of an area and exploitation of foreign tourists. The history is secondary to the renovation of buildings to contain shops.

Tasmania offers a welcome relief from this garish development. Perth in contrast exemplifies it. These highly contrasting areas are at the geographical extremes of Australia:

Perth isolated on the west coast across the huge Nullarbor Plain (a nice way of saying desert) and Tasmania in the southeast, split off from the mainland by the uninviting, often treacherous Bass Strait. The geographic and historic circumstances of the origins of the two locations have led to two distinctly different lines of development. Perth has become known as the "boom and bust" city, a popular mecca for the nouveau rich (as if there were any other kind of rich in Australia), a city of glassy skyscrapers, seeming to rise out of nothing, and a lifestyle conveying a rambunctious demeanor, perhaps a kind of urban frontier spirit.

In the early days of settlement, Tasmania enjoyed considerable prominence as a convict establishment, so that its commercial and penal buildings flourished. However, when gold was discovered on the mainland, the mainstream of Australian life and development passed Tasmania by. The happy result is that many of Tasmania's historic buildings, especially from the colonial and convict periods, are well preserved, sometimes even whole villages.

Perth

The world renowned yachtsman businessman Alan Bond personifies much of Perth. When we were in Australia, the swaggering, cowboy businessman was definitely in his bust phase. Vilified in most of the Australian media, he was selling off his vast empire of estates, mines, breweries and what have you. Aussies had a grudging admiration for this self-made millionaire, mostly because he had indulged in an extravagance that all Aussies love: sport. It was largely through his efforts that Australia captured the America's Cup, with the result that it was run in waters off Perth (and her sister city Fremantle). Bond became a genuine Aussie hero. By drawing an international sporting event to Australia, he proved what Aussies are constantly trying to prove, that Australia is neither backward or isolated, but is at the center of world events.

Unfortunately, another side to the Aussie national character is that they like to see big men fall. Perhaps this attribute harks back to the convict days when most Australians were little men, underdogs, at the mercy of their jailers. They nursed a deep and enduring fantasy to see their masters fall. Aussies watch Bond's financial demise with glee. They relish the thought of his receiving punishment at the hands of the government (even though Australians seem to malign their government to about the same degree).

Perth is the capital of Australia's largest state, Western Australia, which probably constitutes close to a third or more of its area. In the last two decades extensive development of the state's mining resources has led to considerable economical activity in Perth itself, with skyscrapers depicting the growth of a large financial district. The glass and chrome of the downtown area has led one Australian journalist, Andrew Conway in the *Sun Herald,* to describe Perth as a mini Sydney (a characterization which we're sure did not endear Mr. Conway to Perthsiders).

But what sets Perth off from Sydney or any other Australian city for that matter is the way its original designers tried to make it blend with the natural surroundings of the area. There are tall chrome and glass skyscrapers (hardly envisaged by the original planner Captain James Stirling in 1827) it is true, but the way the city begins by hugging the Swan River, then climbs the hill up to beautiful Kings Park, keeps all things, even the downtown development, in perspective. Kings Park is a thousand acres of natural bushland overlooking Perth's center, providing a natural balance to the bustle of the city below. And the city itself seems to be embraced by the Swan River, particularly where it expands almost to the size of a bay called Perth Water.

The colors are excruciatingly bright, for the light in Perth is the brightest of all Australian cities. The sun after all shines down some 350 days a year, and the city glimmers at the edge of the virtual desert interior of the rest of the state. The blues of the bay, river and ocean, the greens of the surrounding parks, the reflections in the glass skyscrapers, all contribute a kind of diamond-like sparkle to this million-person city.

Points of interest include:

Tudor Kitsch. A stroll around the downtown area is a must, but make sure the car is left at the hotel. Driving is congested. Walking is quicker. While there are a number of historic buildings of interest, such as the Old Courthouse and West Australian Museum on Francis Street, or the Old Mill across the Narrows Bridge, the shopping areas are the tourist delights in Perth. Make your way to the Hay Street Pedestrian Mall and London Court that links Hay Street to St. George's Terrace. One is confronted by 1937-mock Tudor, complete with iron portcullises, dungeon towers, even Dick Whittington and his cat. Moving clockwork displays show St. George slaying the dragon, over and over again. The English influence on Australian style was never more apparent.

Black Swans and the River. The Swan River was named after the abundance of the black swans that used to inhabit it (many still do). The river is probably best seen by taking one of the many cruises available. We suggest Captain Cook Cruises (09-3253341). The Metropolitan Transport Trust also offers Swan River ferry cruises, leaving from Barrack Street jetty. For the best view of the black swans and a chance to feed them, take bus #90, 91, or 92 from the central bus station to Lake Monger in the suburbs. This is a haven for black swans and hundreds of other water birds. Take a bag of bread, and the swans will eat out of your hand.

Kings Park. For panoramic views of the city, including smashing views of the Swan River from the top of Mt. Eliza, go to Kings Park. Most of this park is natural bushland, but there are also the usual imported fauna to make the English style botanic gardens, complete with a floral clock and the ubiquitous canon. There is an unusual bubbling and squirting fountain dedicated to pioneer women, and a plantation of gum trees, each one planted for a fallen digger (World War I soldier). An expensive restaurant offers patio dining. We preferred, as usual, the self-service snack terrace that provides tasty Aussie sandwiches, afternoon teas, and little tables at which to enjoy it.

Art Gallery. At 47 James Street is certainly the most magnificent of the art galleries in Australia. Opened in 1979, the building cost $10 million, allowing Perth to brag that she has outdone her big sisters in Sydney and Melbourne. The collection is of high standard, boasting Cezanne, Monet, Renoir and Van Gogh, Whistler and Rembrandt. But one can see these great artists in other places. What one cannot find elsewhere is the excellent display of art of the western desert from the aboriginal Panunya tribe. It is well worth a visit.

Ethnicity. Take a cab to Northbridge, a traditional working class suburb, settled early by first wave immigrants from Italy and Greece. Now, it, like Sydney's Balmain, has become gentrified and has broadened its ethnic diversity. One still finds plenty of souvlaki and cappuccino, but now there are also many Chinese, Vietnamese, and Cambodian shops and restaurants to tantalize the pocketbook and tastebuds. This place comes alive between Thursday and Sunday.

Rats. Well, not exactly. One can take a brief trip out to Rottnest Island, so-called by a Dutch explorer in the 17th century who thought it was swarming with rats. The island is home to the rare and unique marsupials called quokkas which live as tranquil a life as a marsupial could amidst many tourists. It is tranquil because no motorized vehicles of any kind are permitted on the island. Bicycles or bare feet are the preferred mode of transport. This is a fun place, with gorgeous beaches of the finest sand found anywhere, fish leaping out of the water, lots of sport (of course, this is Australia), fishing from boats and rocks. And it's incredibly quiet. Reach this fantasy island via a two-hour ferry ride from Perth's Port city Fremantle, or 65 minutes by hydrofoil.

Fremantle

Fremantle lies at the mouth of the Swan River, some 12 miles downstream. It offers in some ways the reverse of Perth: an attempt (albeit taken over a bit by the commercialization of the area for the America's Cup in 1987) to preserve the charm of its unusual history. Unlike other convict settlements, Fremantle began as a free settlement, but the settlers decided that they could not make out without free labor, so requested the government to send them convicts. They received 10,000. The town sports the first bridge ever built across the Swan River, officially opened in 1866. The bridge is of no special interest except for the circumstances of its official opening: the ribbon was cut by Moondyne Joe, a bushranger who had just escaped from jail! Of interest also is the Fremantle jail, built in 1851 by convicts. Even more amazing is that it is still in use as a jail. Take bus #101 or #103 from St. George's Terrace in Perth to get to Fremantle.

Fremantle Asylum. In the 1860s, the colony's first lunatic asylum was built by convicts at 1 Finnerty Street. It is now the *Fremantle Museum,* and contains an amazing variety of bric-a-brac, weapons, photographs, documents, newspapers, carved whale's teeth. One could browse here for hours, not sure what one was looking for because there is such a variety of stuff. Open seven days until 5 P.M.; admission is free.

Fremantle Markets. If you have never managed to frequent London's east end markets, the Fremantle Markets may be just the thing. Established in 1897 and modeled on the European markets, these are really fun to visit. There are over 100 stalls of antiques, exotic foods, herbs and spices, jewelry, crafts, and just plain junk. Open on Henderson Street and South Terrace, Fridays and Saturday mornings.

A continent away, the history of Australia is enshrined more carefully and more seriously in Tasmania.

Tasmania

Tasmania offers additional contrasts to Western Australia. The latter is a huge sun drenched state. Tasmania is a tiny state by comparison, green, with cloudy skies and frequent rain. A large part of the state is mountainous, filled with tangled bush and vines, some gorges so rugged and dense that they have yet to be explored by man. Because of its enormous and challenging wilderness areas, Tasmania is a great attraction to bushwalkers, rock climbers and mountaineers. The wilderness is so pristine that guidebooks for hikers recommend as a matter of course that hikers drink the water from streams and lakes. There are few wilderness areas left in the world where one can drink the water. Tasmania is one of the best kept secrets of bushwalking. And while some of the best walks are difficult and only for experts, it is a surprising fact that there are a number of bush walks up the slopes of Mount Wellington quite close to the capital city, Hobart.

In 1642, Tasmania was discovered by Dutchman Abel Tasman. And in the 1770s, the French and the British raced to take possession of Van Diemen's Land, as Tasmania was then called. The British won with the help of explorers such as Lieutenant John Bowen and Captain James Cook. Tasmania became the dumping ground for the worst and most recalcitrant criminals from Britain and the rest of Australia for the first half of the 19th century. Conditions were harsh, as men and women alike were shackled and forced to perform hard labor. The major penal settlement was at Point Arthur, some 68 miles south of Hobart.

Hobart, the second-oldest Australian city (15 years younger than Sydney), boasts some of the best examples of early Australian architecture, almost all the result of convict labor. Many relics of the penal settlement have been maintained, serving as a historical treasure chest for everyone to enjoy.

Hobart developed as a major commercial center not only to service the penal colonies but also the thriving fishing and whaling industry. The result was that many buildings were constructed during the Georgian period, and many of these are still standing. These are elegant representatives of that style rendered in local freestone (sandstone). While the inevitable large commercial buildings of the 20th century have sprung up in recent years, there is such a preponderance of historic buildings in Hobart that they still dominate the city, giving it an old world charm largely lost to all other Australian cities on the mainland.

A standard historical walk is that to *Battery Point*. The National Trust conducts walking tours, setting out every Saturday at 9:30 a.m. from Franklin Square, opposite the general post office. The price is $2.50 and includes morning tea. It takes about 3 hours. One walks generally from Franklin Square, past St. Davids Park to Wilmot Street, then left down Hampden to Battery Point, returning around the Castray Esplanade along Salamanca and back to Franklin Square. Along the way one may appreciate the iron railings of St. Mary's Hospital, dating from 1847 and in Battery Point proper, the series of mariners' houses and cottages beautifully preserved. This was an exciting part of town in its heyday, full of pubs, churches, houses and winding streets, all crowded in on top of one another. The district is still so well preserved one can almost feel it come alive. And as one turns each corner, glimpses of the harbor suddenly appear—a little reminiscent of strolling around Sydney's inner suburbs.

Of particular interest is the *Van Diemen Memorial Folk Museum* at 103 Hampden Street. For a small fee one may enter this old colonial home and observe how well the gentry (in contrast to the convicts) lived. This museum recreates the early life of colonial and convict days.

Take a walk across the road and down to the *Barton Cottage,* recognizable by its two small attics. Devonshire teas are served on the verandah and highly recommended.

Battery Point Anglican Church of St. George dominates Cromwell Street and dates from 1836. Note the tapered windows and strange Egyptian-like architecture. Just behind this building is the Tasmanian Maritime Museum.

At 5 Argyle Street, enter the *Tasmanian Museum,* built in 1863. One finds here the tragic story of Tasmania's aboriginals. To put it bluntly, the colonial administration decided that they caused too much trouble, and set out to extinguish them altogether. The last full-blooded Tasmanian aborigine died in 1876. Tasmania's whales were totally demolished too; their story is told here as well.

Up Mount Wellington. As promised, a wilderness walk is possible right out of Hobart. Take a bus from Franklin Square to Ferntree and cross the road from the bus stop to the small park. Select the broad track that runs parallel to the main road towards Silver Falls. Pass the barrier, cross the bridge, and head upstream following the right fork. Already one has passed by eucalyptus forest, a cascading water fall, lush fernery. Climb the track to the right of the falls to reach the Springs. Take it slowly, this is a steep ascent. Follow the track northwards, and turn left at the T junction. One is now some 300 yards from The Springs picnic ground. The main road to the Mount Wellington Lookout passes through here. Take the same route back, except detour at Radfords Monument, taking Fern Glade track. This takes one info rich damp forest and fern glades. Further down the gully is the Huon Highway, and a foot track along the side of the road takes one to the Ferntree bus stop. About two hours.

Port Arthur Sixty-eight miles southeast of Hobart lies the infamous Port Arthur, poised on a craggy headland, joined only by a preciously narrow strip of land to the main island. The convicts who first arrived here in 1833 must have been terror stricken by the sheer wilderness of the place. While some would argue that the penal settlement represented an enlightened treatment of criminals for the times (boys were separated from older hardened criminals, an extensive library was maintained, lessons in reading and writing were given), the fact is that these convicts were ripped from their homes and families, in a country so vastly different from the wilderness they found in Tasmania, that we can hardly begin to appreciate the horror of this punishment. Yet it represented such a neat matching to the contemporary view of criminals as wild and barbarous. How appropriate that they be sent to a wild and primitive land! The books *The Emancipist* and *The Fatal Shore* give graphic portrayals of what life was like for both convicts and freemen.

Vicious dogs guarded Eaglehawk Neck, the narrow entrance to the isthmus of the Tasman peninsula at the location of Port Arthur. The convicts constructed all buildings under the direction of Captain Booth. They even constructed a railway—hacked out of the bush. Convicts were used to power it. They built a large prison, including a chapel specially designed to implement what became known as the silent system. It is a popular view that the silent system—the idea that convicts be kept totally isolated from each other, no talking to each other at all—replaced the lash. The truth is that the lash continued throughout the entire period of the Port Arthur penal colony. The chapel in the prison displays the incredible commitment the British had in their penal treatment. Each place in the chapel is enclosed by a box. A convict sat inside the box totally cut off, forced to suffer in solitary misery.

There is still evidence of suffering and torment. Take the National Park ranger's tour. And to thoroughly absorb the atmosphere, take the small boat trip out to the Isle of the Dead. The experience is something out of a Stephen King novel. There are 1,769 graves on the island—it was where many unfortunate convicts ended their lives, all no doubt, thoroughly wretched lives.

Richmond. This delightful village is a 20-minute drive north of Hobart. There are many early 19th century buildings here. Find in this town the oldest bridge in all Australia. Built in 1823, it spans the Coal River and is still in use today. It was built of the usual sandstone and by convicts, and perhaps contradicts the popular view that prison labor produces substandard products. In fact, there are many well preserved convict built buildings here and elsewhere: churches, jails, graneries, hotels.

Other historic towns may be enjoyed throughout Tasmania. If time permits, a quick visit to *Launceston,* Tasmania's second largest city and port for the ferries which ply the Bass Strait from Melbourne and Sydney is worth seeing. A walk through the historic sections of Launceston, and a look at the nearby Cataract Gorge allows simultaneous enjoyment of history and nature. Nearby, on the main route between Hobart and Launceston lies the well preserved 160-year-old town of *Ross.* It has a famous crossroads known as the Four Corners: Temptation (the hotel), Salvation (the Catholic Church), Recreation (the Town Hall), and Damnation (the jail) are all here. Of most interest, however, is the bridge across the Macquarie River. This bridge, though not as old as that in Richmond, is considerably more interesting. Two convicts sculptured the sandstone to make up the arches, which contain 184 stones depicting Celtic symbols (Governor Macquarie was a Scotsman after all), intersperse with carvings of animals and portraits of various notables. Walk down the steps at either end for the best view. After taking in the historic buildings and streets of the town, wander across to the cemeteries. They are separated by denomination, Church of England, Methodist, Catholic. There are elaborate inscriptions on some markers, others are simple and humble. But they tell much of the hardships of life in the colony, and of the social and religious life of its inhabitants.

One last thing. A couple of miles from the Eaglehawk Neck are a number of striking features of Tasmania's rugged coast:

the Blowhole, Tasman's Arch, the Devil's Kitchen, and a stretch of tessellated pavement. On the way to Port Arthur there is a park that must not be missed: The Tasmanian Devil Park. Talk about Stephen King again! Tasmania is famous for its unique Tasmanian Devil, an evil looking animal that has the head like the devil so often rendered in old European religious paintings. Yet none of them could have known that this animal existed. The Devil used to be widely distributed on mainland Australia, but is now only found in Tasmania. It is one of the few carnivorous marsupials with bone crushing jaws and teeth. And it carries its young in a pouch, some-times up to four at a time. Now that couldn't be a devil, could it?

Books We Enjoyed

If you have time to read a few books in preparation for a trip, we strongly recommend these below. Some of the books are available in the U.S., but many of them are not. Those published only in Australia may be obtained in the U.S. from: Susan Curry, The Australian Book Source, 1309 Redwood Lane, Davis, CA 95616 (tel: 916-753-1519); or Barbara M. Crawford, Books from Australia, 1231 Nyanza Road, S.W., Tacoma, WA 98499

Handy Travel and Fact Books

Australia by Insight Guides, APA Publications. This is a detailed travel guide, with a little something about everything, even lesser known places in Australia. There are interesting essays on Australian life and culture, as well as revealing color photographs. The only drawback is that the book is very large and heavy, printed on thick glossy paper.

Australia on $25 a Day. The Arthur Frommer perennial. Lightweight, with lots of tips on where to stay and quickies on what to do. We found it always useful, and usually accurate.

The Outdoor Traveller's Guide: AUSTRALIA. Gerry Ellis and Sharon Cohen. London: Columbus Books, 1988. For the nature buff who wants to find the best nature-viewing areas.

The Little Aussie Fact Book. Margaret Nicholson. Long Beach: Australia in Print, 1989. A very colorful collection of various Australian facts. $12.95.

The Oxford Literary Guide to Australia. Edited by Peter Price. Exhaustive listing of all Australian literature, criticism and its history.

Creating Australia: 200 Years of Australian Art. The Australian Bicentennial Authority. May be purchased at most Australian art galleries. An excellent collection of key Australian artists, with descriptions of their historical context.

The Illustrated Treasury of Australian Verse. Beatrice Davis. Melbourne: Thomas Nelson Australia, 1986. Beautiful color paintings accompany classic poems. Hardcover, $40.

Place Names of Australia. A. W. Reed. Sydney: Reed Books LTD., 1988. Learn the meanings of Woolloomooloo, Rupanyup, and Wagga Wagga (young kangaroo, tree growing by a swamp, and many crows, not necessarily in that order).

The Dreaming and the Australian Aborigines

Gulpilil's Stories of Dreamtime. Collins, 1979. Stories of the dreamtime illustrated with quality colored photographs of the Australian landscape and authentic aboriginal rock paintings.

Wanamurranganya: The Story of Jack McPhee, Sally Morgan. 1989. $14.95. A very popular novelist explores aboriginal identity and legends.

Tales From the Aborigines. Bill Harney. Rigby, 1959. Delightful collection of aboriginal tales with commentary on the language of the stories and the story tellers themselves.

People of the Dreamtime. Alan Marshall. 1952. A well known and popular traditional Australian author writes poetry inspired by the dreamtime. Gorgeous illustrations by aboriginal artist Miriam-Rose Ungunmerr.

Traditional Bush Medicines. Aboriginal Communities of North America. 1988. Interesting catalog of bush plants, herbs and other substances with medicinal and healing properties.

History and Current Affairs

The Discovery of Australia. Andrew W. Sharp. Oxford: Clarendon, 1963. A technical and detailed account of the many and various discoveries of Australia. For those who like to read about how it was, provides many actual reproductions of ships' logs and diaries of explorers and navigators.

The Timeless Land. Eleanor Dark. 1941. Wonderful construction of the coming of the white man to Australia told from the point of view of an aboriginal boy and his artistic father. The book offers that unmistakable English view of the common Australians.

The Lucky Country. Donald Horne, 1964. Sold millions in Oz. There is now a follow-up called *Ideas for a Nation,* 1988, which states that Oz is no longer so lucky.

A History of Australia. C. M. H. Clark. London and New York: Cambridge University Press, 1962. Scholarly account of the history of Australia written in traditional style. Extremely well documented and researched. Perhaps a little dated by today's standards of history, but non-ideological as far as possible, given the time it was written. Its strength is the early chapters and placing in context of European Christendom and economic history, the discovery and settlement of Australia.

Australia. Russell Ward. Englewood Cliffs, N.J.: Prentice-Hall, 1965. Ward does a great job of showing how the national character of Australians is linked to their past.

Come in Spinner, Dymphna Cusack and Florence James. North Ryde: Angus and Robertson, 1951. The life and loves of three women in a beauty salon in wartime Sydney.

Baby Booms: Growing up in Australia in the 1940's, 50's, and 60's. Helen Townsend. Brookvale: Simon and Shuster, 1988. $19.95. Hilarious and sentimental collection of memories from Australian Baby Boomers (especially if you're one yourself). $19.95.

Songs of a Sentimental Bloke. C. J. Dennis. Poems of greatly loved Australian poet of the war time era. Available in many different editions.

The Fatal Shore. Robert Hughes, 1985. *Time* art critic and expatriot Aussie has written probably the best book that catalogs the ordeals of the first convict settlers in Australia, the injustices, sordid and petty cruelties of the English overseers, and the sheer neglect of the welfare of that great country, by the succession of English governments and administrations.

The Australians. Ross Terrill, 1987. Simon and Schuster. A self conscious account by an accomplished Aussie journalist of the trials and tribulations of modern Australia. Has a lot to say about Australian businessmen and capitalists, a little to say about ordinary Australians, and not much that's nice to say about anybody. A curious book now because it was written before the economic downturn hit the great Aussie entrepreneurs, who have sunk rapidly from boom to bust. One might infer from Terrill's book that he saw the writing on the wall.

A Town Like Alice. Nevil Shute. One of Australia's best known novelists from the 1950s, whose novel, when turned into a TV miniseries, put Alice Springs on the U.S. map. Story of the trek made by Australian wives from town to town under the cruel yoke of the Japanese occupation of Burma in World War II.

On the Beach. Nevil Shute. Made into a movie starring Gregory Peck and Ava Gardner in the 1950s. About the end of life on this planet as a result of a nuclear war. Ava Gardner was said to have observed that Australia was an appropriate place to film a movie about the end of the earth.

The Emancipist. Veronica Sweeney. Bantam, 1989. Enormous tome presenting a fictionalized version of Australia's first 75 years, beginning with the first convict settlement. Stark, evocative and accurate.

The Aussie Character

Waltzing Matilda. A. B. Patterson, Australia's best loved and most widely known poet, better know in the U.S. for his poem "The Man from Snowy River," upon which the movie is based. This poem is available in many different versions and books. There are many Aussies who would have liked this song to become Australia's national anthem to replace "God Save the Queen," which is sung to the tune that Americans know as "My Country Tis of Thee." Australia's anthem is "Australia Fair," only very recently adopted.

Very Rude Places Down Under. John Hilton. North Ryde: Angus and Robertson, 1990. Portrays the kind of rough Aussie sense of humor we have described. Not the type of book we like to recommend, but we are trying to write a book which will aid all types of tourists. $8.95.

Unspeakable Adams. Phillip Adams, with illustrations by Arthur Horner and John Spooner. Sphere Books. Phillip Adams wrote various books which depict Aussie 1970s humor; very political and designed to shock the powers that be, or anyone else within striking distance.

Let Stalk Strine. Afferbeck Lauder, 1965, Ure Smith. Hilarious rendition of how Aussies have murdered the English language, and in so doing created a language all their own.

Death of an Old Goat. Robert Barnard. Penguin, 1977. English murder mystery set in a country campus uncomfortably similar to one in New South Wales. Offers provocative, if a little jaundiced, insights into the Aussie character and lifestyle. Very funny as well.

Great Australian Legends. Frank Hardy (in association with Truthful Jones). Surry Hills: Hutchinson Australia, 1988. Includes legends such as: workers compensation is a God-given right, Australian elections are rigged, the Jolly Swagman wasn't Australian. Illustrated. $12.95.

Kangaroo. D. H. Lawrence. Not one of Lawrence's great books, but offers a view of Australia by a great English writer of this century.

AKUBRA is Australian for Hat. Grenville Turner. Brookvale: Simon and Shuster, 1988. A combination of words and pictures relating the history and lifestyles surrounding the good ol' Aussie hat. $19.95.

Australian Ugliness. Robin Boyd. 1960. Not what it seems. Actually a Post WWII analysis of Oz. Something a little different.

How to Survive in Australia. Robert Treborlang. Potts Point: Major Mitchell Press, 1989. Includes: why Australians don't like to ask questions, putting the locals at ease, how not to dress well, how to make a cup of tea, curbing your generosity, why losers are heroes, cricket. $6.95.

The Dinkum Dictionary. Lenie Johansen. South Yarra: Viking O'Neil, 1988. "A ripper guide to Aussie English." $16.95.

Right Words: A Guide to English Usage in Australia. Stephen Murray-Smith. Ringwood, Penguin Books, 1990. Includes: "Is manageress sexist? Do we eat crayfish or lobster? How much beer is in a schooner? When should I use a pissant?" $12.99.

In the Land of Oz. Howard Jacobsen. Penguin, 1987. An amusingly funny, if not barbed, account of travels throughout

Australia, and the people. A most human analysis of the Aussie character, though touched with only slightly hidden pommie superiority.

The Down Under Cookbook. Graeme Newman, 1986, Harrow and Heston. Cookbook of traditional Australian recipes specially translated and explained for an American cook. Each recipe is accompanied with amusing anecdote of Aussie events. Definitely some tongue in cheek Aussie humor here.

Australia's Natural Wonders, Flora and Fauna

The Australian Geographic. Not widely available in the U.S. but one can subscribe by writing to: Australian Geographic Subscriptons, Freepost 3, P. O. Box 321, Terrey Hills, NSW, 2084, Australia. This is a beautifully illustrated magazine that follows the example of America's *National Geographic.* There are many articles on Australian wildlife, early and modern exploration. Originated by Australia's millionaire electronics retailer Dick Smith.

Australia's National Parks. Michael Morecombe. 1972. Lansdowne. Detailed accounts of all Australian national parks, including beautiful colored photographs of flora, fauna, rock art, and maps.

Outback on a Budget. Brian Sheedy. 1987, Roadwrite. Down to earth how to book on driving and camping in the outback for ordinary people without lots of money to spend.

American (!)

Many Happy Returns. The newsletter of the American Boomerang Society. Yes, if you are turned on by the Aussie mystique, join the society and through their newsletter purchase all manner of boomerangs. Membership package also brings with it a book on how to throw your boomerang so it will come back to you. Better watch out though, or it might come back and clonk you on the head! Much better fun than throwing frisbees, though admittedly antisocial! The American boomerang team recently won the world championship in Boomerang throwing, held in Brisbane, Australia.

Children's Books (Grown-ups like them too)

The Rocks of Honey, 1960. *In an Older Kind of Magic,* 1972. *The Nargun and the Stars,* 1973. Patricia Wrightson. A white child's peek into an aboriginal child's world; each book provides a new and exciting adventure.

Dot and the Kangaroo. Ethel Pedley, 1899. A bushland fantasy.

Possum Magic. Mem Fox. Omnibus Books, 1983. Very young child's story of possums and koalas, delicately illustrated in watercolors. Features not only Aussie animals, but favorite Aussie foods, including vegemite and pavlova.

The Magic Pudding. Norman Lindsay, 1918. Funny even today. The important place of Australian animals in children's stories was established forever with this book.

The *Blinky Bill* series. There are many of these, all starring that mischievous koala, who seems to stumble into trouble no matter how hard he tries to be good.

Playing Beatie Bow. Ruth Park. Puffin Books. 1983. Set in the Rocks area of old Sydney. An exciting tale of mystery and suspense when Abigail plays the scary game of Beatie Bow with her friends and a mysterious kid from the Rocks.

Come Danger, Come Darkness. Ruth Park. Hodder and Stoughton. 1984. Very much a boy's adventure story set in historic Norfolk Island, arguably the most severe of all Australia's convict settlements. The son of a commandant learns of the brutality and cruelty of convict settlements.

By the Sandhills of Yamboorah. Reginald Ottley. Sunbird. 1965. Tale set in the early part of this century, of a boy who ran away into the desert from a huge Australian outback station. He learns about aborigines, but most of all he has a dog. Based on actual real life events, according to the author's note.

The Rainbow Serpent. Dick Roughsey. Collins. 1975. Aboriginal story of the Dreamtime, for young children, unusual illustrations.

Platypus and Kookaburra. Rex Ingamells. Collins. 1987. A fun poem with great illustrations continuing the great Australian romance of its animals. Features a very hungry bunyip.

The Cities

Walking Around Melbourne. De Lacy Lowe, 1989, Leisure Press. Excruciatingly detailed walks telling everything one never wanted to know about even the most insignificant buildings. Very useful guide, nonetheless.

Seven Little Australians. Ethel Turner, 1894. The antics of Seven Little Aussies in suburban Sydney.

Emerald City. David Williamson, 1987. A play contrasting Melbourne and Sydney (read and find out which one the title refers to).

Sydney From Circular Quay. Joan Lawrence. 1987, Hale and Iremonger. Detailed descripton of walks one can take from Circular Quay. Excellent historical detail, helps bring to life Old Sydney.

Sydney Side. Richard Whitaker, 1986, Gregorys. Coffee table hardcover contrasting scenes from modern and old Sydney. Accounts of historical events help create the world of old Sydney. More to the point, the book demonstrates just how drastically Sydney has changed in 200 years.

My Place. Sally Morgan. Freemantle: Freemantle Arts Centre Press, 1987. $12.99

Outback and the Bush

The Thornbirds. Colleen McCullough, 1977. Australia's best known saga about a Catholic family living in the outback.

Picnic at Hanging Rock. Joan Lindsay, 1967. About three schoolgirls who disappear in the outback.

100 Walks In Tasmania. Tyrone Thomas, 1987, Hill of Content Publishing. Dependable account of a wide variety of walks all over Tasmania, from difficult wilderness walks to simple historic strolls in little Tassie villages.

Tin Mosques and Ghantowns. Christine Stevens, Oxford, 1989. Tabloid history revealing the fascinating trials and tribulations of the Afghan camel drivers in central Australia. Expensive, but high quality publication.

The Bush Food Handbook. Vic Cherikoff and Jennifer Isaacs, Ti Tree Press. Glossy but informative account of the foods that grow in Australian bush and can be collected on her shores and rivers, and how to cook them in a bush setting.

Off the Road Again. Bill Bachman, Lothian, no date. Practical down-to-earth advice on how to explore the Australian outback without coming to grief. Strongly recommended for even the most experienced adventurers. Australia's outback can be harsh, unforgiving and brutal. Find out the secret of bull dust and how to deal with it.

Fence People: Yarns from the Dingo Fence. Dinah Percival and Candida Westney, Hutchinson, 1989. The famous dingo fence that stretches right across the Australian center has spawned a folklore of its own. Learn about the sly and thoroughly incorrigible dingo, and the battle of wits he has fought against Australia's outback settlers.

Index

birds, 35-36
Bligh, William, 50, 124
Block Arcade, 156
blowies, *see* flies
Blue Mountains, 43,
   210-215, 219
Bond, Alan, 264-265
Bondi Beach, 138
boomerang, 31
Botanical gardens,
   Brisbane, 258-259;
   Darwin, 238; Melbourne,
   122, 158, 160; Sydney, 120,
   122, 123
Botany Bay, 46-47
bottleshops, 90
Bourke Street Mall, 156-157
breweries, 190
Bribie Island, 256
Brisbane Ranges National
   Park, 193
Brisbane, 217, 256-259
Broken Hill, 219
buffalo, 108
Bundaberg, 252
bunyip, 80
Burley-Griffin, Walter, 202
buses, 117-118, 138, 139
bush walks, 176-177, 178,
   185, 198, 202, 204, 213,
   233, 240, 268, 270
bushranging, 59
busking, 117, 120, 164
butterflies, 160, 215
BYO, 93
Byron Bay, 208

Cadman's Cottage, 116

cafes, *see* coffee shops
camping, 207, 172, 194
Canberra, 201-204
cancer, skin, 40
candy, 102
capital, *see* Canberra
cappuccino, 98-100, 117,
   133, 141-143, 147, 156, *see
   also* coffee, coffee shops
car ferry, 178
Carlton, 156, 169
cars, 9-10
casinos, *see* gambling
cattle, 54
Centrepoint Tower, 116, 129
Chadstone Shopping Mall
   (Melbourne), 96
Chaffey brothers, 216-217
Chamberlain, Lindy, 75, 76,
   226, *see also* Azaria case
chess, 126
Chifley, Ben, 64
Chinatown: Melbourne,
   157; Sydney, 133
Chinese garden, 135
chocolate, 146-147
church, 91, 103, 126, 270
Circular Quay, 116-121,
   133, 138, 142-143
Clarke, Marcus, 17
climate, 12, 19
clothing, 11, 18-21
coffee shops, 208;
   Melbourne, 156, 169-170;
   Sydney, 117, 120, 123, 128,
   130, 136-137, 139-141,
   141-143, 145-147

TRAVEL THE WORLD WITH HIPPOCRENE BOOKS!

HIPPOCRENE INSIDER'S GUIDES:
The series which takes you beyond the tourist track to give you an insider's view:

NEPAL
PRAKASH A. RAJ
0091 ISBN 0-87052-026-1 $9.95 paper

HUNGARY
NICHOLAS T. PARSONS
0921 ISBN 0-87052-976-5 $16.95 paper

MOSCOW, LENINGRAD AND KIEV (Revised)
YURI FEDOSYUK
0024 ISBN 0-87052-881-5 $11.95 paper

PARIS
ELAINE KLEIN
0012 ISBN 0-87052-876-9 $14.95 paper

POLAND (Third Revised Edition)
ALEXANDER T. JORDAN
0029 ISBN 0-87052-880-7 $9.95 paper

TAHITI (Revised)
VICKI POGGIOLI
0084 ISBN 0-87052-794-0 $9.95 paper

THE FRENCH ANTILLES (Revised)
ANDY GERALD GRAVETTE
The Caribbean islands of Guadeloupe, Martinique, St. Bartholomew, and St. Martin, and continental Guyane (French Guiana)
0085 ISBN 0-87052-105-5 $11.95 paper

By the same author:
THE NETHERLANDS ANTILLES:
A TRAVELER'S GUIDE
The Caribbean islands of Aruba, Bonaire, Curacao, St. Maarten, St. Eustatius, and Saba.
0240 ISBN 0-87052-581-6 $9.95 paper

HIPPOCRENE COMPANION GUIDES:

Written by American professors for North Americans who wish to enrich their travel experience with an understanding of local history and culture.

SOUTHERN INDIA
JACK ADLER
Covers the peninsular states of Tamil Nadu, Andhra Pradesh, and Karnataka, and highlights Goa, a natural gateway to the south.
0632 ISBN 0-87052-030-X $14.95 paper

IRELAND
HENRY WEISSER
0348 ISBN 0-87052-633-2 $14.95 paper

POLAND
JILL STEPHENSON and ALFRED BLOCH
"An appealing amalgam of practical information, historical curiosities, and romantic forays into Polish culture"--*Library Journal*
0894 ISBN 0-87052-636-7 $11.95 paper

PORTUGAL
T. J. KUBIAK
2305 ISBN 0-87052-739-8 $14.95 paper

ROMANIA
LYDLE BRINKLE
0351 ISBN 0-87052-634-0 $14.95 paper

THE SOVIET UNION
LYDLE BRINKLE
0357 ISBN 0-87052-635-9 $14.95 paper

GUIDE TO EAST AFRICA:
KENYA, TANZANIA, AND THE SEYCHELLES (Revised)
NINA CASIMATI
0043 ISBN 0-87052-883-1 $14.95 paper

TO PURCHASE HIPPOCRENE'S BOOKS contact your local bookstore, or write to Hippocrene Books, 171 Madison Avenue, New York, NY 10016. Please enclose a check or money order, adding $3 shipping (UPS) for the first book, and 50 cents for each of the others.
Write also for our full catalog of maps and foreign language dictionaries and phrasebooks.